Praise for *Mindfulness in Ea[r]*
Characteristics and Fun[ctions]

Since so few practitioners have the abi[lity] ... Buddhist discourses, which are preserved ... as Pāli, Gāndhārī, Sanskrit, Chinese, and Tibetan, this book, as with the author's other writings, is an important contribution to the topic. Another consequence of letting the primary texts, the discourses attributed to the Buddha, speak for themselves through providing very readable and fluent translations of them, supplemented with the author's commentary and interpretations, is that the book is a delight to read because the early discourses are so varied, fresh, and informative, with teachings liberally illustrated and enhanced through similes, metaphors, and the like. – **Mark Allon**, from the Foreword, author of *Style and Function: A Study of Dominant Stylistic Features of the Prose Portions of Pāli Canonical Sutta Texts and Their Mnemonic Function* and *Three Gāndhārī Ekottarikāgama-Type Sūtras: British Library Kharoṣṭhī Fragments 12 and 14*

In presenting us with this thematic compilation of comparative *Nikāya-Āgama* studies on the topic of mindfulness, Anālayo has once more provided us all with a significant resource that enriches our appreciation of early Buddhist literature and its presentation of mindfulness. And I for one am yet again grateful to Anālayo for his continued dedication to making this overlooked parallel material more easily accessible to scholars and practitioners alike. – **Rupert Gethin**, from the Foreword, author of *The Buddhist Path to Awakening: A Study of the Bodhi-Pakkhiyā Dhammā* and *The Foundations of Buddhism*

Bhikkhu Anālayo's *Mindfulness in Early Buddhism: Characteristics and Functions* is a result of his comparative study of mindfulness in Pāli and Chinese texts. In my view, this is one book that everybody seriously teaching and practising mindfulness meditation should have in their homes as a reference book on various aspects of mindfulness. It can amazingly benefit Buddhists from different traditions who are unfamiliar with each other's meditation practices. Reading this book opens our minds to see various usages, similarities, dissimilarities, and misinterpretations of mindfulness. – **H. Guṇaratana Mahāthera**, author of *Mindfulness in Plain English*

Mindfulness in Early Buddhism: Characteristics and Functions is a treasure trove of teachings, illuminating in depth and detail the many aspects and nuances of mindfulness. Through his own practice and scholarly research, Bhikkhu Anālayo explores the different characteristics and functions of mindfulness and how they lead us on to freedom. A wonderfully deep dive into what liberates the mind. – **Joseph Goldstein**, author of *Mindfulness: A Practical Guide to Awakening*

The definitive resource for scholars, meditation teachers, and those practitioners interested in a high-resolution framing of the meaning and cultivation of mindfulness under a wide variety of life circumstances, as illuminated by a careful and broad-minded exegesis of specific texts (Pāli *Nikāyas* and Chinese *Āgamas*) written down closest to the time of the Buddha. Anālayo here provides a rich framework for examining, reflecting upon, and deepening one's own ongoing practice and understanding in light of these earliest teachings on the cultivation of mindfulness as the direct path for the liberation and the extinguishing of suffering. He ends by offering his own inclusive definition of mindfulness. Much of what is illuminated here may be highly germane to current neuroscience studies of meditation, including brain networks subtending salience, memory (including working memory), proprioception, executive function, emotion regulation, and sense of self. – **Jon Kabat-Zinn**, Founder of MBSR, author of *The Healing Power of Mindfulness* and *Mindfulness for All*

Mindfulness in Early Buddhism: Characteristics and Functions is an invaluable and timely contribution to our understanding of the early Buddhist notion of "mindfulness". Anālayo makes available, through scrupulous translation and astute analysis, the vast scriptural and commentarial literature bearing on the topic in Pāli, as well as the early *Āgama* literature – often ignored – that survives in Chinese. The volume stands as the most comprehensive sourcebook and exhaustive study of the early materials to date, and should be required reading of anyone interested in the Buddhist roots of mindfulness practice. – **Robert Sharf**, author of *Coming to Terms with Chinese Buddhism: A Reading of the Treasure Store Treatise*

MINDFULNESS IN EARLY BUDDHISM

Also by Bhikkhu Anālayo:

Satipaṭṭhāna, The Direct Path to Realization
The Genesis of the Bodhisattva Ideal
A Comparative Study of the Majjhima-nikāya
Excursions into the Thought-world of the Pāli Discourses
Madhyama-āgama Studies
Perspectives on Satipaṭṭhāna
The Dawn of Abhidharma
Compassion and Emptiness in Early Buddhist Meditation
Saṃyukta-āgama Studies
Ekottarika-āgama Studies
The Foundation History of the Nuns' Order
Mindfully Facing Disease and Death
Buddhapada and the Bodhisattva Path
Early Buddhist Meditation Studies
Dīrgha-āgama Studies
Vinaya Studies
A Meditator's Life of the Buddha
Rebirth in Early Buddhism and Current Research
Satipaṭṭhāna Meditation: A Practice Guide
Bhikkhunī Ordination from Ancient India to Contemporary Sri Lanka
Mindfulness of Breathing
Mindfully Facing Climate Change
Introducing Mindfulness: Buddhist Background and Practical Exercises

Bhikkhu Anālayo

MINDFULNESS IN EARLY BUDDHISM

Characteristics and Functions

Windhorse Publications
info@windhorsepublications.com
windhorsepublications.com

As an act of Dhammadāna, Anālayo has waived royalty payments for this book.

The index was not compiled by the author.

Cover design by Dhammarati
Typesetting and layout by Tarajyoti
Printed by Bell & Bain Ltd, Glasgow

British Library Cataloguing in Publication Data:
A catalogue record for this book is available from the British Library.

ISBN: 978-1-911407-55-3

CONTENTS

	ABOUT THE AUTHOR	xii
	ACKNOWLEDGEMENT	xiii
	PUBLISHER'S ACKNOWLEDGEMENTS	xiv
	FOREWORD BY MARK ALLON	xv
	FOREWORD BY RUPERT GETHIN	xxi
	INTRODUCTION	1
	The Source Material	2
	The Chinese *Āgama*s	4
	Oral Transmission Lineages	5
	Conventions	7
Chapter I	**MEMORY DIMENSIONS OF MINDFULNESS**	11
	Recollection of Past Lives	12
	The Function of Recollection	17
	Recollection and Mindfulness	19
	Recollection Counters Fear	20
	Mindful Ascent to a Higher Heaven	20
	Falling Asleep with Mindfulness of the Buddha	22
	Mindfulness and Being Reminded of the Buddha	23
	Mindfully Collecting Oneself	25
	The Path is for One Who is Mindful	26
	Mindfulness and Recollecting Teachings	28

	The Faculty of Mindfulness	28
	Mindfulness as an Awakening Factor	33
	Mindfulness in the Noble Eightfold Path	34
	The Gatekeeper of Mindfulness	36
	The Slow Arising of Mindfulness	41
	Summary	45
Chapter II	**MINDFULNESS OF THE BODY**	47
	Modalities of Cultivating Mindfulness	48
	The Potential of Mindfulness of the Body	53
	Boundless Mindfulness of the Body	56
	The Simile of the Bowl of Oil	57
	The Simile of Six Animals Bound to a Post	62
	The Axle of Mindfulness of the Body	65
	Mindfulness of the Body and Humility	66
	Mindfulness of the Body to Counter Sensuality	67
	Mindfulness of Bodily Postures and Activities	68
	Bodily Dimensions of Absorption	72
	The Constitution of the Body	75
	Mindfulness of Breathing in Sixteen Steps	81
	Summary	84
Chapter III	**ESTABLISHING MINDFULNESS (1)**	85
	The Buddha's Awakening and the Direct Path	86
	The Buddha's Teaching of the Four Establishments	89
	Training in the Four Establishments of Mindfulness	92
	The Path of Mindfulness	94
	Mindfulness and Liberation	94
	The Impermanence of the Objects of Mindfulness	96
	Cultivating the Establishments of Mindfulness	99
	The Wholesome Nature of the Four Establishments	101
	The Inexhaustibility of Teachings on Mindfulness	103
	A Great Person Practises Mindfulness	106
	Shifting Between Concentration and Mindfulness	107
	The Simile of the Cook	111
	The Simile of the Quail	113
	The Simile of the Acrobats	116
	Summary	119

Chapter IV **ESTABLISHING MINDFULNESS (2)** 121
The Simile of the Monkey 122
Newcomers and Seasoned Practitioners 124
Mindful Protection Against Lustful Desires 126
The Moral Foundation for Intensive Practice 129
The Mindful Dwelling of a Trainee 131
Morality is for the Purpose of Mindfulness 133
The Potential of the Four Establishments 134
Emancipation Through Mindfulness 135
Mindfulness in the Gradual Path 137
The Gradual Path and Mindfulness 141
Mindful Reliance on Oneself 147
Mindfully Facing the Death of Others 150
Finding a Mindful Refuge in Oneself 152
Facing Death with Mindfulness 153
Facing Pain with Mindfulness 153
The Buddha Bears Pain with Mindfulness 154
Healing Through the Awakening Factors 155
Summary 159

Chapter V **DIMENSIONS OF MINDFULNESS** 161
Mindfulness in the Noble Eightfold Path 162
The Eightfold Path in Meditation 166
The Charioteer Simile 167
The Wrong and the Right Path 168
The Dire Effects of a Loss of Mindfulness 170
A Cowherd's Mindfulness 171
A Past Buddha's Entry into his Mother's Womb 173
The Buddha's Mindfulness at Conception 174
Overeating and Mindfulness 175
Going to Sleep with Mindfulness 181
Wakefulness 183
Dwelling in a Forest with Mindfulness 184
Mindful Begging for Food 185
Giving Priority to Mindfulness 187
Cultivating Mindfulness Before Teaching Others 188
Mindful Company 189

Mindfulness as a Path of Dharma 190
Mindfulness as a Form of Authority 190
The Ford or Pasture of Mindfulness 191
Bare Awareness 192
Summary 196

Chapter VI **MINDFULNESS AND LIBERATION** 199
Mindfulness and Thinking 200
No Longer Paying Attention 201
Mindfulness Leads to Concentration 203
The Simile of the Elephant 206
Mindfulness and Liberating Insight 206
Mindfulness and the Divine Abodes 207
Great Mental Powers Through Mindfulness 209
The Joy of Purification and Mindfulness 210
Mindfulness Instead of Confusion 211
The Balance of Mindfulness 211
Mindfully Facing an Attack 212
Mindfulness and Criticism 212
Mindful Aloofness From Views 213
Overcoming Anger Through Mindfulness 215
Mindful Removal of Lust 217
Mindfulness in Support of Celibacy 217
Countering Unwholesome Thoughts 218
Mindfully Removing Unwholesome Influences 219
The Treasures of the Awakening Factors 220
The Buddha's Discovery of the Awakening Factors 221
Nutriment for the Awakening Factor of Mindfulness 222
Manifestations of the Awakening Factor of Mindfulness 222
Liberation Depends on Mindfulness 223
Contemplating the Aggregates with Mindfulness 225
Mindfulness is the Path 226
Mindfulness and the Quest For Awakening 226
Mindfulness and Awakening Attained 227
Awakened Ones are Mindful 228

An Arahant's Mindfulness 228
The Buddha's Mindfulness and Insight 229
The Buddha's First Teaching 230
All Buddhas Awaken Through Mindfulness 231
The Buddha's Three Establishments of Mindfulness 232
Summary 236

CONCLUSIONS 237
Characteristics of Mindfulness 237
Functions of Mindfulness 241

ABBREVIATIONS 245
REFERENCES 247
INDEX OF SUBJECTS 259
INDEX LOCORUM 273

ABOUT THE AUTHOR

Born in 1962 in Germany, Bhikkhu Anālayo was ordained in 1995 in Sri Lanka, and completed a PhD on the *Satipaṭṭhāna-sutta* at the University of Peradeniya, Sri Lanka, in 2000 – published in 2003 by Windhorse Publications under the title *Satipaṭṭhāna, The Direct Path to Realization*.

Anālayo is a professor of Buddhist Studies; his main research area is early Buddhism and in particular the topics of the Chinese *Āgamas*, meditation, and women in Buddhism. Besides his academic pursuits, he regularly teaches meditation. He presently resides at the Barre Center for Buddhist Studies in Massachusetts, where he spends most of his time in silent retreat.

ACKNOWLEDGEMENT

I am indebted to Mark Allon, Chris Burke, Bhikkhunī Dhammadinnā, Ann Dillon, Linda Grace, Mike Running, and Bhikṣuṇī Syinchen for commenting on a draft version of this book and to the staff, board members, and supporters of the Barre Center for Buddhist Studies for providing me with the facilities needed to do my practice and writing.

PUBLISHER'S ACKNOWLEDGEMENTS

Windhorse Publications wishes to gratefully acknowledge a grant from the Triratna European Chairs' Assembly Fund and the Future Dharma Fund towards the production of this book.

Triratna European Chairs Assembly

FutureDharmaFund
Transforming Self and World

We also wish to acknowledge and thank the individual donors who gave to the book's production via our "Sponsor-a-book" campaign.

FOREWORD BY MARK ALLON

It is with pleasure that I write this foreword to Bhikkhu Anālayo's most recent book, *Mindfulness in Early Buddhism: Characteristics and Functions*. First, I write in appreciation of the great contribution he has made to scholarship on early Buddhism and in particular, with my own scholarly interests in mind, to research on the origin and development of early Buddhist literature, since these texts are the foundation for our knowledge and understanding of the teaching of the Buddha and of the myriad of expressions of Buddhism that arose as a consequence. Second, I do so in appreciation of his contribution to our understanding of Buddhist meditative practices, in particular of mindfulness practice, the topic of this book, and in appreciation of him as a meditation teacher. I benefited greatly from participating in a week-long meditation retreat he conducted just south of Sydney in July 2018, during which it became apparent to me just how informed his instruction is by his scholarship and by his personal experience as a meditator. Finally, I write this in appreciation of Anālayo as a good friend, a *kalyāṇa-mitra*, I have known for many years.

This interesting book is aimed at practitioners of mindfulness practice who generally do not know much about the context in which mindfulness was taught and practised in the early period of Buddhism and whose understanding of mindfulness, as well as other meditative practices, is generally informed by reading secondary literature mostly written by teachers who set out their own understanding of and method for developing mindfulness. The author rightly believes that modern practitioners would benefit from such knowledge of the primary sources, letting the primary texts which record early Buddhist guidance on understanding and engaging in mindfulness practice speak for themselves. This is a hallmark of Anālayo's work. Both his writings and his meditation retreats are thoroughly grounded in the early Buddhist discourses (Pāli *sutta*, Sanskrit *sūtra*). Since so few practitioners have the ability to access these sources, which are preserved in languages as diverse as Pāli, Gāndhārī, Sanskrit, Chinese, and Tibetan, this book, as with the author's other writings, is an important contribution to the topic. Another consequence of letting the primary texts, the discourses attributed to the Buddha, speak for themselves through providing very readable and fluent translations of them, supplemented with the author's commentary and interpretations, is that the book is a delight to read because the early discourses are so varied, fresh, and informative, with teachings liberally illustrated and enhanced through similes, metaphors, and the like. Similes in particular are a prominent feature of early Buddhist discourses, the Buddha himself reportedly saying that it is through similes that intelligent people better grasp his teachings.

The author has written on the topic of mindfulness for many years, producing four monographs prior to the present one – *Satipaṭṭhāna, The Direct Path to Realization* (2003), *Perspectives on Satipaṭṭhāna* (2013), *Early Buddhist Meditation Studies* (2017), and *Satipaṭṭhāna Meditation: A Practice Guide* (2018) – and many articles whose primary focus is mindfulness, the most recent ones published in the journal *Mindfulness* (see bibliography). This being the case, it is inevitable that there is some repetition amongst these works and reuse of the same material, though usually for different reasons and in different ways. An example is the definition of mindfulness in chapter 1 and its relationship to memory: a reader who is familiar with the author's earlier writings on this topic will get a sense that some passages and arguments are familiar. But, of course, each work has a different purpose and is intended for a slightly different audience. The current work offers much that is new, drawing on both the author's own research, as well as that of others, which has been published since his previous books on this topic. But a major new contribution made by this book is the large number of discourses that are preserved in the Chinese *Āgama* collections that are discussed and translated, most of which have previously not been translated. To date, with the exception in particular of the works of Anālayo himself, discussions of mindfulness have mostly drawn on the more readily available Pāli sources. Although immensely valuable, Pāli texts are but one of several sources we have that attest to the earliest phase of Buddhist thought and practice, others being the rather more fragmentary Sanskrit and Gāndhārī discourses, and the Chinese and occasionally Tibetan translations. Anālayo commands and uses freely all discourse material dealing with mindfulness preserved in these diverse languages. This is relatively rare even for scholars, and I for one envy his command of Chinese sources that are so rich yet so neglected. Such fluency in command of the materials in these languages is even rarer for practitioner-teachers who normally rely on texts in one language, e.g. the Pāli, or translations in modern languages only. But I cannot recall a book dealing with mindfulness in early Buddhism that takes as its primary starting point the Chinese discourses. This is indeed an original approach, one that, judging from the results, is very productive.

As a general rule of methodology, which is the correct one to follow, the author only discusses in detail and translates discourses that are found in both the Chinese *Āgama*s and in the Pāli *Nikāya*s and/or Sanskrit *Āgama*s, rather than say occurring in only one source, believing that such material is most likely to go back to the early common textual inheritance and hence be representative of early Buddhism.

In his far-ranging use of a large number of discourses sourced from different collections preserved in different languages, the author has certainly captured the importance of mindfulness in early Buddhist practice and the profound and diverse benefits of practising it, examples being: that if one is to practise anything it is mindfulness that is most productive (chapter 1); the special status mindfulness has as the first of the seven awakening factors in relationship to the other six (chapter 2); and similarly the special status it has as one of the members of the noble eightfold path in relation to the other seven (chapter 2); its inclusion in many of the lists found in the important *Dasuttara-sutta* and its Chinese parallel (chapter 2); the four establishments of mindfulness being the way to liberation from *dukkha*, to attaining Nirvāṇa, the deathless, and as a direct path to mental purification (chapters 3, 5, 6); that an arahant is one who has completely cultivated the four establishments of mindfulness (chapter 4); that mindfulness can provide vital protection against getting stuck in the world of the senses, aid in facing illness and overcoming physical pain, and in dealing with the death of others and of oneself (chapter 4); the significant role the four establishments of mindfulness have in the cultivation of concentration (chapter 6), and so on. In the course of this book, many less profound, but nonetheless useful, benefits of mindfulness are illustrated, such as the physical and psychological benefits of moderation in eating achieved through eating mindfully, the benefits of falling asleep with mindfulness, and mindfulness as a means of overcoming anger (chapters 5, 6). In his conclusion, the author groups these diverse benefits under the five headings of protective, embodied, attentive, receptive, and liberating, which is quite helpful.

An important point illustrated by several discourse passages discussed at different points in the book is how foundational moral conduct is for the cultivation of mindfulness that leads to liberating insight (e.g. chapters 3, 4). In the modern practice of mindfulness in non-Asian countries this is commonly either lightly touched on or not mentioned at all. This may in part be due to a general dislike of "moralizing" and rules for behaviour that characterizes the modern age. Yet as here, time and again in early Buddhist texts the importance of moral conduct as foundation for practice is emphasized. We see many modern applications of what is called "mindfulness practice" aimed at improving performance in activities that from a Buddhist perspective are ethically problematic, such as in military training, or are quite contrary to its Buddhist applications, such as in marriage counselling or in enhancing sensual experience and appreciation. In this connection, an interesting fact noted by the author (chapter 3) is that in early Buddhist thought mindfulness itself is considered to be an ethically indeterminate quality, in contrast to some later Buddhist traditions where mindfulness is invariably a wholesome quality.

As in the author's numerous other publications, the value of taking all versions of a given discourse into account, texts that are preserved in different languages and have different transmission lineages, is amply illustrated throughout this book, exposing developments and likely transmission errors in each version. For example, in the Chinese version of a particular discourse (SĀ 1319) mindfulness is said to be the means by which the mind can overcome anger, where the Pāli version (SN 10.4) gives the impression that mindfulness alone is not enough to do so. The author argues that, in light of the Chinese version, the Pāli version is likely to have suffered from a textual corruption, where the conjunction *ca*, "and", was confused with the negative particle *na*, "not" (chapter 6).

The book has a user-friendly structure: each chapter introduces the discourses and topics that will be discussed, with subheadings for the discussion of the discourses at hand, and concludes with a summary of the main ideas and arguments.

Having thought about and translated for us an enormous amount of early Buddhist discourses on mindfulness, the author ends the book with a provisional definition of mindfulness: "An openly receptive presence that enables a full taking in of information, resulting in an awake quality of the mind that facilitates clarity and recollection by monitoring, in the present moment and without interfering, the internal and external repercussions of whatever is taking place." This subtle and perceptive definition may well serve the test of time.

I believe the reader and particularly the practitioner will find much in this book that is useful and inspiring.

Mark Allon

FOREWORD BY RUPERT GETHIN

For the last fifteen years Bhikkhu Anālayo has devoted most of his very considerable scholarly energies to exploring the parallel versions of the surviving Buddhist *Nikāya-Āgama* literature. In particular he has published numerous studies comparing the suttas of the four primary Pāli *Nikāya*s – the *Dīgha-*, *Majjhima-*, *Saṃyutta-* and *Aṅguttara-nikāya*s – preserved by the Theravāda tradition, with the parallel versions preserved by other ancient Indian Buddhist traditions that survive in Chinese translation. In doing this Anālayo has contributed to something of a revolution in the study of the earliest stratum of Buddhist literature.

Twenty years ago there were, of course, a number of studies available that made some of the rich source material surviving in Chinese translation available to scholars of early Buddhist literature working on the Pāli and Sanskrit sources. But to those of us with little or no knowledge of Buddhist Chinese and without access to a library that held the Taishō edition of the Chinese Tripiṭaka, the Chinese *Āgama* translations remained largely a closed book. Then, at the beginning of the new millennium, through the efforts of the Chinese Buddhist Text Association (CBETA) in Taiwan and the SAT Daizōkyō Text Database project in Japan, the Chinese text of the Taishō edition of the Chinese Tripiṭaka began to become widely available in a digital form. Following this, Anālayo embarked on his work providing English translations and studies of material from the Chinese *Āgama*s. More than any other single scholar, he has worked to make the repository of early Buddhist literature found in the Chinese Tripiṭaka more accessible and more familiar to scholars and meditators used to relying on the Pāli *Nikāyas* for their understanding of early Buddhism. Anālayo has challenged us all to consider what light the many parallels surviving, especially in Chinese translation, shed on the early history and development of Buddhist literature and thought. Anālayo's output is prodigious. In a series of over 300 articles as well as a number of books and studies, he has discussed parallel after parallel. Anālayo suggests that the close scrutiny of the parallel versions of an early discourse provides a means of approaching more closely the authentic teaching of the Buddha himself. He believes that where we find variant parallel presentations, we can in many cases determine with some degree of probability which is the earlier. Whether or not we are always persuaded by his judgement in this regard, there can be no doubt that the great quantity of material that Anālayo has brought to the scholarly community's attention in itself provides an invaluable resource to be pondered and considered. The sheer volume of his work provides us with a solid basis for the task of forming a properly rounded and balanced appreciation of the breadth and depth of the earliest Buddhist literary tradition.

In addition to presenting us with parallel versions of *Nikāya-Āgama* materials generally, Anālayo's scholarly output has also frequently had a particular focus on the way the practice of mindfulness is presented in the earliest Buddhist sources. The present volume thus brings his method of comparing parallel versions of *Nikāya-Āgama* discourses to bear once more on the topic of mindfulness. Each chapter is devoted to considering parallel versions of a series of passages related to a particular topic. The first chapter is prompted by the fact that the word we have come to translate as "mindfulness" is more literally rendered as "remembering": how then is the relationship between mindfulness and remembering understood in the early literature? The second chapter focuses on mindfulness of the body. Chapters three and four consider the presentation of the four establishments of mindfulness in *Nikāya-Āgama* material apart from the *(Mahā-)Satipaṭṭhāna-sutta* and its parallels (which Anālayo has considered in previous studies); the focus here is on the Chinese parallels to the discourses of the *Satipaṭṭhāna-saṃyutta*. Chapter five considers miscellaneous material on mindfulness. Finally, chapter six turns to the manner in which the early literature relates mindfulness to liberation itself.

In presenting us with this thematic compilation of comparative *Nikāya-Āgama* studies on the topic of mindfulness, Anālayo has once more provided us all with a significant resource that enriches our appreciation of early Buddhist literature and its presentation of mindfulness. And I for one am yet again grateful to Anālayo for his continued dedication to making this overlooked parallel material more easily accessible to scholars and practitioners alike.

Rupert Gethin

INTRODUCTION

The present book has its origin in a retreat I taught together with Jon Kabat-Zinn at the Insight Meditation Society (IMS) in Massachusetts. Based on our personal friendship and within the setting of an intensive meditation retreat, we opened up a space for a practice-oriented dialogue on the topics of disease and death between teachers of Mindfulness-Based Stress Reduction (MBSR) and teachers or practitioners of traditional insight meditation.

The experience of this retreat made me realize that those involved in the current mindfulness movement would benefit from more detailed information on the nature and purposes of mindfulness in the Buddhist traditions. This inspired me to start working immediately by contributing from my own area of research, which is early Buddhism. In addition to a series of articles relating specific aspects of early Buddhism to current mindfulness-based interventions or programmes, with the present book and its companion, *Introducing Mindfulness* (2020f), I hope to offer a starting point for an exchange of information, dialogue, and further research.

Whereas *Introducing Mindfulness* is aimed at a more general readership and meant to provide an easy and practical approach to mindfulness, the present book has a more scholarly orientation. The ensuing pages in a way put mindfulness in the early discourses under the microscope, providing a sourcebook that brings together a range of different aspects to enable an appreciation of the wealth of information available on early Buddhist mindfulness and its versatility.

My presentation is based mainly on selected excerpts translated from the four Chinese *Āgama*s that mention mindfulness and have a Pāli parallel. The choice of such excerpts is based on my impression that their presentation is in some way relevant to an understanding of early Buddhist mindfulness. Even though I have endeavoured to be fairly comprehensive in my survey, my presentation is necessarily incomplete. Mindfulness is often implicit in passages where it is not explicitly mentioned. Yet, in order to avoid too much of an influence by my personal judgement, it seemed wise to restrict myself to only those passages where mindfulness is explicitly mentioned in at least one of the parallel versions.

One of the discourses taken up proclaims that the Buddha would have been able to give uninterrupted teachings on the cultivation of mindfulness for even a hundred years without running out of material (see below p. 103). Thus the topic of mindfulness was already in ancient times considered inexhaustible. Hence the present book, although building on three monographs dedicated to *satipaṭṭhāna* meditation (Anālayo 2003b, 2013b, and 2018i), can at best only be a starting point for further discussion. For this reason, even though I have tried to the best of my abilities to put into perspective the extracts chosen for translation, the present survey can only be an interim stage in our ongoing attempts to understand and practise the various dimensions of mindfulness.

THE SOURCE MATERIAL

The discourses found in the Pāli *Nikāya*s and their Chinese *Āgama* parallels are the final results of centuries of oral transmission, involving texts which according to tradition were spoken originally by the Buddha and his disciples. One lineage of these orally transmitted discourses eventually reached Sri

Lanka and was subsequently committed to writing. According to the Sri Lankan chronicles, the writing down of the texts occurred shortly before the beginning of the Common Era. By then, several centuries had passed since the time when the Buddha would have lived. Other Buddhist traditions in India also preserved their records of the Buddha's teachings and, probably at about the time of the writing down of the Pāli canon in Sri Lanka or soon thereafter, these other transmission lineages were also committed to writing.

Due to the climatic conditions in most of the Indian subcontinent, written records of the teachings, made on material such as palm leaves, were sooner or later in need of being copied again. With the eventual disappearance of Buddhism from India, the process of copying manuscripts came to an end in the Buddha's home country, and much of the written material produced there has been lost. In Sri Lanka and other Southeast Asian countries, however, the Pāli manuscript tradition continued. Moreover, collections of discourses from different Buddhist traditions had been brought from India and Central Asia to China and translated into Chinese. As far as we know, early discourse collections also reached Tibet, but these appear to have been lost during a period of persecution of Buddhism. The present-day Buddhist canon preserved in Tibetan translation does not contain counterparts to the four main discourse collections, the Pāli *Nikāya*s or the Chinese *Āgama*s, but only some selected discourses preserved on their own or as citations in exegetical treatises.

Other sources of early Buddhist discourse material can be found in manuscripts that come from Gandhāra (present-day eastern Afghanistan and northern Pakistan) and Central Asia. Due to the dry climatic conditions in these regions, texts written on material like birch bark endure much longer than manuscripts in the tropical climates of Sri Lanka or South India. Even in recent years substantial manuscript finds have made headlines.[1]

1 A survey of Gāndhārī fragments and their particular significance can be found in Salomon 2018.

THE CHINESE *ĀGAMAS*

The Chinese *Āgama*s stem from various oral transmission lineages that attempted to preserve the teachings of the Buddha. Such transmission lineages became part of the canonical textual collection of particular Buddhist monastic traditions that had developed over time.[2]

In the case of discourses preserved in Chinese, there is of course the problem of translation errors. Rendering an Indic text into Chinese involves bridging two languages that are substantially different from each other, making it a rather demanding task to transform a text from one language to the other without a change or even loss of meaning. Nevertheless, the discourses in the Chinese *Āgama*s are not themselves products of Chinese culture, but are testimonies of Indian Buddhism. By way of illustration, they could be compared to an Indian wearing traditional Chinese dress. However much the clothing is Chinese, the person inside remains an Indian.

Recourse to the Chinese *Āgama*s (or other parallels, when extant) enables comparing different versions of a particular discourse and thereby assessing the earliest strata of Buddhist teachings that are still accessible today. A basic principle here is that, if material is found in similar ways in different versions, such passages can be more confidently relied upon for reconstructing early Buddhist thoughts and ideas. When differences manifest, often (but not always) it is possible to determine with some degree of probability which of the variant presentations is the earlier one.

The vision of early Buddhism that emerges from such comparative study can at times be quite different from the doctrinal position of the Theravāda tradition, which has developed since the transmission of Buddhism to Sri Lanka during the time of the reign of King Asoka in India. The expression "early Buddhism", in contrast to Theravāda, stands for the preceding period of time, from the Buddha

2 On the notion of transmission lineages as monastic ordination lineages, rather than being doctrinal schools, see also Anālayo 2020g.

until King Asoka, spanning roughly from the fifth to the third century before the Common Era. Thus what follows in the ensuing chapters of this book is meant to offer source material and observations that enable an appreciation of the "early Buddhist" perspective on mindfulness, as distinct from the perspectives of later traditions as presented in Abhidharma and exegesis.

ORAL TRANSMISSION LINEAGES

Whereas the four Pāli *Nikāya*s were transmitted by a single tradition, commonly called Theravāda, the *Āgama*s to which we have access in Chinese translation stem from different transmission lineages. Such lineages are usually distinguished by the name of the ordination tradition within which the respective monastic reciters went forth.[3] In the case of the Pāli *Nikāya*s, the reciters were ordained according to Theravāda monastic discipline. This does not mean that the Pāli discourses are themselves the product of Theravādins; in fact, as already mentioned above, they can at times differ considerably from Theravāda doctrine. It only means that those responsible for the oral transmission of this particular set of discourses were Theravāda monastics. In the case of the Chinese *Āgama*s, relevant monastic ordination lineages are known by the names of Dharmaguptaka, Mahāsāṅghika, Mūlasarvāstivāda, and Sarvāstivāda.

Translations taken from the collection of long discourses, the *Dīrgha-āgama* (DĀ), can fairly confidently be identified as representing a Dharmaguptaka transmission lineage.[4] From the viewpoint of the history of the different Buddhist traditions, resulting from geographical separation and the coming into being of different monastic observances, texts from the

3 For a brief survey see Anālayo 2015a.
4 The Chinese *Dīrgha-āgama* has been translated into English by Ichimura 2015, 2016, and 2018. Unfortunately, his translations are unreliable; see Anālayo 2020e. Hence in what follows I provide my own translations. Out of the *Dīrgha-āgama* discourses taken up in the course of my study, partial translations of DĀ 1 and DĀ 21 can also be found in Anālayo 2017a: 74–83 and 2017b: 122–174.

Dharmaguptaka tradition tend to be close to those transmitted by Theravādins.

Although the lineage responsible for transmitting the collection of medium-length discourses, the *Madhyama-āgama* (MĀ), has been a matter of debate, it seems to me fairly certain that it can be assigned to a Sarvāstivāda line of transmission.[5] Texts passed down by the Sarvāstivāda tradition(s) tend to differ more markedly from their Theravāda counterparts than Dharmaguptaka texts.

The reciter tradition of the topic-wise discourses contained in the *Saṃyukta-āgama* (SĀ) can with a high degree of certainty be identified as being Mūlasarvāstivāda.[6] This discourse collection, which also tends to differ considerably from its Theravāda parallels, is particularly rich in material relevant to an understanding of mindfulness and for this reason is the source of most of my translations.[7]

Identifying the reciter lineage responsible for transmitting the Indic original of the numerical collection, the *Ekottarika-āgama* (EĀ), is complicated by the fact that this collection appears to have undergone a process of reworking in China, leading to the integration of material that did not belong to the original.[8] As far as the Indic original is concerned, it seems to me quite

5 Anālayo 2017g. Out of the *Madhyama-āgama* discourses taken up, complete translations of MĀ 189 and MĀ 198 can also be found in Anālayo 2012: 294–307 and 395–410 and a partial translation of MĀ 163 in Anālayo 2013b: 240f.

6 See in more detail Anālayo 2020d.

7 Out of the *Saṃyukta-āgama* discourses taken up, complete translations of SĀ 265, SĀ 271, SĀ 272, SĀ 575, SĀ 619, SĀ 638, SĀ 727, and SĀ 803 can also be found in Anālayo 2013a: 34–40, 2013a: 55–60, 2013a: 60–64, 2016c: 187–190, 2015c: 311–314, 2016c: 119–123, 2017b: 210–214, and 2013b: 228f. Partial translations of the relevant parts in SĀ 312, SĀ 541, SĀ 615, SĀ 616, SĀ 617, SĀ 620, SĀ 623, SĀ 639, SĀ 713, SĀ 715, SĀ 1150, SĀ 1171, SĀ 1175, and SĀ 1319 can be found in Anālayo 2018a, 2017b: 218, 2015c: 294f, 2013b: 239, 2013b: 26f, 2013b: 24f, 2013b: 56f, 2017f: 212f, 2013b: 209f, 2013b: 206, 2018e: 1649, 2013b: 56, 2013b: 28, and 2018f: 1967 respectively. As evident from this list, there is some overlap between translations included in the present book and those found in other publications of mine. On reflection, it seemed to me preferable to present all the relevant material here together, rather than directing the reader each time to these other publications for consultation of a translated passage.

8 See Anālayo 2016b: 51–112, 165–214, 443–472.

probable that this was transmitted by Mahāsāṅghika reciters. The Mahāsāṅghika tradition formed at an early point in the history of the different Buddhist traditions. Texts preserved by the corresponding transmission lineages have for a long time been transmitted independently and can therefore at times be markedly different from their Pāli counterparts. This in turn means that, when *Ekottarika-āgama* texts agree with their Pāli counterpart, such concordance is fairly strong evidence for the earliness of the respective passage. Only a few instances from that collection will be taken up in the following chapters, as it contains relatively less relevant material.[9]

Besides these four main *Āgama*s, partial discourse collections have also been preserved in Chinese translation. In the course of my study, I will refer to a partial *Saṃyukta-āgama* (SĀ²) and a partial *Ekottarika-āgama* (T 150A), and also to single discourses translated in Chinese as well as other relevant material in Gāndhārī, Sanskrit, or Tibetan translation.

CONVENTIONS

In my annotations, I provide abbreviated references to relevant Pāli discourses. Here abbreviations that have an "N" as their second letter denote the four main Pāli collections, referred to as the Pāli *Nikāya*s: the collection of long discourses (DN: *Dīgha-nikāya*), the collection of medium-length discourses (MN: *Majjhima-nikāya*), the collection of topic-wise assembled discourses (SN: *Saṃyutta-nikāya*), and the collection of numerical discourses (AN: *Aṅguttara-nikāya*). Their Chinese parallels can be discerned by the fact that the second letter of the abbreviation is instead an "Ā", representing the term *Āgama*. These are similarly collections of long (DĀ), medium-length (MĀ), topic-wise (SĀ), and numerical discourses (EĀ). The first occurrence of each reference to a Pāli discourse comes with information about an English translation that, in case of interest, could be consulted. To date no reliable complete translation of any of the

9 Out of the discourses taken up, a complete translation of EĀ 19.2 can be found in Anālayo 2016b: 268f.

four Chinese *Āgamas* has been published,[10] which is why in what follows I provide my own translations from these collections.

What I present here is meant as a sourcebook, wherefore in the ensuing pages my exploration of the material and its relevance to understanding mindfulness in early Buddhism alternates between renditions from the Chinese *Āgamas* and my own comments on the translated excerpts in light of their Pāli discourse parallels. Reading through all of the material assembled will not necessarily be an attractive prospect to all readers. For this reason, the introductions to each chapter are meant to provide an initial brief survey of the topics covered. Any point of particular interest could then be followed up by proceeding to the relevant discourse, whose number is given in brackets in the introduction and again in the headers to the respective section. Summaries at the end of each chapter are meant to highlight key points that emerged from the passages surveyed and bring the various perspectives together.

In an attempt to string together the wealth of material available on mindfulness in the early discourses, I will be referring recurrently to five qualities of mindfulness (Anālayo 2018i: 213). These simply reflect my personal understanding and are just one of several possible ways in which key aspects of mindfulness could be summarized. The five qualities that I have chosen are: protective, embodied, attentive, receptive, and liberating.

In the first of the altogether six chapters of my exploration, I begin with a topic that has been a perennial challenge for the understanding of mindfulness, namely its relationship to memory. I will relate this in particular to the "attentive" dimension of mindfulness (although the "protective" dimension also emerges in the context of the practice of recollection, also discussed in this chapter). With the second chapter I turn to mindfulness of the body, which reflects in particular an "embodied" aspect of mindfulness. The four establishments of mindfulness are the theme of the third and fourth chapters.

10 As mentioned above in note 4, the only complete translation of an *Āgama* into English is unfortunately unreliable.

These rely on the "receptive" nature of mindfulness, which in turn has a "liberating" effect. In addition, the four establishments of mindfulness also serve a "protective" function. The last two chapters cover the remaining relevant material, which due to its variety is not easily assigned to a single topic. The fifth chapter somewhat loosely assembles passages that reflect various "dimensions" of mindfulness. In the sixth chapter, the "liberating" potential of mindfulness is fairly prominent, as most of the passages here provide perspectives on the relationship between mindfulness and liberation.

I

MEMORY DIMENSIONS OF MINDFULNESS

In the present chapter I explore passages that in one way or another have a bearing on the relationship between mindfulness and memory, and thereby to what I would consider to be an "attentive" dimension of mindfulness. I begin my exploration with an instance that involves mindfulness in the role of recalling things from the past, which is the practice of recollection of past lives (DĀ 9). Mindfulness also relates to other forms of recollection (MĀ 202 and SĀ 930), the practice of which can counter fear (SĀ 981) or lead to a higher rebirth (DĀ 14). Mindfulness of the Buddha can have a relation to the future, in the sense of being mindful of him in anticipation of meeting him for the first time the next day (SĀ 592). In addition to its role in the context of recollection, a closely related aspect emerges when someone is reminded of the Buddha by external circumstances (DĀ 28).

Some references relating mindfulness to a form of memory are not supported by their parallels (DĀ 10, MĀ 74, and DĀ 2). A similar disagreement among parallel versions can be seen in relation to definitions of mindfulness as a faculty or power (SĀ 646 and SĀ 647) and as an awakening factor (SĀ 711). In each case, only some parallel versions refer to the ability to remember what happened a long time ago. Of relevance to this discussion are also some definitions of mindfulness as a factor of the path to liberation (MĀ 31 and SĀ 784).

Nevertheless, at least in the context of a simile of a gatekeeper, the parallels do agree in defining mindfulness as the ability to recall the past (MĀ 3). Another simile involving the same imagery of a gatekeeper in a different context, however, instead speaks of the four establishments of mindfulness (SĀ 1175). The variations that emerge between parallel discourses in this way show the memory nuance to be less central to an understanding of mindfulness than might be expected on consulting only the Pāli discourses and thus just a single reciter tradition (in this case that of the Theravādins).

The final passage taken up in this chapter describes a slow arising of mindfulness (SĀ 1173 and MĀ 192). A similar description, found in a Pāli discourse, has a close relationship to memory. Terminology found in this passage has significantly influenced the understanding of mindfulness in the Theravāda tradition, leading to the idea that mindfulness plunges into its objects.

RECOLLECTION OF PAST LIVES (DĀ 9)

The Pāli or Sanskrit term usually translated as "mindfulness", *sati/smṛti*, has etymological connections to memory. However, already in the most ancient of sacred Indian scriptures, which predates the Buddhist material by centuries, the term occurs occasionally to designate an activity related to the present rather than the past.[1] Hence Klaus (1993: 78) reasons:

> from an etymological point of view, "attention, awareness" is not necessarily a new connotation of *sati* attached to it at the rise of Buddhism, but one that might have belonged to it all along.

Besides regularly referring to memory, *smṛti* also stood for the body of sacred texts that were memorized (as distinct from *śruti*, texts received by direct revelation). Gethin (1992: 36) explains:

---

1 One example provided by Klaus 1993: 79 is found in *Ṛgveda* X.106.9, Aufrecht 1877: 410,7: *ánu hí smárāthaḥ* (based on the same verbal root as *smṛti*), conveying the sense "give heed", in that those addressed in this way should listen carefully.

> Sanskrit *smṛti* can be both an act of "remembering" or "bearing in mind", and also what is remembered – hence the brahmanical use of *smṛti* to characterize the body of received tradition as what has been remembered, as opposed to what has been directly heard (*śruti*) from the vedic seers. In Buddhist literature, however, it is the bare aspect of "remembering" or "having in mind" that is focused upon to the exclusion of other meanings: memory as the act of remembering, not what is remembered.

In the ancient Indian oral setting, young brahmins were trained from their early youth onwards in learning by rote texts whose contents they did not yet understand. From the viewpoint of current research in psychology, the precise textual recall achieved with this mode of learning appears to be precisely because the text is not understood, due to which no inferences are drawn during its processing.[2] As no inferences are drawn, the text can be remembered precisely as it was heard.

This in turn suggests that the type of textual memory trained in ancient India requires avoiding additional associations and instead endeavouring as much as possible to stick to just what has been actually experienced. This in a way points to a feature of mindfulness that is quite prominent in the early Buddhist discourses, which is just being with what is rather than reacting to it and proliferating it in various ways.

Another form of memory, of the episodic type, comes to the fore in one of the three higher knowledges the Buddha reportedly acquired during the night of his awakening: recollection of past lives.[3] This refers to the ability, based on the previous cultivation of a high degree of concentration, to direct the mind in such a way that one can remember circumstances of one's own former lives. The standard description of such abilities mentions the recollection of a range of details from such previous lives, for example the place where one was born, one's earlier name and family, the kind of food eaten,

2 See in more detail Anālayo 2019b.
3 Anālayo 2017f: 96–100 and 2018g: 18f.

and the pleasure or pain experienced. The ability to remember such details from even a long time ago involves mindfulness:[4]

> [Through] mindfulness one realizes [recollection of] one's former lives.

This is a good example of an "attentive" function of mindfulness that is clearly related to memory of the past. Such ability to recall the distant past is considered available to anyone who cultivates the mind accordingly. Examples for such ability can be found in the *Brahmajāla-sutta* and its parallels, which report various views about the nature of the world that can arise if someone has developed this ability and then draws unwarranted conclusions from it.[5]

Now the role of mindfulness in the context of such recollection does not appear to be related to the storing of information, but to its recall. In other words, the idea is probably not that one must have been mindful at the time of a particular event in a past life for it to be recalled now. The Buddha himself is on record for having remembered certain details of a great number of past lives. It would hardly do to assume that, for him to remember various details from those past lives, mindfulness must have been invariably established on each occasion.

Of course, had mindfulness been present at a certain time in the past, it would have enhanced the storing of that particular event in memory. But the same is also possible without it.

Thus, attending with mindfulness to something from the past will facilitate the recalling of what happened at that time. Nevertheless, the same is also possible without mindfulness, as the arising of distracting memories during meditation shows. Such memories are due to a loss of mindfulness rather than being one of its modalities. It follows that memory can function

4 DĀ 9 at T I 51a12, parallel to DN 33 at DN III 230,7 (translated by Walshe 1987: 492); see also the Sanskrit fragments in Stache-Rosen 1968: 103, where only the commentary, found in the *Saṅgītiparyāya*, T 1536 at T XXVI 395b2, spells out what is to be realized through mindfulness, namely recollection of past lives.

5 For a comparative study see Anālayo 2017b: 115–178.

on its own even when mindfulness was not present at the time of the event to be recalled and is also not present now, at the time of recalling the past event. Memory will certainly be enhanced through mindfulness, but it does not require it in order to function.

The impression that emerges in this way can be contrasted with reflections on the role of mindfulness in relation to memory in some later Buddhist exegetical traditions. Cox (1992/1993: 83) explains that, according to strands of Sarvāstivāda exegetical thought,

> mindfulness functions to cause the nonloss (*asampramoṣa*) of the object, and the fixing and noting (*abhilapana*) by the mind of the object ... there is some evidence to indicate that such a definition of mindfulness refers explicitly to the ordinary psychological event of recollection ... [in that] mindfulness performs the functions of retention, noting or fixing, and stabilizing that are requisite for recollection.

On the above reasoning, mindfulness becomes indispensable for memory. According to Cox (1992/1993: 84f), from the viewpoint of an exegete in a Sarvāstivāda scholastic tradition,

> in the absence of this activity of mindfulness, which fixes or notes the present object in each and every moment, subsequent recollection would be impossible ... [thus mindfulness] operates on present objects in each and every moment; it is this present functioning of fixing or noting that enables the subsequent event of recollection.

Once mindfulness had become invested with such a function, it unavoidably came to be considered a quality present in every state of mind. Only such continuous presence throughout could ensure that any past state of mind could in principle be recollected later. This differs from the early Buddhist notion of mindfulness, which does not connote a quality present in any state of mind.

Drawing such a distinction does not imply that the Sarvāstivādins somehow got it wrong, but only clarifies that the idea that mindfulness is indispensable for memory involves an understanding of mindfulness that differs from the early Buddhist position on the matter. In fact, understanding how the relationship to memory impacts mindfulness practice has been a subject of continuous discussion. For a proper appreciation of this topic, there is a need to distinguish clearly between the different constructs of mindfulness that have arisen throughout the history of Buddhism.

The early Buddhist notion of mindfulness does not equal memory, be it of the episodic, working, or semantic type.[6] Whereas recollection of past lives involves the intentional recalling of memories of past events, memories can also arise in the form of distractions during meditation and in such a case involve a loss of mindfulness, as already mentioned above. Similarly, one might be doing a daily chore in autopilot mode or carrying on a conversation quite absent-mindedly, which would be examples that involve working and semantic memory but take place without mindfulness being present. In sum, although early Buddhist mindfulness has indeed an important relationship to memory, at the same time it is not simply the same as memory.

Mindfulness being part of a recollection of past events somehow needs to be bridged with the general emphasis in the cultivation of the four establishments of mindfulness on attending to the present moment. This could be achieved by considering an enhanced mental presence to be characteristic of mindfulness.[7] Such "attentive" mental presence through mindfulness has a natural relationship to the present moment, but can also be exercised when trying to recall something that happened earlier. The attentiveness of mental presence would also serve to distinguish intentional recall of the past from distractions during meditation that involve memories, as the latter arise when the mental presence has been lost.

---

6 The present summary is based on more detailed discussions of the memory nuance of mindfulness in Anālayo 2003b: 46–49, 2013b: 30–36, 2016a: 1273–1275, 2017c: 26–34, 2018c, 2018d, 2018h, 2018i: 3–6 and 173f, and 2019d.

7 For a discussion of the emphasis on the present moment evident in the instructions on *satipaṭṭhāna* meditation see Anālayo 2019d.

THE FUNCTION OF RECOLLECTION (MĀ 202)

Of relevance to the role played by mindfulness in the actual event of recollection are also descriptions of the practice and benefits of recollecting the Buddha or his teaching. In what follows, I will take up several passages related to this topic. Recollection of the Buddha is one of six types of recollection regularly recommended in the early discourses. The six recollections take the following themes:

- the Buddha,
- the teaching (Dharma) of the Buddha,
- the community of his noble disciples,
- one's own accomplishment in morality,
- one's own accomplishment in generosity,
- one's own accomplishment in qualities similar to those of celestial beings.

The passage below outlines the first of these six, recollection of the Buddha, who is here referred to with the epithet "Tathāgata":[8]

> One mindfully recollects the Tathāgata: "That Blessed One, the Tathāgata, is free from attachment, fully awakened, accomplished in knowledge and conduct, a Well-gone One, a knower of the world, an unsurpassable person, a leader on the path of Dharma,[9] a teacher of celestials and human beings, called a Buddha, an Exalted One."
>
> One who has mindfully recollected the Tathāgata in this way will in turn gain the ceasing of any bad inclination, and will also

8 MĀ 202 at T I 771a26 to 771b1, parallel to AN 3.70 at AN I 207,5 (translated by Bodhi 2012: 295); see also T 87 at T I 911b14. On the term *tathāgata* see also Anālayo 2017h.

9 The counterpart to the two expressions "unsurpassable person" and "leader on the path of Dharma" in AN 3.70 is the single expression "unsurpassed trainer of persons to be tamed", *anuttaro purisadammasārathi*. Nattier 2003: 227 explains that the Chinese translation is based on taking the Indic counterparts to the Pāli terms *anuttaro* and *purisa* as a separate title. The remainder of the compound became a second title of the Buddha, with a change of *damma* to become *dhamma*. As a result, the qualification "to be tamed", *damma*, became "the Dharma", and the whole title was then understood to convey the sense that the Buddha was a leader or charioteer, *sārathi*, in relation to the Dharma.

gain the ceasing of any defiled, bad, and unwholesome mental state.

In agreement with its Pāli parallel, the *Madhyama-āgama* discourse continues by depicting similar benefits to be gained by recollecting the Dharma, the community, one's own morality, and celestial beings (thus not explicitly covering the topic of generosity).[10] The Pāli version additionally mentions the arousing of gladness in the mind as a beneficial effect of such recollection.

The expression translated in the above extract as "mindfully recollecting" combines two Chinese characters, one of which stands for recollection and the other for mindfulness. This conveniently exemplifies the close interrelation between the two. Their combination could perhaps be captured with the expression "keeping in mind" (or even "holding in mind") as a key aspect of recollection. In this way the impression could be avoided that such recollection is invariably concerned only with what is past. In fact, as becomes evident in a passage to be taken up below (p. 23), instances in the discourses where someone is reminded of the Buddha are not limited to remembering something from the past.

The same holds in general, as the practice of recollecting the Buddha does not necessarily involve remembrance of something that happened in the past. The description in the passage above is much rather about bringing to mind certain qualities of the Buddha. Its function is also related to the present, as the inspiration to be gained from bringing such qualities to mind is meant to overcome unwholesome mental conditions that have manifested or might manifest now.

Harrison (1992/1993: 228) explains that

> if we look at the traditional subjects of *anusmṛti* [recollection], we can see quite clearly that personal recollection of past experience is not involved ... we are dealing with a "calling to mind" rather than recollection in the strict sense, which, as far as *buddhānusmṛti*

10 For the case of contemplating one's own morality see Anālayo 2017f: 21.

[recollection of the Buddha] is concerned, would clearly have been impossible within a generation of Gautama's death.

RECOLLECTION AND MINDFULNESS (SĀ 930)

A practical modality of recollection comes to the fore in a passage in which a disciple of the Buddha describes his experience when, after having paid a visit to the Buddha, he has to return home:[11]

> Often I have encounters with mad elephants, mad people, and mad chariots. I become afraid for myself and concerned whether, with all these mad ones, I am encountering life or encountering death, and I forget to be mindful of the Buddha, mindful of the Dharma, and mindful of the monastic community.

The Pāli parallel similarly uses just the term "mindfulness" to refer to this disciple's recollection of the Buddha, the Dharma, and the community.[12] In a traditional context, such recollection usually involves the recitation of formulaic phrases.[13] However, such recitation is not mentioned in the present passage.

The import of the passage translated above appears to be that he was so worried about his present predicament that he was no longer able to keep in mind the Buddha, etc. In other words, fear here apparently overwhelmed the ability to relate mentally to these three objects of inspiration. This supports the suggestion made above that the memory dimension of recollection could perhaps be captured with the idea of "keeping in mind". Such keeping in mind can of course take the form of remembering something from the past or else employing formulaic phrases memorized earlier. At the same time, however, it can also involve simply maintaining an object in the range of one's awareness.

---

11 SĀ 930 at T II 237b25 to 237b26, parallel to SN 55.21 at SN V 369,13 (translated by Bodhi 2000: 1808), SĀ² 155 at T II 432b17, and EĀ 41.1 at T II 744a8 (which only mentions his fear, without referring to mindfulness or recollection).

12 The same is the case for SĀ² 155 at T II 432b19.

13 See Anālayo 2017f: 231.

RECOLLECTION COUNTERS FEAR (SĀ 981)

Whereas the previous discourse depicted a situation in which the arising of fear led to a loss of the ability to keep in mind the Buddha, etc., the passage below clarifies that the very presence of fear in the mind can in turn be countered by the practice of recollection:[14]

> At the time of being afraid, being so scared that the hairs stand on end, one should be mindful of the topic of the Tathāgata, the topic of the Dharma, and the topic of the monastic community.

The Pāli parallel provides the full formula for recollection of each of these topics. The present instance thereby complements the theme of the previous passage, according to which a fearful situation can cause loss of mindfulness of the Buddha, etc. Read in conjunction with the present discourse, the remedy is then simply to make an effort to re-establish one's mindful recollection of the Buddha, etc. In other words, the very experience of a loss of mindfulness due to external challenges that provoke fear can, on being recognized, become an opportunity to return to the presence of mindfulness and thereby avoid being overwhelmed by fear. This in turn points to a "protective" dimension of mindfulness, which in the present case takes the form of recollection.

MINDFUL ASCENT TO A HIGHER HEAVEN (DĀ 14)

The uplifting potential of mindfulness, when cultivated as a form of recollection of the teachings, the Dharma, can even result in ascending to a higher heavenly realm. The relevant episode, found in the *Sakkapañha-sutta* and its parallels, describes a lay woman who had been reborn in a higher heavenly realm than

---

14 SĀ 981 at T II 255a27 to 255a28, parallel to SN 11.3 at SN I 219,27 (translated by Bodhi 2000: 319), Sanskrit fragments, Waldschmidt 1932: 48 and 1959/1967: 379 (see also Sander 1987: 136), SHT XI 4496, Wille 2012: 90, Or. 15003/171, Wille 2006: 118, Or. 15004/79+80, Wille 2009: 92, Or. 15007/288, Wille 2015: 83, Or. 15009/352, Kudo 2015: 234, Or. 15009/536, Nagashima 2015: 368, a Tibetan parallel, Skilling 1994: 292, and EĀ 24.1 at T II 615a18.

the three Buddhist monastics whom she had supported during her human life. Realizing where the monastics had been reborn, she scolded them. On hearing her rebuke, two of the former Buddhist monastics recollected the teachings they had earlier received and by putting these into practice were able to ascend to a higher heavenly realm. The relevant line in the Chinese *Dīrgha-āgama* version indicates:[15]

> The two men strove with energy, giving attention to the teachings of the Tathāgata.

The text continues by indicating that their striving was aimed at removing affectionate attachment and contemplating sensual pleasures as unattractive. A verse in the Pāli parallel similarly describes their dispassion on seeing the disadvantages of sensuality, which here is based on effort and "recollecting" the teachings of Gotama.[16] Another parallel in the *Madhyama-āgama* speaks also of "recollecting" the teachings and the monastic discipline (taught) by Gotama.[17] The same holds for a Sanskrit fragment, which parallels a reference to such recollection found a little later in the Pāli version.[18]

At an earlier point, the prose of the *Sakkapañha-sutta* speaks of these two as just regaining their "mindfulness".[19] Another two Chinese parallels use the term "mindfulness" in their description of what the earlier-mentioned versions consider to be a form of recollection.[20]

The terminological variations that emerge in this way point again to the close relationship between mindfulness and recollection, already evident from the passages surveyed earlier. This is the case to such a degree that in the *Sakkapañha-sutta* the two terms can be used alternatively to describe what is

---

15 DĀ 14 at T I 63c25; the Chinese characters, used here to convey the sense "giving attention", often serve to render *manasikāra*.

16 DN 21 at DN II 274,1: *anussarā gotamasāsanāni* (translated by Walshe 1987: 327).

17 MĀ 134 at T I 634c8.

18 SHT V 1421 V3, Sander and Waldschmidt 1985: 252: *padānusāriṇau*, parallel to DN 21 at DN II 275,3: *sambodhi-pathānusārino*.

19 DN 21 at DN II 272,14: *satiṃ paṭilabhiṃsu*.

20 T 15 at T I 247c23 and T 203 at T IV 477a9.

basically the same mental event. Here mindfulness and memory in combination make the two monastics realize the contrast between their present situation and the teachings they earlier followed, as a result of which they are sufficiently stirred to let go of attachment to sensuality and are able to ascend to a higher heavenly realm.

FALLING ASLEEP WITH MINDFULNESS OF THE BUDDHA (SĀ 592)

Mindfulness directed to the Buddha could also be cultivated when falling asleep. The narrative setting of the relevant discourse describes a householder who had only heard about the Buddha but not yet met him. In anticipation of meeting him the next day, he went to sleep:[21]

> Then, in that night, the householder Anāthapiṇḍika directed his mind to be mindful of the Buddha and because of that was able to fall asleep.

The Pāli version similarly describes that he went to sleep with his "mindfulness" directed towards the Buddha. Both versions report that he was so eager to meet the Buddha that he arose far earlier than needed. In this way, just having heard about the Buddha had been sufficient for arousing deep inspiration that then led to cultivating mindfulness of the object of such inspiration.

The case of Anāthapiṇḍika is of interest as he had as yet only heard about the Buddha. Whereas the two monastics able to ascend to a higher heavenly realm, mentioned in the previous passage, might have met the Buddha personally when hearing the teachings which they later remembered, so far Anāthapiṇḍika had not met the Buddha. Keenly anticipating his future meeting with the Buddha, he even got up too early. In his case, being mindful of the Buddha was not just related to

---

21 SĀ 592 at T II 157c12 to 157c13, parallel to SN 10.8 at SN I 211,4 (translated by Bodhi 2000: 311); another parallel, SĀ² 186 at T II 440b24, describes him paying attention to the Blessed One.

recalling a personal encounter with him. He was not so much "remembering" the Buddha, whom he was rather "keeping in mind".

MINDFULNESS AND BEING REMINDED OF THE BUDDHA (DĀ 28)

Another modality of being mindful of the Buddha emerges in a description of someone who witnesses other practitioners giving various conflicting answers to a question about the cessation of perception. This person then is reminded of the Buddha:[22]

> For this reason, mindfulness arose in me; mindfulness of the recluse Gotama who certainly knows this matter.[23]

The Pāli parallel also refers to the arising of mindfulness.[24] Another similar instance can be found in a discourse in the *Madhyama-āgama* and its *Majjhima-nikāya* parallel. Both versions describe a king who sees a secluded place suitable for meditation. The vision brings the Buddha to his mind. To describe this, both versions use the term "mindfulness", which the *Madhyama-āgama* combines with a character that conveys the sense of "remembering".[25] A parallel in the *Ekottarika-āgama*, however, only uses this character and thus does not refer to mindfulness.[26]

These two instances of being reminded of the Buddha, one due to a discussion and the other due to seeing a secluded place, further help to bridge a recalling of something from the past with mindfulness of the present moment. In the first case, the speaker in fact hopes that subsequently he might get an

22 DĀ 28 at T I 110a12 to 110a13, parallel to DN 9 at DN I 180,24: *bhagavantaṃ yeva ārabbha sati udapādi*, translated by Walshe 1987: 160 as "I thought of the Lord"; a more literal translation would be "mindfulness arose concerning the Blessed One".

23 The translation "certainly" is based on adopting a variant reading.

24 The same is not the case for the corresponding passage in a Sanskrit fragment parallel, Melzer 2006: 252.

25 MĀ 213 at T I 795b23 and MN 89 at MN II 118,19: *bhagavantaṃ yeva ārabbha sati udapādi* (translated by Ñāṇamoli 1995/2005: 728); see also Anālayo 2011: 511.

26 EĀ 38.10 at T II 724c5.

explanation of the matter from the Buddha. In the other passage, the king associates secluded places with the Buddha's lifestyle and this then motivates him to pay a visit to the Buddha. In both cases, even though these are clear instances of being "reminded" of the Buddha as someone both had met earlier, such reminding is not confined to a recollection of things past.

Already Rhys Davids and Rhys Davids (1910: 322), responsible for popularizing the translation "mindfulness" for *sati*, pointed out that a rendition of this term as just a form of memory would be an "inadequate and misleading translation", although *sati* has of course some specific functions related to recall. Commenting on the same term a hundred years later, Bhikkhu Bodhi (2011: 22) concurs that in its early Buddhist usage

> *sati* no longer means memory ... it would be a fundamental mistake to insist on reading the old meaning of memory into the new context.

As part of an exploration of mindfulness in classical Yogācāra, Griffith (1992/1993: 111) reasons that *smṛti*

> has by itself nothing essentially to do with the remembering of some past object of cognition; it can operate just as well in the present as in the past, and it is perhaps more natural to take its primary sense as having a present reference. The fact that *smṛti* notes ... objects, however, makes possible their preservation as objects of consciousness ... and thus explains the extension of the term to cover at least some of the same semantic ground as the English word *memory* and its cognates. In other words, I suggest that the basic meaning of *smṛti* and derivatives in Buddhist technical discourse – basic in the sense that this meaning is both temporally and logically prior to other meanings – has to do with observation and attention, not with awareness of past objects.

In the context of a survey of relevant material from the tradition of the Great Perfection, Kapstein (1992/1993: 249) concludes that

> it appears not at all strange that memory and mindfulness have often been gathered together under a single lexical head ...

> although the normal temporal reference of memory to the past is sometimes not a feature of the codesignated phenomena in question.

Based on the clarification that the memory dimension of mindfulness does not imply that the activity described must invariably concern the past, I now turn to passages where some versions have a description that relates mindfulness to recollecting the past, but the same is not found in the respective parallels.

MINDFULLY COLLECTING ONESELF (DĀ 10)

One of the passages relating mindfulness to recollecting the past occurs in the context of a listing of ten beneficial qualities in a *Dīrgha-āgama* discourse and its Pāli parallel. One of these qualities involves mindfulness in the following form:[27]

> One constantly collects oneself with mindfulness, without having another perception, recollecting one's former wholesome conduct.

The Pāli parallel instead describes the ability to remember what was done or said long ago. In the listing of beneficial qualities in both versions, mindfulness is preceded by energy (in the sense of making an effort) and followed by wisdom, two qualities of decisive importance for progress on the path. In this context, the idea of recollecting one's former wholesome conduct is not entirely clear, but could perhaps be taken as a more specific modality of what the Pāli version describes as remembering what was done long ago. In spite of differing in details, both versions clearly agree in relating mindfulness to the ability to remember something from the past. Such an ability features repeatedly in definitions of mindfulness in other Pāli discourses, and in what follows I will explore such occurrences from a comparative perspective.

27 DĀ 10 at T I 57a16, parallel to DN 34 at DN III 290,14 (given in abbreviation; translated by Walshe 1987: 520).

THE PATH IS FOR ONE WHO IS MINDFUL (DĀ 10 AND MĀ 74)

Another relevant instance occurs in the context of an enumeration of eight thoughts of a "great person" (*mahāpurisa*), a term that in the ancient Indian setting carried connotations of being a hero or a very exceptional person. These eight thoughts enshrine foundational principles of the path to liberation. One of these thoughts relates to mindfulness. A *Dīrgha-āgama* version of these eight thoughts presents the matter in this way:[28]

> One on the path should collect mindfulness; being often forgetful is not the path.

The *Dīgha-nikāya* parallel to this discourse makes basically the same point by stating that this teaching is for one who establishes mindfulness, not for one who has lost mindfulness.[29]

The original occasion for the delivery of this particular teaching on eight thoughts of a great person is recorded in a discourse in the *Madhyama-āgama* and its *Aṅguttara-nikāya* parallel. These offer additional information on the type of mindfulness that is required. According to the *Madhyama-āgama* account, the reference is to the four establishments of mindfulness:[30]

> How is the path to be attained through right mindfulness, not wrong mindfulness? That is, a monastic contemplates the body as a body internally ... contemplates feeling tones internally ... the mind ... dharmas as dharmas.[31] This is reckoned to be attaining the path through right mindfulness, not wrong mindfulness.

A similar reference can be found in another parallel extant in Chinese.[32] The *Aṅguttara-nikāya* parallel differs, as it instead

28 DĀ 10 at T I 55c24 to 55c25.
29 DN 34 at DN III 287,21 (translated by Walshe 1987: 518).
30 MĀ 74 at T I 541c26 to 541c28.
31 The abbreviation in the original implies that the same mode of contemplation is to be practised externally as well.
32 T 46 at T I 836a28; this reference actually expounds on the quality of concentration, which in MĀ 74 and AN 8.30 comes next. The previous quality in T 46 lists the four absorptions, which are mentioned in the

mentions the ability to remember mindfully what was done or said long ago.[33]

When examined in its context, it is noteworthy that the preceding and following qualities of being energetic and concentrated are described in the *Madhyama-āgama* and *Aṅguttara-nikāya* discourses in the standard way by listing the four types of effort and the four absorptions. On following this precedent, it would be more natural for their description of mindfulness to take up the four establishments of mindfulness.

From the viewpoint of the path to liberation, the cultivation of the establishments of mindfulness has a major contribution to offer, highlighted similarly in the *Satipaṭṭhāna-sutta* and its Chinese *Āgama* parallels.[34] In contrast, remembering what one did or said long ago does not necessarily offer a comparable contribution and would therefore not really merit being one of eight foundational principles of the path to liberation. In other words, the original point of the reference to mindfulness, as part of the eight thoughts of a great person, would more probably have been the cultivation of the four establishments of mindfulness as an indispensable practice for attaining the path.

This in turn suggests that the reference in the *Aṅguttara-nikāya* discourse to recalling the past could be the result of a later change. This suggestion finds further support in the circumstance that the *Dīrgha-āgama* and *Dīgha-nikāya* versions of the eight thoughts of a great person also do not mention remembering what was done or said long ago. Perhaps an increasing concern with memory and its relationship to mindfulness in later exegesis influenced the oral transmission of the discourse and led to an introduction of the ability to remember the distant past in the *Aṅguttara-nikāya* discourse.

---

two parallels under the heading of concentration. This makes it safe to assume that the explanations of these two qualities have been accidentally exchanged and that the reference in T 46 to the four establishments of mindfulness corresponds to the presentation in MĀ 74. Another parallel, EĀ 42.6 at T II 754b16, provides a detailed exposition only of the quality of being energetic, not of the others.

33 AN 8.30 at AN IV 234,16 (translated by Bodhi 2012: 1164).

34 See Anālayo 2013b: 8–12.

MINDFULNESS AND RECOLLECTING TEACHINGS (DĀ 2)

The *Dīrgha-āgama* parallel to the *Mahāparinibbāna-sutta* refers to mindfulness, in the context of a list of altogether seven states that prevent spiritual decline, in the following way:[35]

> What one has formerly learned, one mindfully recollects it without loss.

The corresponding listing of seven qualities in the Pāli parallel just refers to establishing mindfulness, without any reference to what one has formerly learned.[36] The same holds for a Sanskrit fragment parallel.[37] Three Chinese parallels instead refer to training in reciting, to reciting without remiss, and to delighting in hearing the teachings.[38]

In conjunction with the passage just examined above, the variations found in the present case make it possible that in the course of oral transmission brief references to mindfulness might at times have been supplemented with more detailed indications, by adding a description of remembering something from the past or even training in recitation. Such a type of supplementation would not be uncommon in oral transmission and a fairly natural occurrence. On consulting parallel versions, transmitted by different reciter lineages, such potential supplementations can be detected. The possibility of such an occurrence during oral transmission is of further relevance for examining definitions of mindfulness as a spiritual faculty.

THE FACULTY OF MINDFULNESS (SĀ 646 AND SĀ 647)

The discourses regularly mention five mental qualities designated as spiritual "faculties" (at times also called

35 DĀ 2 at T I 11c19.

36 DN 16 at DN II 79,1: *upaṭṭhitasatī bhavissanti*, "they will be with mindfulness established" (also translated in Walshe 1987: 233).

37 Waldschmidt 1951: 126.

38 T 5 at T I 161a22, T 6 at T I 176c11, and T 7 at T I 194a21 (the identification of these passages as "parallels" comes with some degree of uncertainty, as other items in the respective listings differ).

"powers"), which support progress on the path to liberation.[39] These comprise confidence (or "faith"), energy (in the sense of making an effort), mindfulness, concentration, and wisdom.[40] The faculty of mindfulness receives the following definition in a discourse in the *Saṃyukta-āgama*:[41]

> The faculty of mindfulness should be understood to be the four establishments of mindfulness.

The Pāli version makes the same basic point, stating that the faculty of mindfulness is to be seen in the four *satipaṭṭhānas*.[42] The next discourse in the *Saṃyukta-āgama* provides the same correlation in more detail:[43]

> What is the faculty of mindfulness? Suppose a monastic dwells [mindfully] contemplating the body [in relation to] the body internally, with ⟨diligent⟩ effort,[44] right knowing, and right mindfulness, overcoming greed and discontent in the world ... the body externally ... the body internally and externally ... feeling tones ... the mind ... dwells mindfully contemplating dharmas [in relation to] dharmas *should also be recited like this*. This is called the faculty of mindfulness.

In this case, however, the Pāli parallel rather defines the faculty of mindfulness in terms of remembering what was done or said long ago.[45] The next discourse in the Pāli *Saṃyutta-nikāya* then combines both definitions, perhaps the result of a conflation that occurred during oral transmission.[46] This is followed by another *Saṃyutta-nikāya* discourse which defines the faculty

---

39 See in more detail Gethin 1992: 104–145.

40 A variant listing in verse form in AN 6.54 at AN III 373,20 (translated by Bodhi 2012: 932) refers to the last two of the five faculties as "tranquillity" and "insight"; the parallel MĀ 130 at T I 620a28 has "right concentration" and "right insight".

41 SĀ 646 at T II 182b20.

42 SN 48.8 at SN V 196,16 (translated by Bodhi 2000: 1670).

43 SĀ 647 at T II 182c4 to 182c7.

44 The translation "diligent" is based on emending the original, in line with the formulation found elsewhere in the *Saṃyukta-āgama* for this type of description.

45 SN 48.9 at SN V 197,10 (translated by Bodhi 2000: 1671).

46 SN 48.10 at SN V 198,16 (translated by Bodhi 2000: 1672).

of mindfulness by referring to the four establishments of mindfulness.[47]

Definitions of the faculty of mindfulness in another two discourses in the *Saṃyukta-āgama* likewise equate it with the four establishments of mindfulness.[48] In this way, the *Saṃyukta-āgama* never defines the faculty of mindfulness in terms of remembering what was done or said long ago.[49]

The same situation repeats itself with the five powers (*bala*), which are basically the same five mental qualities under a different name. *Saṃyukta-āgama* discourses define the power of mindfulness consistently in terms of the four establishments of mindfulness.[50] Pāli discourses, found in the *Aṅguttara-nikāya*, instead vary between this definition and the definition by way of remembering the past.[51]

In this way, the elevation of the ability to remember what was done or said long ago to the position of a spiritual faculty or power, found in some Pāli discourses, is not corroborated by their *Saṃyukta-āgama* parallels. In evaluating this significant difference, the question would be whether the memory nuance of mindfulness plays a large enough role to become one of the

---

47 SN 48.11 at SN V 200,1 (translated by Bodhi 2000: 1673).

48 SĀ 655 at T II 183b29 and SĀ 658 at T II 184a4. In addition to these, a definition of the faculty of mindfulness can be found in SĀ 659 at T II 184a14, which speaks of the mindfulness of the Tathāgata's first arousal of an awakened mind, thereby employing a phrase that, with some slight variation, is applied to each of the five faculties. A possible parallel in SN 48.50 at SN V 225,23 (translated by Bodhi 2000: 1694) instead presents the other faculties as being based on the confidence one has gained in the Tathāgata and his teaching, hence here the faculty of mindfulness is just the outcome of the energy that has been aroused through such confidence. SN 48.50 then defines such mindfulness in terms of remembering what was done or said long ago, which has no counterpart in SĀ 659.

49 See also Anālayo 2018h: 1988.

50 SĀ 675 at T II 185c12, SĀ 691 at T II 188a27, and SĀ 698 at T II 188c14; the last two cover a set of seven powers, which add a sense of shame and conscience to the five powers that correspond to the five spiritual faculties.

51 AN 5.15 at AN III 12,7 (translated by Bodhi 2012: 637) refers to the four establishments of mindfulness, whereas AN 5.14 at AN III 11,8 (translated by Bodhi 2012: 637) and AN 7.4 at AN IV 4,9 (this involves the same set of seven powers as mentioned in the previous footnote; translated by Bodhi 2012: 999) mention the ability to remember the distant past.

faculties or powers that are to be cultivated for progress towards awakening. For such progress, the four establishments of mindfulness clearly play a prominent role, and their cultivation is predominantly concerned with the present moment rather than with what happened long ago. This can be seen through a closer survey of the exercises common to the *Satipaṭṭhāna-sutta* and its parallels, which shows that the cultivation of the four *satipaṭṭhāna*s comes with a clear emphasis on staying in the present moment, mindful of what is taking place here and now.[52]

A relationship between progress towards awakening and the ability to remember what happened long ago is less self-evident.[53] Of course, a cultivation of the four establishments of mindfulness relies to some degree on a prior acquaintance with the relevant instructions, hence one might suppose that the memory connotation reflects the need to allow for the input provided by the instructions.[54] Such input is indeed crucial for insight meditation to issue in liberation and I will come back to this topic below, in relation to the simile of the gatekeeper (see p. 38).

From the viewpoint of the definition of the faculty or power of mindfulness in some Pāli discourses, however, it needs to

---

52 See also Anālayo 2017c: 34, 2018c, 2018d, and in particular 2019d.

53 Ditrich 2016: 14f argues that "the predominant occurrences of *sati* in meditation contexts reflect the main ... focus on the soteriological goals to be achieved through ethical and meditative training", which "is not much concerned with mundane events and their remembrance. Although the conditions for recollective memory and mindful awareness are linked within the semantic range of *sati* ... *sati* occurs in the Pāli Canon primarily as a meditational term."

54 Ṭhānissaro 2012: 1 and 13 argues that right mindfulness is "a faculty of active memory, adept at calling to mind and keeping in mind instructions and intentions that will be useful on the path", hence mindfulness, "as a factor in the path to the end of suffering and distress, brings memories from the past to bear on ... events and actions in the present". In the same vein, Levman 2017: 145 proposes that "*sati* is that special faculty of memory ... which bears in mind the Buddha's teachings and their relevance to one's own personal spiritual quest." According to Levman 2018: 1044, "*sati* is recollection with wisdom, that is, recollecting the Buddha's teaching and their applicability to one's own personal sufferings and problems and reinterpreting, transforming and extinguishing them through the catalyst of the *buddhadhamma*"; for a critical reply see also Mattes 2019.

be noted that these speak of remembering "what was done or said long ago", *cirakataṃ cirabhāsitaṃ*. Had the intention been to refer to doctrinal teachings, it would have been more straightforward to mention these explicitly. Instead, the phrase in question seems to be just about memory abilities in general, stressing the fact that even what happened long ago will be recalled and not forgotten.

As far as progress on the path to awakening is concerned, defining the faculty or power of mindfulness in terms of the four establishments of mindfulness is more to the point. Given that this definition is found in both the *Saṃyutta-nikāya* and the *Saṃyukta-āgama* traditions, it seems fair to assume that the reference to memory in definitions of the faculties and powers could well be a later development.

This conclusion ties in with a suggestion made above in relation to the eight thoughts of a great person, where the Pāli version's reference to the ability to remember something from the distant past is neither supported by the Chinese parallel nor fits the context too well.

Besides the occurrences already discussed, several other discourses in the Pāli *Nikāya*s that relate mindfulness to remembering the distant past lack a parallel in the Chinese *Āgama*s.[55] It is only in relation to a simile of a gatekeeper that the Chinese *Āgama* parallel agrees with the Pāli discourse in linking mindfulness to the ability to remember what was done or said long ago. I will come back to the simile of the gatekeeper below (see p. 36).

One of these references to memory in a Pāli discourse without a parallel in the Chinese *Āgama*s occurs in the *Aṅguttara-nikāya*.[56] In this discourse the relationship between mindfulness and

55 DN 33 at DN III 268,11 (translated by Walshe 1987: 508), in which case the corresponding set of qualities is not found in DĀ 9; DN 34 at DN III 286,2 (translated by Walshe 1987: 518), in which case the corresponding quality in DĀ 10 at T I 55a3 does not mention mindfulness; MN 53 at MN I 356,17 (translated by Ñāṇamoli 1995/2005: 463), of which no parallel is known; AN 10.17 at AN V 25,6, AN 10.18 at AN V 28,18, and AN 10.50 at AN V 91,12 (translated by Bodhi 2012: 1356, 1359, and 1401), of which no parallels are known.

56 AN 4.35 at AN II 35,23 (translated by Bodhi 2012: 423).

remembering the past is part of a brahmin's proposition of the qualities that make up a great person. The discourse continues with the Buddha explicitly stating that he neither approves nor disapproves. Then he presents his definition of a great person, a definition that does not refer to the ability to remember the past.

In this discourse, the relationship between mindfulness and remembering the distant past is presented as a brahminical notion. In contrast, according to a passage to be taken up below (see p. 86) the four establishments of mindfulness should be considered an outcome of the Buddha's own distinct realization of the potential of mindfulness. Moreover, according to another passage to be studied in a subsequent chapter, from an early Buddhist perspective the way to become a great person is to cultivate *satipaṭṭhāna* until the mind is liberated from all defilements (see below p. 106). These passages support the impression that the four establishments of mindfulness are a more natural fit for definitions of the faculties and powers than the ability to recall what happened in the distant past.

MINDFULNESS AS AN AWAKENING FACTOR (SĀ 711)

Nevertheless, the relationship of mindfulness to remembering the past is reflected in a different context in the *Saṃyukta-āgama*. This context concerns mindfulness as the first of the seven factors of awakening. These seven are mindfulness, investigation-of-dharmas, energy, joy, tranquillity, concentration, and equipoise. The relevant discourse in the *Saṃyukta-āgama* describes the first of these, the awakening factor of mindfulness, as follows:[57]

> Brahmin, suppose one has singularly superior mindfulness, is decidedly accomplished in it, capable of mindfully recollecting according to what has been done a long time ago and what has been said a long time ago. At that time, one arouses the mindfulness awakening factor and, having cultivated the

57 SĀ 711 at T II 190c12 to 190c15, parallel to SN 46.56 at SN V 128,1 (translated by Bodhi 2000: 1616).

> mindfulness awakening factor, the mindfulness awakening factor becomes fulfilled.

In this case, the Pāli version does not refer to remembering the past. Instead, it describes the cultivation of mindfulness in dependence on seclusion, dispassion, and cessation, ripening in letting go.

As with the passages involving the faculties and powers, the definition by way of memory seems less straightforward from the perspective of progress towards awakening. From that viewpoint, the description of the cultivation of mindfulness in the form found in the Pāli version appears more meaningful. In other words, here, too, the topic of memory could be a later intrusion. The only difference from the case of the faculties and powers is that in the present instance it would be the Pāli version which, if the above reasoning should be correct, does not reflect such apparent intrusion.

MINDFULNESS IN THE NOBLE EIGHTFOLD PATH (MĀ 31 AND SĀ 784)

Right mindfulness is the seventh factor in the noble eightfold path, which is the key framework for the cultivation of mindfulness in early Buddhist soteriology. This noble eightfold path places the practice of mindfulness on a foundation of ethical conduct and endows it with a proper sense of direction. The definition of right mindfulness in a discourse in the *Madhyama-āgama* proceeds as follows:[58]

> What is right mindfulness? That is, when a noble disciple is mindful of *dukkha* as *dukkha* ... of its arising as arising ... of its cessation as cessation, and when being mindful of the path as path; or on

58 MĀ 31 at T I 469b19 to 469b24, parallel to MN 141 at MN III 252,5 (translated by Ñāṇamoli 1995/2005: 1100), T 32 at T I 816c7, and EĀ 27.1 at T II 643b24 (translated by Anālayo 2016b: 241), which just mentions right mindfulness without providing any further details. Such a brief reference might have been the common starting point of the parallel versions, which in the course of oral transmission then fleshed out this reference in different ways.

> contemplating one's former deeds; or on training to be mindful of formations; or on seeing the disadvantage in formations; or on seeing Nirvāṇa as peace; or when being free from attachment and mindfully contemplating the well liberated mind – herein the mind's being adapted to mindfulness, its turning away from being dissociated from mindfulness, its being with mindfulness that is pervasive, mindfulness that recollects and again recollects with a straight mind,[59] the mind being appropriately without forgetfulness: this is called right mindfulness.

The Pāli parallel instead just lists the four establishments of mindfulness. The presentation in the above passage reflects the impact of emerging Abhidharma thought, where interest proceeds from the practical role of mindfulness as a path factor to an analysis of what mental quality or set of mental factors is present when the path factor is being cultivated.[60]

The same tendency at work can be seen in a definition of the implications of each factor of the noble eightfold path in a discourse in the *Saṃyukta-āgama*. Whereas the Pāli parallel mentions the four establishments of mindfulness when defining right mindfulness, the *Saṃyukta-āgama* discourse offers the following perspective on it:[61]

> What is right mindfulness? It is reckoned to be mindfulness that is concordant, mindfulness that is not lost and not in vain.

Regarding the apparent tendency to shift from concern with the practice of mindfulness to describing the quality of mindfulness in terms of its mental properties, Cox (1992/1993: 78) explains:

---

59 The translation "straight" is based on adopting a variant.

60 See also Anālayo 2011: 807 and 2014: 95f.

61 SĀ 784 at T II 203a15 (the translation assumes that the three qualifications render equivalents to what in Pāli are *anuloma*, *muṭṭha*, and *tuccha*), parallel to SN 45.8 at SN V 9,28 (translated by Bodhi 2000: 1529) and T 112 at T II 505b10. SĀ 784 and T 112 combine what in the *Saṃyutta-nikāya* are two discourses, as their exposition of each path factor parallels SN 45.8, but their introductory exposition rather parallels SN 45.21 at SN V 17,23 (translated by Bodhi 2000: 1535). A similar definition of right mindfulness can be found in SĀ 785 at T II 203c28 and 204a3; on the significance of this mode of presentation for appreciating the evolution of Abhidharma thought see in more detail Anālayo 2014: 136–140.

> Psychological description becomes the norm in Abhidharma definitions of the praxis-related modes of mindfulness and largely displaces the previously cited definitions of mindfulness in terms of the four applications [*satipaṭṭhāna*].

The same influence of emerging Abhidharma thought, evident in the two passages just surveyed, might also have been responsible for an increasing tendency in descriptions of mindfulness to shift from its four establishments to a focus on the mental quality of remembering what happened a long time ago, in line with a general interest in the topic of memory, evident in Abhidharma texts.

THE GATEKEEPER OF MINDFULNESS (MĀ 3 AND SĀ 1175)

With the next passage I turn to a simile that describes a gatekeeper in a border town. A version of this simile, found in a *Madhyama-āgama* discourse and its *Aṅguttara-nikāya* parallel, stands out for being an instance where a Pāli discourse and its Chinese *Āgama* parallel agree in relating mindfulness to the ability to remember what was done or said long ago. The gatekeeper image recurs also elsewhere in a slightly different form, which I will take up next.

The simile in the *Madhyama-āgama* discourse and its *Aṅguttara-nikāya* parallel describes several endowments of a border town that will prevent it from being easily assailed by external enemies, one of which is having a capable gatekeeper:[62]

> It is just like a high-ranking officer who has been appointed as the gatekeeper in a border town of the king, one who is sharp-witted and wise in making decisions, brave and resolute, of excellent counsel, who allows the good to enter and arrests the bad, for the sake of peace within and to control outside enemies.

---

62 MĀ 3 at T I 423c14 to 423c19, parallel to AN 7.63 at AN IV 110,28 (translated by Bodhi 2012: 1078). Another parallel, EĀ 39.4 at T II 730b5, does not mention a gatekeeper. A gatekeeper is mentioned in yet another parallel found in an *Udāna* collection, T 212 at T IV 652c9.

> In the same way a noble disciple constantly practises mindfulness, is accomplished in right mindfulness, always recollecting without loss what has been practised long ago and what has been heard long ago. This is reckoned to be a noble disciple's attaining of mindfulness, a high-ranking officer, as a gatekeeper, to remove what is bad and unwholesome and to develop wholesome states.

The description of the gatekeeper in the Pāli version is closely similar. A difference is that it speaks simply of remembering what a long time ago was said (*bhāsita*) instead of what was heard. In this way, the formulation in the Pāli version could also refer to remembering what one earlier said oneself.[63] In contrast, the *Madhyama-āgama* version's reference to what has been "heard" could be referring to teachings. In the oral setting of ancient India, teachings were invariably heard, so much so that the quality of being learned finds expression in the qualification of someone as having "heard much".

However, the recall of such learning is usually described with more specific terms like "to retain" (*dhāreti*). To describe the role of the gatekeeper of mindfulness, the Pāli discourse rather uses the more general verb "to remember" (*sarati*). This conveys the idea of a general remembering, rather than the specific recall of teachings learned earlier.

This impression receives further support from the fact that in both versions acquaintance with the teachings finds illustration in a different aspect of the border town, which is its varied weaponry.[64] In this way, mindfulness and remembering the teachings are listed separately and compared to different aspects of the frontier town. Needless to say, they interact and support each other, just as the different endowments of the frontier town are related to each other. Yet, mindfulness and remembering the teachings are sufficiently distinct to be

---

63 See in more detail Anālayo 2019d: 579.

64 MĀ 3 at T I 423c8 and AN 7.63 at AN IV 110,4.

associated with diverse aspects of the frontier town, namely the gatekeeper and the weaponry.[65]

This relates back to a topic taken up earlier in this chapter, namely the idea that the memory connotation of mindfulness could be related to the input provided by relevant teachings (see above p. 31). This does not seem to be what the gatekeeper simile is concerned with, otherwise recall of the teachings would not have been listed separately. Instead, the imagery seems to be about the monitoring role of mindfulness in making one aware of the presence of unwholesome mental conditions, thereby furnishing the indispensable foundation for taking the appropriate action. This role requires constant vigilance, comparable to the gatekeeper's task in keeping out the bad.

The less absent-minded one is when doing or saying something, the higher in turn are the chances that one will later remember it. Understood in this way, it indeed makes sense to describe the quality of mindfulness by indicating an outcome to be expected from its cultivation, namely improving the ability to remember what one did or said even long ago.

The comparison of mindfulness to a gatekeeper at a frontier town recurs also in a *Madhyama-āgama* discourse without Pāli parallel,[66] and in a discourse in the *Saṃyukta-āgama*, where it takes the following form:[67]

> "It is just as a border-country king who has the walls of the city kept well in order, the gates with a firm foundation, and the access roads level and straight. He has placed four gatekeepers at the four city gates, all of whom are clever and wise, knowing those who come and go. In that city there are four access roads

65 See also Anālayo 2019d.

66 MĀ 69 at T I 519a15 (translated by Bingenheimer et al. 2013: 479), where the simile serves to illustrate various accomplishments of male and female monastics, one of which is having the gatekeeper of right mindfulness that enables them to abandon what is bad and cultivate what is good. The text does not spell out what form such right mindfulness takes and thus has a reference neither to the four establishments of mindfulness nor to the ability to recall things from the past.

67 SĀ 1175 at T II 315c19 to 316a5, parallel to SN 35.204 at SN IV 194,10 (translated by Bodhi 2000: 1252, given as number 245) and a Tibetan parallel, Up 6073 at D 4094 *nyu* 43a3 or Q 5595 *thu* 82b1.

towards the couch that has been prepared for the lord of the city to sit on.[68]

"Suppose from the eastern direction a messenger comes and asks the gatekeeper: 'Where is the lord of the city?' He answers: 'The lord is in the middle of the city, at the end of the four access roads, seated on a couch.' Having heard this, that messenger approaches the lord of the city. He receives an instruction and returns again by the road.

"From the southern ... western ... northern direction a messenger comes and asks the gatekeeper: 'Where is the lord of the city?' He also answers: 'In the middle of the city, at the end of the four access roads.' Having heard it, those messengers all approach the lord of the city, receive an instruction, and each of them returns to their former place."[69]

The Buddha said to the monastics: "Having spoken this simile, I will now explain its meaning. What is called 'the city' serves to exemplify the human body, made of coarse material form (*as described in the discourse with the simile of the chest of poisonous snakes*). The walls of the city that are kept well in order are reckoned to be right view. The level and straight access roads are reckoned to be the six internal sense-spheres. The four gates are reckoned to be the four establishments of consciousness.[70] The four gatekeepers are reckoned to be the four establishments of mindfulness. The lord of the city is reckoned to be the consciousness aggregate of clinging. The messengers are reckoned to be ⟨tranquillity⟩ and insight.[71] A statement that

---

68 In SN 35.204 at SN IV 194,11 the city wall has instead six gates. Up 6078 at D 4094 *nyu* 43a4 or Q 5595 *thu* 82b1 agrees with SĀ 1175 in speaking of four gates.

69 In SN 35.204 at SN IV 194,14 and in the Tibetan parallel, Up 6078 at D 4094 *nyu* 43a5 or Q 5595 *thu* 82b2, a pair of messengers approaches the gatekeeper.

70 According to SN 35.204 at SN IV 194,32, the gates (here counted as six) represent the six sense-spheres. Up 6078 at D 4094 *nyu* 43b3 or Q 5595 *thu* 83a2 agrees with SĀ 1175.

71 The translation is based on adopting an emendation suggested in the CBETA edition of the original reading "right insight"; the emendation is supported by a reference to "tranquillity" and insight found in SN 35.204 at SN IV 195,1 and in Up 6078 at D 4094 *nyu* 43b4 or Q 5595 *thu* 83a3.

> accords with truth is reckoned to be the four noble truths.[72] Again, the path of return is by way of the noble eightfold path."[73]

The Pāli parallel speaks of a single gatekeeper, which here represents mindfulness.[74] A third parallel, preserved in Tibetan translation, also has only a single gatekeeper, which according to its presentation stands for mindfulness of the body.[75]

The overall concern of the gatekeeper imagery appears to be again the function of mindfulness as the mental quality that monitors progress on the path to liberation and thereby protects one from taking the wrong route. It is through mindfulness that a practitioner of the noble eightfold path is able to recognize the correct route to be taken in the cultivation of insight and tranquillity.

Alongside some variations regarding the field of application of mindfulness, the parallels agree that the meditative practice of mindfulness corresponds to the role played by the gatekeeper. This differs from the other gatekeeper simile examined above, which relates mindfulness instead to remembering what was done or said long ago. Perhaps this reflects the somewhat different tasks of the respective gatekeepers. In the present context, the gatekeeper simply furnishes information about the correct road to be taken. This role is close to the monitoring function that mindfulness can acquire in the context of its four establishments or else in relation to the body. In the other gatekeeper simile, however, the task is to ensure peace in the town and protect its inhabitants by allowing only trustworthy people to enter the town and prevent or even arrest bad persons.

---

72 In SN 35.204 at SN IV 195,8 the message is Nirvāṇa. SN 35.204 at SN IV 195,5 additionally specifies that the place in the middle of the city represents the four elements.

73 According to SN 35.204 at SN IV 195,10, the noble eightfold path is the way by which the messengers *arrived*; Up 6078 at D 4094 *nyu* 43b5 or Q 5595 *thu* 83a4 also speaks of their path of entry. The reference to their way of return in SĀ 1175 might be due to the slightly different depiction of the messengers' task, which in SN 35.204 is to deliver a message to the lord of the city, whereas in SĀ 1175 they receive an instruction from him, which they are then perhaps expected to deliver to someone else.

74 SN 35.204 at SN IV 194,34.

75 Up 6078 at D 4094 *nyu* 43b3 or Q 5595 *thu* 83a2.

In line with the more active responsibility of the gatekeeper in this other context and the need to remember people's appearance, mindfulness relates to remembering what was done or said long go.

It is already remarkable that the Pāli discourses and their Chinese *Āgama* parallels agree only in the previously discussed instance of the gatekeeper simile in defining mindfulness as the ability to remember the distant past. Moreover, a recurrence of the motif of a gatekeeper, found in the present discourse, instead stands for the meditative cultivation of mindfulness. In this way the comparative perspective shows that the memory nuance of mindfulness, although an important dimension, is considerably less prominent than its functions related to the present moment.

From the viewpoint of practice, it also needs to be kept in mind that the relationship established in the first gatekeeper simile between mindfulness and memory concerns a mental ability of retention. It describes the results of practice, rather than how actual mindfulness practice should be undertaken. In other words, the suggestion is not that one should go on remembering what was said or done long ago. Instead, the ability to remember what was said or done long ago is a result of having cultivated mindfulness.

In sum, the memory nuance can perhaps best be taken to point to the qualities of increased attentiveness and enhanced mental presence as important dimensions of mindfulness. Being fully attentive and mentally present now, it will be easy to remember later what happened. Again, at the time of wanting to recall, full attention and mental presence will ensure remembrance. But the actual cultivation of mindfulness is not about continuously remembering things from the past. Instead, its overarching concern is with what arises in the present.

THE SLOW ARISING OF MINDFULNESS (SĀ 1173 AND MĀ 192)

The next two passages have a more distant relationship to the topic of memory. Their relevance emerges when considering another Pāli passage without a parallel; I will discuss this immediately after the two passages to be taken up now, which are found in the *Saṃyukta-āgama* and the *Madhyama-āgama* respectively.

The relevant discourse from the *Saṃyukta-āgama* describes a situation when unwholesome thoughts arise in the mind. If mindfulness is lost, such arising is not recognized right away. Yet, even though mindfulness arises only slowly, once this has happened, a quick response is possible. This finds illustration in a simile of drops of water sprinkled on hot iron:[76]

> It is just like an iron ball that is burning so that it has become very hot and a few drops of water are sprinkled on it: they immediately evaporate. In the same way, a learned noble disciple with dull faculties, on arousing mindfulness, immediately extinguishes [unwholesome thoughts] like this.

The Pāli version similarly relates the manifestation of unwholesome thoughts to an earlier loss of mindfulness, which only re-arises slowly. Once mindfulness has arisen, however, a quick response will occur, comparable to two or three drops of water falling onto a heated iron plate.

The same imagery is found in another Pāli discourse, which has a parallel in the *Madhyama-āgama*:[77]

> It is just like an iron ball or an iron ploughshare that has been heated and been on fire for a whole day. Suppose a person puts two or three drops of water on it; the drops [fall] slowly and separately and the water is in turn quickly extinguished ...
>
> It is the same way with a monastic's practice of abandoning [sensual thoughts]. After having practised abandoning, suppose there is a time when, the mind being forgetful, one is with thoughts related to sensuality and one is bound by craving and delight. One is slow in observing it, but quick in eradicating them.

76 SĀ 1173 at T II 314b10 to 314b13, parallel to SN 35.203 at SN IV 190,12 (translated by Bodhi 2000: 1250, given as number 244), and Up 6066 at D 4094 *nyu* 35b5 or Q 5595 *thu* 73a1.

77 MĀ 192 at T I 743a3 to 743a6, parallel to MN 66 at MN I 453,26 (translated by Ñāṇamoli 1995/2005: 556); see also Anālayo 2011: 366.

Although the *Madhyama-āgama* version does not explicitly mention mindfulness, it can safely be assumed to be implied, an impression supported by its explicit occurrence in the Pāli parallel.

A third occurrence of this imagery is found in a discourse in the *Aṅguttara-nikāya*, of which no parallel is known. Since the passage in question is of considerable significance for understanding a development in the Theravāda understanding of mindfulness, I will take it up in detail, on the understanding that this is meant to show the starting point of a later development and not a reflection of the early Buddhist conception of mindfulness.

The passage in question describes someone who has memorized the teachings of the Buddha, later passes away with a loss of mindfulness, and is reborn in a celestial realm.[78] The discourse continues with a somewhat obscure description that involves a term found only in this instance among the Pāli discourses. The import of the passage appears to be that the celestials in that realm recite some extract from the teachings of the Buddha in the presence of the one recently reborn there. This has the same result as in the passages just surveyed above, which illustrate the slow arising of mindfulness leading to a quick reaction with the example of the slow falling of water drops on a heated piece of iron and their quick evaporation. In the present context, the arising of mindfulness in the one just reborn in that celestial realm is similarly slow, but then the teachings are quickly remembered (which the discourse refers to in terms of this person quickly "reaching distinction").

The importance of this discourse lies in the somewhat obscure passage just mentioned, which employs the verb *apilapati*.[79] Cone (2001: 174) explains that the corresponding noun *apilāpana* conveys the sense of "enumerating; reminding or remembering by reciting or enumerating." Norman (1988: 50) notes that later texts reflect an alternative understanding of the term. Instead of the correct derivation as *api* + *lāpana*, the term was seen as

---

78 AN 4.191 at AN II 185,7 (translated by Bodhi 2012: 561).

79 On the phrase see also the comments in Bodhi 2012: 1714n904 and Anālayo 2019e.

combining *a* + *pilāpana* and thus as "not floating". Gethin (1992: 38 and 40) explains that

> *apilāpana* seems to have been misunderstood – or at least reinterpreted – by the Pāli Abhidhamma tradition ... the *Dhammasaṅgaṇī* creates a pair of opposites, *apilāpanatā* and *pilāpanatā*, which are used to explain *sati* and *muṭṭha-sati* ("lost mindfulness") respectively. Now *apilāpanatā* would seem to mean "not floating [on the object of the mind]" and *pilāpanatā* "floating [on the object of the mind]". This, at least, is evidently how the commentarial Abhidhamma tradition took the terms ...
>
> It seems that because the commentaries fail to recognize *api-lapati* (= *abhi-lapati*), they therefore make use of a rather different image: *sati* is the mental quality that submerges itself in the objects of the mind; when there is no *sati* the mind floats or drifts on the objects of the mind.

The description of how someone forgets teachings due to a loss of mindfulness when passing away and then regains mindfulness and therewith memory of the teachings would naturally have attracted the attention of later exegesis, in particular for its potential to illustrate the relationship between mindfulness and memory. It seems obvious that, when drawing up listings of near-synonyms of *sati*, the *Aṅguttara-nikāya* passage was consulted and the term *apilāpana* added to such listings.

The basic procedure in the canonical Abhidharma of presenting pairs of opposites, such as contrasting mindfulness established to mindfulness lost, appears in turn to have led to creating another pair of opposites with this particular term. This pair of opposites, however, was based on an incorrect derivation of the term in question, resulting in associating the idea of "not floating" to mindfulness. As a final result, mindfulness was understood as a quality that, rather than "floating", "plunges into" its objects.

This idea in turn has influenced Theravāda conceptions of mindfulness practice. From the viewpoint of insight meditation taught in the Mahāsi tradition, U Sīlananda (1990: 21) explains:

> Mindfulness is something like a stone hitting a wall. In order to throw a stone, you must put out energy. You throw the stone with energy and it hits the wall. Like the stone hitting the wall, mindfulness hits the object. Whatever the objects are – the breath, or the movements of the abdomen, or the activities of the body – your mind, as it were, goes to the objects. That hitting of the object is mindfulness.

U Paṇḍita (1992/1993: 99) reasons:

> "Mindfulness" has come to be the accepted translation of *sati* into English. However, this word has a kind of passive connotation which can be misleading. "Mindfulness" must be dynamic and confrontative. In retreats, I teach that mindfulness should leap forward onto the object ... if we throw a cork into a stream, it simply bobs up and down on the surface, floating downstream with the current. If we throw a stone instead, it will immediately sink to the very bed of the stream. So, too, mindfulness ensures that the mind will sink deeply into the object and not slip superficially past it.

In this way, the impact of the nuances called up by the term *apilāpana*, understood to imply a plunging into the object, has in turn influenced how the functioning of mindfulness has been understood in the cultivation of contemporary Theravāda insight meditation.

SUMMARY

The passages surveyed in this chapter place into perspective the indubitable relationship of *sati*/*smṛti* to memory. Although this relationship is evident in practices of recollection, the assumption that the same holds for the role of mindfulness in the context of other mental qualities and meditative practices related to progress towards awakening is not borne out by a comparative study. A net result of the above comparative survey is that, at least in early Buddhist thought, the memory nuance of mindfulness is less central than has at times been assumed. The concern with the memory nuance of mindfulness, so pervasive in later exegesis, has in the case of the Theravāda tradition triggered a re-interpretation of mindfulness, now seen as a quality that actively plunges into its objects.

When viewed from the perspective of cognitive psychology, the relationship between mindfulness and recalling what happened long ago does not equal the functions of memory anyway. Episodic memory of the type described in the relevant passage, although certainly benefiting from the presence of mindfulness at the time of the event to be recalled as well as when trying to remember it, is also possible without mindfulness. Any attempt at meditating will soon show that the mind can get completely lost in various memories of the past, precisely because of a loss of mindfulness. Similarly, working memory and semantic memory can operate when mindfulness is not present, therefore they cannot be equated with it.

Giving due recognition to the memory dimension of mindfulness could be achieved by placing emphasis on its "attentive" potential that facilitates "keeping in mind" and hence recall. On this understanding, mindfulness in turn can be considered to point to a type of attentiveness and mental presence that would make it easier to recall later what happened. Thus memory is an important dimension but not an exhaustive account of mindfulness. Understood in this way, memory and mindfulness could be seen to converge on "keeping in mind" through "attentiveness" and "mental presence".

II

MINDFULNESS OF THE BODY

In the course of the last chapter, several passages came up in which the role of mindfulness in key teachings of the early Buddhist path to liberation (such as the five faculties, the five powers, and the noble eightfold path) takes the form of the four establishments of mindfulness. This makes it an obvious choice to continue from the topic of memory to these four in the next three chapters. The first of these establishments, mindfulness of the body, occurs on its own in a range of passages. Hence in what follows I will first explore mindfulness of the body and its relation to an "embodied" dimension of mindfulness, and in the next two chapters then turn to the whole set of four establishments of mindfulness.

Before getting into my main topic of mindfulness of the body, by way of introduction I take up a discourse that recommends several modes of cultivating mindfulness (DĀ 10). Here mindfulness of the body features as the one thing that one should cultivate.

A range of benefits can be expected from mindfulness of the body (EĀ 2.19), one of which is the experiencing of a boundless mental condition (MĀ 201). Similes illustrating mindfulness of the body employ the images of carrying a bowl of oil (SĀ 623), of tying six animals to a post (SĀ 1171), and of the axle of a chariot (SĀ 566).

Mindfulness of the body can foster humility (MĀ 24) and support overcoming sensuality (SĀ 1214). Actual practice of mindfulness of the body can involve bodily postures, various activities, breathing, the embodied experience of absorption, contemplation of the components of the body, and of its eventual decay (MĀ 81).

The last passage taken up in the present chapter presents mindfulness of breathing in sixteen steps of practice (SĀ 803). This serves as a bridge between the present chapter and the next, as it shows how a bodily object of meditation, the breath, can be employed to cultivate all four establishments of mindfulness.

MODALITIES OF CULTIVATING MINDFULNESS (DĀ 10)

Various forms of cultivating mindfulness feature in a *Dīrgha-āgama* discourse and its Pāli parallel, the *Dasuttara-sutta*. Such a survey of different modalities of mindfulness comes in conveniently as a first introduction to what I will be exploring in subsequent chapters. The two discourses have as their main structural element a progression of topics comprising sets from ones to tens. In this context, mindfulness occurs repeatedly; in fact, it features right away in the first category of ones. According to both discourses, the one thing to be cultivated is mindfulness of the body:[1]

> What is the one thing to be cultivated? It is reckoned to be constant mindfulness of one's own body.

It is almost as if saying: if you want things to be simple and practise just one thing, then choose mindfulness of the body. The Pāli parallel makes the same statement, offering an additional qualification of such mindfulness of the body: it should be accompanied by delight.[2]

Leaving for a moment the *Dasuttara-sutta* and its parallel to pursue this topic further, the qualification of mindfulness of the body as a practice related to delight recurs in the Pāli version of an instruction given by the Buddha to one of his

1 DĀ 10 at T I 53a5.
2 DN 34 at DN III 272,18: *kāyagata sati sātasahagatā* (translated by Walshe 1987: 511).

disciples renowned for his ascetic tendencies, Mahākassapa.[3] A Chinese parallel to this discourse has a similar reference to delight, which here should accompany the cultivation of all four establishments of mindfulness:[4]

> Dwell with right mindfulness and joy in the four establishments of mindfulness.

Yet another parallel, also extant in Chinese, speaks of dwelling in the four establishments of mindfulness with a "peaceful mind".[5] These qualifications bring out dimensions shared by mindfulness of the body and the four establishments of mindfulness as a whole, namely their potential to lead to joy and peace of mind.

Returning to the *Dasuttara-sutta* and its *Dīrgha-āgama* parallel, in both discourses the topic of mindfulness recurs in a description of four things to be cultivated. Perhaps hardly surprisingly, these are the four establishments of mindfulness:[6]

> What are the four things to be cultivated? They are reckoned to be the four establishments of mindfulness. A monastic contemplates the body [in regard to] the body internally with untiring energy and recollective mindfulness that is not lost, removing greed and discontent in the world. One contemplates the body [in regard to] the body externally with untiring energy and recollective mindfulness that is not lost, removing greed and discontent in the world. One contemplates the body [in regard to] the body internally and externally with untiring energy and recollective mindfulness that is not lost, removing greed and discontent in the world. Contemplation of feeling tones ... the mind ... and dharmas *is also like that*.

The passage in a way fleshes out various dimensions of *satipaṭṭhāna* meditation. It shows that this is to be applied

3 SN 16.11 at SN II 220,28 (translated by Bodhi 2000: 678); see also the *Mahāvastu*, Senart 1897: 52,16 (translated by Jones 1956/1978: 52).
4 SĀ 1144 at T II 303b17 to 303b18.
5 SĀ[2] 119 at T II 418b29.
6 DĀ 10 at T I 53b10 to 53b14; parallel to DN 34 at DN III 276,9 (translated by Walshe 1987: 514).

internally and externally and that it requires combining mindfulness with energy. Moreover, it points to the overarching aim of mindfulness practice: removing greedy desire and discontent. This "liberating" potential of mindfulness applies to contemplation of the body and in the same way to feeling tones, the mind, and dharmas, given in the above passage only in abbreviation. Together these cover the different dimensions of experience that can become a fertile field for mindful exploration.

The Pāli parallel mentions an additional requirement for cultivating the four establishments of mindfulness: clear knowing. In this way, mindfulness collaborates with energy, in the sense of making an effort by applying oneself to the task at hand, and clear knowing, in the sense of understanding and insight.[7]

Another difference is that the Pāli discourse does not explicitly distinguish between contemplation undertaken internally, externally, and both. Nevertheless, this distinction is found in the Pāli *Satipaṭṭhāna-sutta*, reflecting the same need to apply mindfulness internally, externally, and both.[8] This shows that the basic idea of cultivating mindfulness in this way is shared by the different traditions, even though they differ in the extent to which they explicitly draw attention to it.

In the course of subsequent chapters, I will examine the implication of this distinction between internal and external mindfulness in more detail (see below pp. 90 and 234). Suffice it for now to note that, as far as I am able to see, the most straightforward interpretation of this distinction would be as referring to mindfulness applied to oneself (internally) and to others (externally).[9] This would then reflect in particular a "receptive" dimension of mindfulness, in the sense of staying receptively open to the repercussions of whatever happens in relation to oneself as well as to others.

7 On clear knowing see in more detail Anālayo 2020c.
8 Anālayo 2013b: 15f.
9 Gethin 1992: 53 comments that "the significance of the terms *ajjhattaṃ* and *bahiddhā* is clear enough from the Abhidhamma texts onwards: that which refers to oneself is 'within' and that which refers to other beings and persons (*para-satta*, *para-puggala*) is 'without'. There seems to be little reason to suppose that their significance is any different in the Nikāyas."

The *Dīrgha-āgama* parallel to the *Dasuttara-sutta* next mentions the five spiritual faculties in its exposition of five items that are to be cultivated.[10] Mindfulness is the third of these five mental qualities of central importance for progress towards awakening. In this case, however, the Pāli version differs and does not refer to the faculties in its list of five qualities that should be cultivated. The two versions agree again in mentioning the six recollections as six things that should be cultivated:[11]

> What are the six things to be cultivated? They are reckoned to be the six recollections: recollection of the Buddha, recollection of the Dharma, recollection of the community, recollection of morality, recollection of generosity, and recollection of celestial beings.

As already explored in the previous chapter, the practice of recollection has a close relationship to mindfulness. In fact the passage translated above uses the same Chinese character, usually employed for translating "mindfulness" (Pāli *sati*), to render "recollection" (Pāli *anussati*). Thus a literal translation would actually result in six types of "mindfulness", these being "mindfulness" of the Buddha, etc.

When it comes to seven things to be cultivated, the two parallel versions agree in featuring mindfulness again, here as the first of the seven factors of awakening:[12]

> What are the seven things to be cultivated? They are reckoned to be the seven factors of awakening. Hence a monastic cultivates the mindfulness awakening factor in dependence on dispassion, in dependence on cessation, and in dependence on seclusion. One cultivates [investigation] of dharmas ... one cultivates energy ... one cultivates joy ... one cultivates tranquillity ... one cultivates concentration ... one cultivates equipoise in dependence on

---

10 DĀ 10 at T I 53c3. DN 34 at DN III 277,25 instead presents five aspects of right concentration as something to be cultivated; for a discussion of which see Anālayo 2019c: 15.

11 DĀ 10 at T I 54a19 to 54a20, parallel to DN 34 at DN III 280,3 (translated by Walshe 1987: 515).

12 DĀ 10 at T I 54b16 to 54b19, parallel to DN 34 at DN III 282,7 (translated by Walshe 1987: 516).

> dispassion, in dependence on cessation, and in dependence on seclusion.

The Pāli parallel simply lists the seven awakening factors, without explicitly relating their cultivation to dispassion, cessation, and seclusion. In other contexts, the Pāli discourses similarly indicate that each of the awakening factors should be cultivated in dependence on seclusion, in dependence on dispassion, and in dependence on cessation, adding that they should culminate in letting go. This is how the potential of the awakening factors can be actualized.

Among these seven awakening factors, mindfulness serves as the foundation for the other six. Mindfulness therefore is the one quality out of the whole set that is equally required at all times. The other six fall into two groups of three. Investigation of dharmas, energy, and joy are particularly appropriate at times when the mind is sluggish and needs to be energized. Tranquillity, concentration, and equipoise are particularly commendable when the mind is agitated and needs to be calmed. In this context, the "liberating" dimension of mindfulness is prominent, in the sense of leading towards awakening.

Under the heading of eight things to be cultivated, the *Dasuttara-sutta* and its *Dīrgha-āgama* parallel mention the noble eightfold path, where mindfulness features as the seventh factor, a role that also relates to its "liberating" potential:[13]

> What are the eight things to be cultivated? They are reckoned to be the [factors] of the noble eightfold path: right view, right intention, right speech, right action, right livelihood, right effort, right mindfulness, and right concentration.

The eightfold path sets the context for the cultivation of mindfulness, by endowing it with a sense of proper direction through right view, which in turn via right intention informs the ethical foundation for mindfulness practice, covering the domains of speech, action, and livelihood. Based on these and

---

13 DĀ 10 at 55a7 to 55a8, parallel to DN 34 at DN III 286,14 (translated by Walshe 1987: 518).

with the right effort to emerge from unwholesome mental conditions and cultivate wholesome ones, the cultivation of mindfulness comes fully into its own and will in turn enable the gaining of right concentration.[14]

Looking back over the exposition in the *Dasuttara-sutta* and its *Dīrgha-āgama* parallel, the two discourses agree in mentioning mindfulness among the ones, fours, sixes, sevens, and eights out of altogether ten items to be cultivated. In other words, a considerable portion of their recommendations for what one should cultivate involves mindfulness in one way or another. The occurrence among the ones covers the "embodied" dimension of mindfulness and the one among the sixes relates to its "attentive" dimension, whereas the remaining occurrences reflect its "liberating" potential.

The overall impression conveyed by both discourses is a clear emphasis on the importance of cultivating mindfulness as a crucial quality in the early Buddhist scheme of mental culture. Out of these different modalities of mindfulness that emerge in this way, in the remainder of the present chapter I explore what these two discourses present as the one thing to be cultivated: mindfulness of the body. I begin with the potential of such an "embodied" type of mindfulness practice.

THE POTENTIAL OF MINDFULNESS OF THE BODY (EĀ 2.19)

A discourse in the *Ekottarika-āgama* highlights the potential of cultivating mindfulness of the body in the following manner:[15]

> You should cultivate one thing, you should make much of one thing, and in turn you will accomplish supernormal powers, discard all distracting perceptions, gain the fruits of recluse-ship, and reach Nirvāṇa yourselves. What is that one thing?

14 For a discussion of right concentration as the culmination of the cultivation of the other seven path factors see Anālayo 2019c.

15 EĀ 2.19 at T II 553b16 to 553b21 (translated in an abbreviated manner by Huyên-Vi 1986: 31), parallel to AN 1.20 at AN I 43,14 (translated by Bodhi 2012: 129). For a similar highlight on mindfulness of breathing see Anālayo 2019j: 227f.

> It is reckoned to be mindfulness of the body as being impermanent, which you should cultivate well, you should make much of, and in turn you will accomplish supernormal powers, discard the mass of distracting perceptions, gain the fruits of recluse-ship, and reach Nirvāṇa yourselves.
>
> For this reason, monastics, you should cultivate [this] one thing, you should make much of [this] one thing. In this way, monastics, you should train yourselves.

The Pāli parallel lists a broad range of benefits to be expected from cultivating mindfulness of the body, with the difference that it does not explicitly specify such practice to be concerned with the impermanent nature of the body. Nevertheless, directing mindfulness to the body will sooner or later reveal evidence of its impermanent nature, hence from a practical viewpoint the additional stipulation in the above passage is certainly meaningful.

Of further interest for appreciating the role of mindfulness in the present context is that the above passage appears in a list of ten recollections. In this way, mindfulness of the body comes under the same heading as the six recollections (of the Buddha, etc.), discussed in the previous chapter. Another member of this list is mindfulness of breathing, to which I will turn at the end of the present chapter.

The flexible usage of the term "recollection" here ties in with the finding above regarding the six things to be cultivated, where the *Dīrgha-āgama* version employed the term "mindfulness" for what is in fact a recollection. A discourse in the *Aṅguttara-nikāya*, parts of which have been preserved in a Gāndhārī fragment, lists a range of contemplations of the body under the heading of subjects for recollection, including contemplation of the anatomical constitution of the body, of a corpse in decay, and of postures.[16]

Although I will examine each of these three practices in more detail below, the last one mentioned, which is also the one

16 AN 6.29 at AN III 323,20 (translated Bodhi 2012: 890) and fragment a r1–2, Jantrasrisalai et al. 2016: 17.

preserved in the Gāndhārī fragment, is particularly noteworthy. It requires simply being mindful of one's own bodily posture as involving walking, standing, sitting, or lying down. Out of the different modalities of contemplation of the body, this is the one most directly related to an "embodied" form of mindfulness.

The fact that such a mode of practice can come under the explicit heading of "recollection" is telling. In line with what already emerged in the last chapter, this instance serves to underline again the need to handle terms like "recollection" and "memory" with circumspection if we are to understand what their ancient Indian equivalents were meant to convey. Clearly these did not refer only to activities and practices that must involve a recall of the distant past. Instead, the spectrum that ranges from "memory" via "keeping in mind" to "present-moment awareness" is a continuum.

In her discussion of mindfulness in Sarvāstivāda Abhidharma thought, Cox (1992/1993: 67) speaks of what at first sight might appear to be

> two distinct functions of *smṛti*: first, as a technique central to religious praxis; and second, as an aspect of ordinary psychological processes ... [which] appears to coincide with some of the psychological operations normally associated in the West with memory: specifically, retention and recollection. Such a twofold distinction, though appealing in its descriptive simplicity, obscures a complex historical evolution.

Instead, Cox (1992/1993: 67f) proposes an alternative model,

> whereby the apparent twofold distinction in the functioning of *smṛti* does not represent a semantic bifurcation, but rather an interrelated semantic complex ... the various meanings of the term *smṛti* suggested by the dichotomous framework reflect an underlying unity and interaction between models of memory and religious practice and not a secondary and thereby negligible semantic overlap. For this reason, the inclusive and initially ambiguous term *mindfulness* has been chosen to translate *smṛti* in all of its contexts. Mindfulness is chosen here not, as in many cases, to avoid confusion with the psychological function of

> *smṛti* as memory, but precisely for the opposite reason; that is, to indicate at the outset ... that the contexts for the operation of *smṛti* suggested by the term *mindfulness* actually encompass the psychological functions of memory as they were understood in Indian Buddhism.

BOUNDLESS MINDFULNESS OF THE BODY (MĀ 201)

The next passage to be taken up relates mindfulness of the body to a boundless condition of the mind. This qualification points to a similarity between the state of mind when practising mindfulness of the body and the cultivation of the *brahmavihāras*, which are regularly qualified in the same way.[17] The passage in question occurs in the *Madhyama-āgama* parallel to the *Mahātaṇhāsaṅkhaya-sutta* and concerns sense restraint:[18]

> On seeing a form with the eye, one does not delight in or become attached to beautiful forms and does not detest ugly forms, being with mindfulness of the body established and with a boundless mind, and one understands, as they really are, liberation of the mind and liberation by wisdom [whereby] one eradicates without remainder whatever bad and unwholesome states arise, demolishing them without remainder.

In agreement with its Pāli parallel, the *Madhyama-āgama* discourse continues by applying the same treatment to the other sense doors, where in each case the establishing of mindfulness of the body leads to a boundless condition of the mind. The same relationship between mindfulness of the body and a boundless state of mind recurs in other Pāli discourses and their parallels.[19]

This is of considerable significance for an appreciation of mindfulness. The setting concerns a situation where one is

---

17 See Anālayo 2019f.

18 MĀ 201 at T I 769c14 to 769c17, parallel to MN 38 at MN I 270,9 (translated by Ñāṇamoli 1995/2005: 360); see also Anālayo 2011: 255.

19 See, e.g., SN 35.132 at SN IV 120,20 (translated by Bodhi 2000: 1204) and its parallel SĀ 255 at T II 64b2 (translated by Anālayo 2020h) or SN 35.202 at SN IV 186,15 (translated by Bodhi 2000: 1246, referred to as number 243) and its parallel SĀ 1176 at T II 316b29.

exposed to a variety of experiences at any of the sense doors, which could in principle provoke attraction or dislike. Being rooted in the body through an "embodied" form of mindfulness makes it possible to avoid being carried away by such reactions and instead remain with a broad mind. Such a broad-angled mental perspective seems to reflect a distinct dimension of mindfulness when cultivated on its own and not in conjunction with other factors of the mind that result in a narrowed focus.[20]

THE SIMILE OF THE BOWL OF OIL (SĀ 623)

The early discourses abound in the use of similes or metaphors, several of which relate to the topic of mindfulness. Such similes can best be appreciated by keeping in mind their employment in an oral setting in ancient India. This can help to avoid too literal an interpretation or an attempt to match every minor item in a particular image with a specific doctrinal element. At times, such as in the case taken up below, aspects of the description may strike a discordant note for a modern reader sensitive to gendered discourse or appear somewhat violent and unrealistic. Yet, at the time of their original delivery, the similes would probably not have called up such associations. It can be helpful to keep this in mind in order to arrive at a balanced appreciation of the message a simile was originally meant to convey. This holds for the simile to be taken up now, which involves carrying a bowl of oil through a crowd that watches a beautiful girl singing and dancing. The main import of this illustration would have been to illustrate the "protective" potential of mindfulness of the body in relation to potential distractions:[21]

> At that time the Blessed One said to the monastics: "[Suppose a girl] is called 'the beauty of the world'. Is the beauty of the world able to get many people to gather and look at her?"

---

20 See also Anālayo 2019k.

21 SĀ 623 at T II 174b16 to 174c19, parallel to SN 47.20 at SN V 170,2 (translated by Bodhi 2000: 1649).

The monastics said to the Buddha: "It is like this, Blessed One."[22]

The Buddha said to the monastics: "Suppose there is this beauty of the world. Is the beauty of the world able to get even more people to gather and look at her if she is able to sing and dance in various ways?"[23]

The monastics said to the Buddha: "It is like this, Blessed One."

The Buddha said to the monastics: "Suppose there is this beauty of the world. This beauty of the world is in one place and smilingly performs various kinds of singing, dancing, and merriment. Moreover, a great crowd has gathered in that one place. Suppose there is a man who is not foolish and not silly, who likes joy and is averse to pain, who wants to live and is afraid of death.

"A person says to him: 'Man, you take this bowl full of oil and pass through between the beauty of the world and the great crowd. I am sending a capable executioner to follow you with drawn sword. If you lose one drop of the oil, right away your life will be cut off.'

"Monastics, what do you think, will that man carrying the bowl of oil be able to be without mindfulness of the bowl of oil, without mindfulness of the executioner, and look at the dancing girl and at the great crowd?"

The monastics said to the Buddha: "No, Blessed One.[24] Why is that? Blessed One, that man sees for himself that at his back there is a person with a drawn sword and he constantly has the thought: 'Suppose I lose one drop of the oil, that person with the drawn sword will cut my head off.' His mind is solely with collected mindfulness while walking with the bowl of oil between the beauty of the world and the great crowd and getting past them; he does not dare to look around."

---

22 In SN 47.20, the Buddha does not engage the monastics in a question-and-answer exchange, but just relates the whole situation and then asks them if the carrier of the oil would be negligent in such a situation.

23 SN 47.20 at SN V 170,3 reports a gradual building up of the great crowd, which first just gathers to look at the beautiful girl, but when she starts singing and dancing more people come to join the crowd.

24 The remainder of SĀ 623 is without a parallel in SN 47.20.

[The Buddha said]: "Monastics, in the same way, suppose there are recluses and brahmins who rightly conduct themselves with bodily dignity, with single-minded mindfulness, not paying attention to voices and forms, being well collected with regard to all objects of the mind, dwelling in the establishment of mindfulness of the body; they are indeed my disciples who follow my teaching.

"How do monastics rightly conduct themselves with bodily dignity, with single-minded mindfulness, not paying attention to voices and forms, being [well] collected with regard to all objects of the mind, and dwelling in the establishment of mindfulness of the body?

"Monastics, it is in this way: one mindfully contemplates the body [in regard to] the body with diligent effort, with right knowing, and right mindfulness, overcoming greed and discontent in the world. *It is also like this for* feeling tones ... the mind ... and for dwelling mindfully contemplating dharmas [in regard to] dharmas.

"This is reckoned how monastics rightly conduct themselves with bodily dignity, with single-minded mindfulness, not paying attention to voices and forms, being well collected with regard to [all] objects of the mind, dwelling in the four establishments of mindfulness."

At that time the Blessed One spoke in verse:

"Single-mindedly with right mindfulness
He guardedly carried the bowl of oil
And accordingly guarded his own mind
So that it never went in [any] direction,
It being very difficult to cross.

"Most excellent and subtle
Are the teachings of all Buddhas
Whose instructions are [like] sharp swords.

"One should be single-minded
Focused on keeping up one's guard,

> Not being [like] those ordinary persons
> Who are engaged in negligence.
>
> "In this way one will be able to undertake
> The teaching on diligence."

The verses in the above discourses are without a parallel in the Pāli version. Conversely, the explanation given in the Pāli discourse that the bowl of oil stands for mindfulness of the body is not found in the Chinese. Although the *Saṃyukta-āgama* version does not have such an explanation of the simile, it clearly places a similar spotlight on mindfulness of the body as the means for avoiding distraction.

This comes out nicely in the first verse, which relates the guardedness with which the bowl of oil is carried to guarding the mind. The somewhat dramatic nature of the simile finds explicit recognition in the verses, which compare the Buddha's instructions to sharp swords. Again, the point need not be taken too literally. The implication appears to be simply that the simile and the instructions given can have a stirring effect and serve to encourage the listener to make an effort to cultivate mindfulness of the body. This receives further emphasis through the contrast drawn with others who are negligent. In contrast to such negligent persons, by being firmly established in mindfulness of the body one puts into practice the frequent encouragement in the early discourses to be diligent.

Notably, the *Saṃyukta-āgama* version translated above conveys the possibility that the man carrying the bowl might forget about his task or the presence of the executioner with a reference to the absence of "mindfulness". In order to draw this out, I have adopted a literal translation which reads: "without mindfulness of the bowl of oil, without mindfulness of the executioner". The Pāli parallel expresses the same sense, here only in relation to the bowl of oil, with the help of the phrase "not paying attention" or "not attending" to it, *amanasikāra*.[25] This minor variation in

25 SN 47.20 at SN V 170,14 speaks of no longer attending to the bowl and, out of negligence, turning attention outwards.

terminology reflects a wider topic, namely the interrelation and partial overlap in meaning between mindfulness (*sati*) and attention (*manasikāra*), a topic to which I will return in more detail in a subsequent chapter (see below p. 202).

In the Pāli version the listening monastics do not describe in detail why the man carrying the oil would not stop paying attention to the bowl, in fact it has no counterpart at all to the latter section of the above *Saṃyukta-āgama* discourse. In the Pāli account, the Buddha just asks the monastics if the carrier would stop paying attention to the bowl, and when they deny, he draws out the significance of the bowl of oil in the simile by explaining that it stands for mindfulness of the body. The discourse comes to a close with the Buddha enjoining the monastics to train themselves in mindfulness of the body.

The additional description in the passage translated above, although in view of its absence in the Pāli version probably a later addition, helps to visualize the situation more clearly and better discern the function performed by mindfulness of the body in this respect. The carrier's mindfulness of the body operates in conjunction with his clear awareness of the swordsman at his back. He knows very well that, if he spills a single drop of oil, his head will be cut off. For this reason, he does not dare to look around.

The rather vivid illustration given in this way compares to rightly conducting oneself with bodily dignity. This serves to balance the effect of the dramatic description by showing that it is meant to convey not a sense of agitation and fear, but simply a strong effort to avoid distraction. In the passage translated above, this has its external and internal dimensions. The external dimension is exemplified by voices and forms, appropriate to the situation of a heterosexual male walking past a beautiful girl who is singing. The internal dimension involves being well collected in relation to whatever may become an object of the mind. The groundwork for nurturing such ability is then the cultivation of the four establishments of mindfulness. In other words, the emphasis on the first of these, mindfulness of the body, is not meant to exclude the others.

In fact, an exclusive focus on the body would not be appropriate in the context of the simile. The man has to pass between the girl and the crowd without running into anyone, as that would result in a loss of oil and therewith loss of his head. He can only get through if he keeps a wide attentional field that is centred sufficiently on the body such that no distraction occurs. This suggestion concurs with the passage taken up previously, according to which mindfulness of the body can result in a broad, even boundless condition of the mind (see above p. 56). Thus mindfulness of the body here is not about cultivating an exclusive focus on the body. Much rather, it is about a grounding in an "embodied" form of mindfulness, an anchoring that can serve as a reference point for an inclusive and wide-angled mental attitude that can even become boundless.

THE SIMILE OF SIX ANIMALS BOUND TO A POST (SĀ 1171)

Another and complementary perspective on the cultivation of mindfulness of the body takes the form of a simile that describes six animals bound to a post:[26]

> It is just as a person on a journey who, being in an empty house, had caught six types of animals: first he caught a dog, and taking hold of the dog he bound it to one spot. Then he caught a bird, then he caught a poisonous snake, then he caught a jackal, then he caught a crocodile, and then he caught a monkey. Having caught these animals, he bound them all to a single spot.[27]
>
> That dog desires to enter the village, that bird constantly wishes to fly up into the sky, that snake constantly wishes to enter a cave, that jackal delights in approaching a cemetery, the crocodile continuously wishes to enter a large lake, and the monkey wishes to enter a mountain forest.

---

26 SĀ 1171 at T II 313a15 to 313b12, parallel to SN 35.206 at SN IV 198,3 (translated by Bodhi 2000: 1255, given as number 247), EĀ 38.8 at T II 723c17, and Up 9006 at D 4094 *nyu* 80a2 or Q 5595 *thu* 125b6.

27 The sequence of listing the animals and the places to which they wish to go differ in the parallel versions.

These six animals, being all bound to a single spot, with their different preferences, each wishing to reach a peaceful place, are each in that place against their likes, because they are firmly bound. Each uses its strength to approach the direction it likes, yet, they are unable to get free.

In the same way the six faculties have different domains, each seeking to find delight in its respective domain and not delighting in other domains. With the eye faculty one constantly seeks forms that are lovable and one gives rise to disgust in relation to forms that are not attractive. With the ear faculty one constantly seeks sounds that are attractive and one gives rise to disgust in relation to sounds that are not attractive. With the nose faculty one constantly seeks for odours that are attractive and one gives rise to disgust in relation to odours that are not attractive. With the tongue faculty one constantly seeks for flavours that are attractive and one gives rise to disgust in relation to flavours that are not attractive. With the body faculty one constantly seeks for tangibles that are attractive and one gives rise to disgust in relation to tangibles that are not attractive. With the mind faculty one constantly seeks for mental objects that are attractive and one gives rise to disgust in relation to mental objects that are not attractive.

Each of these six faculties, which have different areas of functioning and different domains, does not seek the domain of another faculty. These six faculties have strength and ability in accordance with their own power and comprehension of their domain, which is just as the six animals who were bound together by that person to a firm post. They properly manifest the use of their force to leave according to their intentions, moving forward and backward. Because of being bound by the rope, they become very tired. In the end, they have to comply with the post.

Monastics, having spoken this simile, I wish to clarify to you its meaning. The six animals exemplify the six faculties. The firm post exemplifies the establishment of mindfulness of the body. If one well cultivates the establishment of mindfulness of the body, whether one is [intentionally] mindful or not [intentionally] mindful of forms, on seeing forms that are lovable one does not

> give rise to attachment and with forms that are not lovable one does not give rise to disgust. With the ear and sounds ... the nose and odours ... the tongue and flavours ... the body and tangibles ... the mind and mental objects one does not seek and desire attractive mental objects and does not give rise to disgust for unattractive mental objects. For this reason, monastics, you should diligently cultivate and often dwell in the establishment of mindfulness of the body.

The Pāli version presents two different situations in regard to the six animals. At first, they are just bound together but not yet bound to a post. As each animal tries to pull towards its respective domain, eventually they are all dragged along by the one strongest among them.[28] This illustrates the situation when mindfulness of the body has not been cultivated. Each of the six senses exerts its pull, the eye pulls one in the direction of visible objects, the ear pulls one towards sounds, etc. In each case, the pull can take the form of liking what is agreeable or disliking what is disagreeable, as in the passage translated above. The predicament of being in this way pulled here and there illustrates the fragmentation of experience and the concomitant mental reactivity.

The situation changes, however, once the six animals are not just bound together, but are also bound to a firm post. At first the animals might still be pulling, but sooner or later they will realize its futility and just stand or sit near the post. This illustrates the situation when mindfulness of the body is established. At such a time, the senses will no longer be able to pull one towards their respective objects.

The two-stage presentation in the Pāli version helps to get a clearer sense of the implications of the simile, through the contrast between the absence or the presence of the strong post. Similar to the passage translated above, the Pāli parallel also identifies this firm post, to which the six animals are bound, as mindfulness of the body. In this way, an "embodied" form of mindfulness can provide a centring force that enables meeting

28 SN 35.206 at SN IV 199,10.

variegated experiences in daily life situations without being pulled along.

THE AXLE OF MINDFULNESS OF THE BODY (SĀ 566)

Whereas the previous similes drew out in complementary ways the potential of an "embodied" form of mindfulness to provide an anchor in the body that enables handling sensory experience with breadth of mind, other aspects of mindfulness come to the fore in several similes related to a chariot. One of these illustrates key aspects of the path with parts of such a chariot. The part that illustrates mindfulness is its axle:[29]

> The single axle [of the chariot] is mindfulness of the body.

The Pāli parallel identifies the single axle with mindfulness in general.[30] Since in its presentation the chariot stands for the body, however, the implications of the axle of mindfulness appear to be similar to those in the extract translated above. The point of this imagery could be to place a highlight on mindfulness as the central factor around which progress on the path to liberation revolves.

Mindfulness recurs in another simile in relation to a chariot. In this case the *Saṃyukta-āgama* discourse refers to the halter, whereas the Pāli version identifies mindfulness as the chariot's upholstery.[31] The nuances conveyed by the *Saṃyukta-āgama*

29 SĀ 566 at T II 149b15, parallel to SN 41.5 at SN IV 292,4 (translated by Bodhi 2000: 1321).

30 The expression *ekāra* (on which see also the gloss at Ud-a 370,11) and its Chinese translation rather convey the idea of a "single spoke". In fact, descriptions of a wheel with a thousand spokes take the form of qualifying the *cakka* as *sahassāra*, e.g., MN 129 at MN III 172,16. From a practical viewpoint, however, this is a less straightforward interpretation of the same term in the present context, as a wheel would require more than just a single spoke in order to function well. For this reason, it seems to me preferable to take the expression to convey the sense of the "axle" when it relates to the whole chariot, rather than a wheel, following the translation adopted by Hecker et al. 2003: 159f (Woodward 1927/1980: 199 rather translates *ekāra* as "one-wheeled" and Bodhi 2000: 1321 as "one-spoked").

31 SĀ 587 at T II 156a20 and SN 1.46 at SN I 33,11 (translated by Bodhi 2000: 122).

simile's reference to a halter could be taken to convey the ability of mindfulness to keep mental reactivity in rein and provide the proper direction in which to proceed. The Pāli version's reference to the upholstery could in turn be understood to express a "protective" dimension of mindfulness, which can cushion against the impact of the potholes of life, in the sense that its presence will diminish the tendency towards strong reactivity when facing any vicissitude.

Be it as the single axle, the halter, or the upholstery, each of these aspects of a chariot can exemplify a dimension of mindfulness that enables the chariot to move on smoothly. In this way mindfulness, as a single source of strength, can rein in reactivity, help to keep going in the right direction, and cushion the impact of life's vicissitudes. The last of these comes up in the next passage, which relates mindfulness to humility.

MINDFULNESS OF THE BODY AND HUMILITY (MĀ 24)

Mindfulness of the body can lead to the absence of the type of arrogance that could make one slight another and then just leave without apology. The accusation of having acted in such a way had been levelled against the monastic Sāriputta, a chief disciple of the Buddha. In order to clarify in front of the Buddha that he was incapable of intentionally slighting another and then leaving, Sāriputta refers to his possession of mindfulness of the body:[32]

> Suppose someone is without mindfulness of the body [in regard to] the body, such a one might in turn slight a companion in the celibate life and then go travelling among the people. Blessed One, I possess proper mindfulness of the body [in regard to] the body, how could I slight a companion in the celibate life and then go travelling among the people?

The Pāli parallel similarly establishes a connection between a lack of mindfulness of the body and the possibility that one

---

32 MĀ 24 at T I 453a1 to 453a4, parallel to AN 9.11 at AN IV 374,22 (translated by Bodhi 2012: 1262). Another parallel, EĀ 37.6 at T II 713a5, does not have a counterpart to this part of the discourse.

might slight another and then just walk off. The presentation in both versions points to a relationship between the cultivation of mindfulness of the body and the absence of arrogance. This could be simply an extension of rootedness in the body through mindfulness, leading to the absence of reactivity. Yet, given the narrative setting it may well imply more, namely an insight into the nature of the body as something that instils humility rather than arrogance. On this interpretation, with the present passage the depiction of mindfulness of the body moves from its somatic dimension of being rooted in the body through an "embodied" form of mindfulness to the insight dimension of understanding the body as it is, which relates to the "liberating" dimension of mindfulness. The same two aspects appear to be relevant to the next passage.

MINDFULNESS OF THE BODY TO COUNTER SENSUALITY (SĀ 1214)

A brief reference to contemplation of the body occurs in the *Saṃyukta-āgama* as part of a set of recommendations for how to counter sensual desire:[33]

> With mindfulness collected, rightly contemplate the body.

The parallels tend to speak just of having mindfulness of the body, which leaves open the possibility that the reference above to "right" contemplation was added by the Chinese translator in order to arrive at a count of five characters per line, the standard form taken by a verse.

The overall point made by the passage continues on the theme already evident in the descriptions of mindfulness of the body as what enables maintaining breadth of the mind amidst various

33 SĀ 1214 at T II 331b5, parallel to SN 8.4 at SN I 188,22 (translated by Bodhi 2000: 284), a Sanskrit fragment, SHT V 1140 R3, Sander and Waldschmidt 1985: 137 (which has preserved *smṛtiṃ kāyagatāṃ kṛtvā*, see also Enomoto 1989: 25), SĀ² 230 at T II 458b13, and Up 5010 at D 4094 *ju* 271a4 or Q 5595 *thu* 14b3. Another parallel, EĀ 35.9 at T II 701a28, recommends mindfulness of the Buddha as one who is free from sensual desire.

experiences, illustrated with the similes of carrying a bowl of oil and of six animals bound to a post. In addition, the present passage also relates to the cultivation of insight into the nature of the body itself. This is a "liberating" dimension of mindfulness of the body that forms a recurrent theme in a whole discourse dedicated to various modalities of contemplating the body, which I examine next. The detailed analysis provided by this discourse is precisely about different modalities of mindfulness of the body that range from somatic anchoring in the body to insightful non-attachment towards the body. Due to the length of this discourse, I will take up its presentation in several sections.

MINDFULNESS OF BODILY POSTURES AND ACTIVITIES (MĀ 81)

The *Kāyagatāsati-sutta* and its *Madhyama-āgama* parallel take their occasion from a group of monastics speaking in praise of the Buddha's instructions on mindfulness of the body.[34] Being informed of the topic of their discussion motivates the Buddha to give a detailed exposition on the subject. The first exercise in the *Madhyama-āgama* discourse concerns bodily postures:[35]

> Walking one knows one is walking, standing one knows one is standing, sitting one knows one is sitting, lying down one knows one is lying down, [falling] asleep one knows one is [falling] asleep, waking up one knows one is waking up, [falling] asleep [or] waking up one knows one is [falling] asleep [or] waking up.

The Pāli parallel has the present exercise as its second contemplation. The two versions agree in indicating that such a practice leads to concentration. In terms of training in mindfulness, this exercise requires cultivating a proprioceptive type of awareness. This enables one to remain grounded in the somatic experience of the body in whatever way it is disposed, combined with a clear recognition of how it is disposed. Out

34 For a comparative study see Anālayo 2011: 673–678.

35 MĀ 81 at T I 555a12 to 555a14 (already translated by Kuan 2008: 156), parallel to MN 119 at MN III 89,25 (translated by Ñāṇamoli 1995/2005: 950).

of the different practices surveyed in the *Kāyagatāsati-sutta* and its parallel, the present one is most directly related to the cultivation of an "embodied" form of mindfulness.

The *Kāyagatāsati-sutta* does not refer to falling asleep and waking up in the present context, but only in relation to the next exercise, which in both versions takes the form of clear or right knowing in relation to various activities:[36]

> One is with right knowing when going out and coming in, properly contemplating and distinguishing when bending, stretching, lowering, or raising [a limb]; with appropriate deportment well wearing the double robe, [other] robes, and the bowl; always being with right knowing when going, standing, sitting, lying down, [falling] asleep, waking up, speaking, and being silent.

The *Kāyagatāsati-sutta* additionally mentions eating, drinking, consuming food, tasting, defecating, and urinating as activities during which one should possess clear knowing. In the present context, such clear or right knowing stands in particular for being circumspect in relation to the activities listed.

Out of the body contemplations listed in the *Kāyagatāsati-sutta* and its parallel, the cultivation of clear or right knowing is the one that recurs regularly in accounts of the gradual path of practice in other discourses.[37] Descriptions of this gradual path take up key aspects of conduct and cultivation that lead a practitioner, who has gone forth from the lay life and become a Buddhist monastic, gradually to the realization of awakening. Such descriptions do not mention other exercises found under the heading of contemplation of the body in either the *Kāyagatāsati-sutta* and its parallel or in the *Satipaṭṭhāna-sutta* and its parallels, such as contemplation of the anatomical parts of the body or its elements, or else of a corpse in decay (to be studied below).

This suggests that cultivating mindfulness of the body through clear or right knowing of various bodily activities is of prime relevance to a practitioner of this gradual path. Mindfulness of

---

36 MĀ 81 at T I 555a18 to 555a20, parallel to MN 119 at MN III 90,1.
37 Anālayo 2017c: 80–90.

the bodily postures could also be included here, since from a practical viewpoint this is required in order to be able to execute the present exercise. Without the type of embodied mindfulness that comes from being aware of the position of one's body, it would be difficult to cultivate clear or right knowing when walking, standing, sitting, or lying down, etc.

On this understanding, then, the circumstance that the *Madhyama-āgama* parallel to the *Kāyagatāsati-sutta* begins its exposition with these two exercises could be read as reflecting their importance in building a foundation in mindfulness (the *Kāyagatāsati-sutta* instead begins with mindfulness of breathing).

Another reason for such explicit mention in accounts of the gradual path could be related to the function of such descriptions, which are often given to outsiders in order to convey to them some idea of the kind of training a Buddhist practitioner undertakes. Here the composed and circumspect behaviour that is cultivated with the present practice is a good illustration, something that can easily be visualized and even witnessed when encountering well-behaved Buddhist monastics. In contrast, a person unfamiliar with meditation practice will hardly be able to know if someone else is at that time undertaking mindfulness of breathing or other *satipaṭṭhāna* exercises.

When evaluated from a practical perspective, these reasons could be combined in considering composed and circumspect bodily behaviour to be a key aspect of training in embodied mindfulness as a foundational practice for progressing on the gradual path to liberation.

The *Madhyama-āgama* discourse continues with two exercises that do not have a parallel in the Pāli version and which describe abandoning unwholesome thoughts and forceful mind control.[38]

38 MĀ 81 at T I 555a24: "[When] bad and unwholesome thoughts arise, one rectifies, abandons, eradicates, and stops them by wholesome states and thoughts. It is just like a carpenter or a carpenter's apprentice who might apply an inked string to a piece of wood [to mark a straight line] and then cut the wood with a sharp adze to make it straight ... With teeth clenched and tongue pressed against the palate one uses [the willpower of] the mind to rectify the mind, to rectify, abandon, eradicate, and stop [bad thoughts]. It is just like two strong men who might grab a weak man and, turning him this way and that way, might beat him up as they wish."

In line with a standard procedure for each exercise covered in the discourse, these two are presented as instances of mindfulness of the body. Yet, both exercises clearly do not fit in this context, as they do not take the body as their object. This makes it safe to conclude that, during the course of oral transmission, the overall topic of concentration mentioned after each exercise would have led to the addition of these two practices as they can also help to steady the mind.[39]

The next exercise, also found in the *Kāyagatāsati-sutta*, relates mindfulness to the experience of the breath:[40]

> Being mindful of breathing in, one knows to be breathing in mindfully; being mindful of breathing out, one knows to be breathing out mindfully. Breathing in long, one knows to be breathing in long; breathing out long, one knows to be breathing out long. Breathing in short, one knows to be breathing in short; breathing out short, one knows to be breathing out short. One trains [in experiencing] the whole body when breathing in; one trains [in experiencing] the whole body when breathing out.[41]

---

39 Kuan 2008: 86–90 discussed the probable provenance of these two passages from MN 20 at MN I 119,5 and 120,35 (translated by Ñāṇamoli 1995/2005: 211), with a parallel in MĀ 101 at T I 588a10 and 588c17 (he also includes the refrains made in this discourse and MN 119 in his discussion, yet these do not seem to be borrowings). He sums up (p. 90) that "it may be concluded that ... the third and fourth practices in the Chinese version of the *Kāyagatāsati Sutta* come from the *Vitakkasanthāna Sutta/*Adhicitta Sūtra*. This strongly suggests that those two practices in the Sarvāstivāda version ... were originally included in the antecedent version of the *Kāyagatāsati Sutta* ... those two practices which do not look like mindfulness of the body were omitted by the Theravādins." Yet, once the two passages clearly have a natural home in MN 20 and MĀ 101, where they fit the context, and given that they do not fit the context in MĀ 81 and are absent from the Pāli parallel MN 119, it would be more reasonable to conclude that during the transmission of the *Madhyama-āgama* these two passages were added to MĀ 81. Having become part of MĀ 81, the same two exercises would then have naturally become part also of MĀ 98, the parallel to the *Satipaṭṭhāna-sutta*, during oral recitation of the *Madhyama-āgama*.

40 MĀ 81 at T I 555b10 to 555b15, parallel to MN 119 at MN III 89,12 (here serving as the first exercise).

41 On different interpretations of how far this step concerns the physical body see Anālayo 2019j: 37–39 and 2020b: 198–201.

> One trains in calming bodily activity when breathing in; one trains in calming ⟨bodily⟩ activity when breathing out.[42]

Despite appearing in both versions, based on a study of the full exposition of mindfulness of breathing in sixteen steps and the occurrence of a similar excerpt of just the first part of these instructions in the *Satipaṭṭhāna-sutta*, it seems probable that the present passage is a later addition to the exposition on contemplation of the body.[43] I will return to the topic of mindfulness of breathing at the end of this chapter, based on a translation of the whole scheme of sixteen steps of mindfulness of breathing, of which the above is just an extract of the first part.

BODILY DIMENSIONS OF ABSORPTION (MĀ 81)

The next set of exercises in the *Kāyagatāsati-sutta* and its *Madhyama-āgama* parallel concerns the bodily experience of absorption:[44]

> One completely drenches and pervades the body with joy and happiness born of seclusion [experienced in the first absorption], so that there is no part within the body that is not pervaded by joy and happiness born of seclusion.
>
> It is just like a bath attendant who, having filled a vessel with bathing powder, mixes it with water and kneads it, so that there is no part [of the powder] that is not completely drenched and pervaded with water ...
>
> One completely drenches and pervades the body with joy and happiness born of concentration [experienced in the second absorption], so that there is no part within the body that is not pervaded by joy and happiness born of concentration.
>
> It is just like a mountain spring that is full and overflowing with clear and clean water, so that water coming from any of the four directions cannot enter it, with the spring water welling

42 The original speaks of verbal activity when breathing out, which clearly is a textual error.
43 See Anālayo 2013b: 45–50 and 2019j: 165–170.
44 The translated parts are found between MĀ 81 at T I 555b19 and 555c21, parallel to MN 119 at MN III 92,23.

> up from the bottom on its own, flowing out and flooding the surroundings, completely drenching every part of the mountain so that there is no part that is not pervaded by it ...
>
> One completely drenches and pervades the body with happiness born of the absence of joy [experienced in the third absorption], so that there is no part within the body that is not pervaded by happiness born of the absence of joy.
>
> It is just like a blue, red, or white lotus which, being born in the water and having come to growth in the water, remains submerged in water, with every part of its roots, stem, flower, and leaves completely drenched and pervaded [by water], so that there is no part that is not pervaded by it ...
>
> One mentally resolves to dwell having accomplished a complete pervasion of the body with mental purity [experienced in the fourth absorption], so that there is no part within the body that is not pervaded by mental purity.
>
> It is just like a person covered from head to foot with a cloth measuring seven or eight units, so that no part of the body is not covered.

The inclusion of the somatic dimension of absorption experience under the header of mindfulness of the body points again to an embodied form of mindfulness. The respective illustrations in the Pāli parallel come with a few variations.

The simile for the bodily experience of the first absorption describes a ball of soap that does not ooze. This appears to reflect a way of bathing in ancient India by going to a river to take a bath out in the open. In such a situation, the soap powder needs to be kneaded in such a way that it will not be scattered by the wind and also not become so liquid that it will be carried away by the river. This can be achieved by moistening it and then forming it into a firm ball that does not ooze. In this way, it can be handled easily and fulfil its function when one bathes.

In the case of the bodily experience of the second absorption, the Pāli version speaks of a lake that has water welling up from within, instead of the mountain spring mentioned in the *Madhyama-āgama* discourse translated above.

To illustrate the bodily dimension of entry into the third absorption, the *Kāyagatāsati-sutta* uses the same imagery of lotuses submerged in water, adding that the water is cool. Needless to say, in the often hot climate of India, cool water will be perceived as attractive.

When it comes to illustrating the bodily dimension of the experience of the fourth absorption, the Pāli description does not stipulate the size of the cloth used by the person as a cover. It adds that the cloth is white. In both versions, the description of being covered completely by a cloth exemplifies the imperturbable nature of this absorption experience. Keeping in mind the ancient Indian setting, where sitting outside exposes one to the sun and bites from mosquitoes or gadflies, the idea of being completely covered in this way conveys clear positive nuances.

Another and more substantial difference is that the Pāli parallel also mentions the mental factors and qualities that lead to the actual attainment of the four absorptions. Although this is standard procedure in other contexts, here it obfuscates to some extent the significance of the present description. The main point of the exposition is not so much about how absorption is attained, but rather how the bodily dimension of absorption is experienced.[45] During oral transmission, the standard listing of mental factors could easily have been added to the Pāli discourse.

The *Madhyama-āgama* version continues with two exercises that have no parallel in the *Kāyagatāsati-sutta* and which refer to the perception of light and the reviewing sign.[46] Similar to

---

45 Kuan 2008: 94 reasons that "even though *kāyagatā sati* may lead to the *jhāna*s, it is not *jhāna* or any other meditative attainment as such." This is indeed the case, but the bodily experience of the *jhāna*s can become an object of cultivating mindfulness of the body. Together with his reasoning mentioned above in note 39, Kuan 2008: 97 then arrives at the conclusion that "when the *Kāyagatāsati Sutta* was first composed, *kāyagatā sati* was not considered to be mindfulness of the physical body alone, and *kāya* obviously had a much broader sense than the physical body." Although in other contexts *kāya* can indeed refer to one's whole being, covering body and mind, in the context of *kāyagatā sati* the term rather seems to refer to being mindful of one's physical body.

46 MĀ 81 at T I 555c27: "One is mindful of the perception of light, properly taking hold of it, properly retaining it, and properly recollecting what one is mindful of, [so that] what is behind is like what is in front, what is

the earlier case of two contemplations not found in the Pāli parallel, in the present case it seems also fair to conclude that these two exercises are later additions, given that they have no real relationship to being mindful of the body. The descriptions of the absorptions and the recurrent reference to concentration would have attracted these two passages during the course of oral transmission.

THE CONSTITUTION OF THE BODY (MĀ 81)

The next contemplation in the *Kāyagatāsati-sutta* and its *Madhyama-āgama* parallel concerns the anatomical constitution of the body:[47]

> One contemplates this body, according to its position and according to what is attractive and what is repulsive, from head to foot, seeing that it is full of various unclean parts, namely: "Within this body there are head hairs, body hairs, nails, teeth, rough and smooth epidermis, skin, flesh, sinews, bones, heart, kidneys, liver, lungs, large intestine, small intestine, spleen, stomach, lumps of faeces, brain and brain stem,[48] tears, sweat, saliva,[49] pus, blood, fat, marrow, mucus, phlegm, and urine."[50]
>
> It is just like a clear-sighted person who, on seeing a vessel full of various seeds, clearly distinguishes them all, namely: "there is rice, millet seed, barley, wheat, big and small sesames and beans, turnip seed, and mustard seed."

---

in front is like what is behind, night is like day, day is like night, what is above is like what is below, and what is below is like what is above. In this way, with an undistorted and undefiled mind one cultivates a mind that is bright and clear, a mind that is not at all obscured by impediments ... One properly takes hold of and properly retains [in mind] the reviewing sign, recollecting properly what one is mindful of. It is just like a person who is seated and contemplates another person who is lying down, or while lying down contemplates another person who is seated."

47 MĀ 81 at T I 556a12 to 556a18, parallel to MN 119 at MN III 90,12.

48 Kuan 2008: 211n28 notes an explanation according to which the characters rendered above as "brain stem" would refer to the occipital bone.

49 My rendering follows a suggestion by Glass 2007: 162 to read as one anatomical part what, according to the punctuation in the Taishō edition, would be two parts.

50 With the translation "phlegm" I follow Kuan 2008: 213n16.

Leaving aside some minor differences in the listing of bodily parts and seeds, the two parallels agree on the main points of the present contemplation. From the viewpoint of actual practice, the evaluative element found in both versions, referring to the unclean or even impure nature of the body, can be placed into perspective through the additional reference in the *Madhyama-āgama* to contemplating the body "according to what is attractive and what is repulsive". On following this indication, the aim would be to recognize both what is seen generally as beautiful (such as well-kept head hairs, properly trimmed nails, and even teeth) alongside what is usually perceived as disgusting (such as faeces, pus, mucus, and urine). In the end, both are simply aspects of the human body.

From the viewpoint of mindfulness practice, it is nevertheless remarkable that such an evaluative element is found at all. Now mindfulness itself is highly adaptable and can function in conjunction with a range of other mental qualities, enhancing them through sustained mental presence. In such a collaboration, not all of the qualities of mindfulness itself are as clearly discernible as they would be when it is deployed on its own. Hence there is no problem in principle in mindfulness taking part in an evaluative contemplation, even though such active evaluation is not a prominent characteristic of mindfulness cultivated on its own.

Another perspective on the nature of the human body emerges with the next exercise, which concerns its material elements:[51]

> One contemplates the body's elements: "Within this body of mine there are the earth element, the water element, the fire element, the wind element, the space element, and the consciousness element."
>
> It is just like a butcher who, on having slaughtered and skinned a cow, divides it into six parts and spreads them on the ground [for sale].

The *Kāyagatāsati-sutta* speaks of only four elements. In the case of the *Satipaṭṭhāna-sutta*, the same difference recurs between the Pāli

51 MĀ 81 at T I 556a26 to 556a28, parallel to MN 119 at MN III 91,1.

version and its *Madhyama-āgama* parallel. In this case, another parallel in the *Ekottarika-āgama* also has only four elements.[52] A reference to consciousness as the sixth element does in fact not fit the heading of contemplation of the body. This makes it fairly probable that an original reference to four elements was, in the course of oral transmission, expanded to six, a form of analysis found in other discourses in contexts concerned with the whole of subjective experience and not only the body. This apparent replacement led to an adjustment of the simile as well, which now speaks of "six" parts of the slaughtered cow.

The present exercise is yet another analytical contemplation that involves mindfulness, although with less of an evaluative tone than the preceding one. Both have in common that mindfulness is employed for the sake of cultivating insight into the nature of the body, be it from the perspective of its anatomy or its elements.

The next exercise comprises a series of contemplations of a corpse in various stages of decay:[53]

> One contemplates a corpse dead for one or two days, or up to six or seven days, that is being pecked at by crows, devoured by jackals and dogs, burned by fire, or buried in the earth, or that is completely rotten and decomposed ...
>
> Similar to what one has formerly seen in a charnel ground, so one [recollects] a carcass of bluish colour, decomposed and half eaten [by animals], with the bones lying on the ground still connected together ...
>
> Similar to what one has formerly seen in a charnel ground, so one [recollects a skeleton] without skin, flesh, or blood, held together only by sinews ...
>
> Similar to what one has formerly seen in a charnel ground, so one [recollects] disconnected bones scattered in all directions: foot bones, shin bones, thigh bones, a hip bone, vertebrae, shoulder bones, neck bones, and a skull, all in different places ...

---

52 EĀ 12.1 at T II 568a24 (translated by Anālayo 2013b: 288).

53 The extracts are found between MĀ 81 at T I 556b5 and 556c5, parallel to MN 119 at MN III 91,14.

> Similar to what one has formerly seen in a charnel ground, so one [recollects] bones white like shells, or bluish like the colour of a pigeon, or red as if smeared with blood, rotting and decomposing, crumbling to dust.
>
> Having seen this, one compares oneself to it: "This present body of mine will also be like this. It is of the same nature and in the end cannot escape [this fate]."

The instruction to compare oneself to the condition of a corpse applies to each of the stages of decay described above. From the viewpoint of the distinction between internal and external forms of mindfulness, it is worth noting that the present exercise already involves an interrelation between one's own body and that of others. The external apperception of the dead condition of another body should be applied to one's own body with the understanding that both bodies share the same nature (an understanding that could then be again applied externally to other bodies that are still alive).

The purpose of the employment of mindfulness in the practice described above can be considered as twofold. One would be revealing the lack of attractiveness of the body once it begins to fall apart. This would complement the earlier contemplation of its anatomical constitution. Another purpose would be to drive home the truth of the mortality of the body. Mindfulness can indeed serve as a powerful tool to face death, a topic to which I will return in a subsequent chapter (see below p. 153).

Having completed their survey of different modalities of mindfulness of the body, the two versions proceed to illustrate the potential of such practice:[54]

> If mindfulness of the body is cultivated in this way, widely [cultivated] in this way, then all wholesome states are completely comprised by it, namely the states that pertain to awakening. Whatever state of mind one resolves on will be penetrated.
>
> It is just like the great ocean; all minor rivers are completely contained in the ocean.

---

54 MĀ 81 at T I 556c9 to 556c12, parallel to MN 119 at MN III 94,22.

The *Kāyagatāsati-sutta* has the same comparison, with the minor difference that the image of the ocean containing all minor streams comes with the additional specification that this refers to encompassing the whole ocean with one's mind. In other words, once one has taken the whole ocean as the object of one's mind, any stream that flows into it will automatically be included. This in itself minor detail helps to relate the simile to the potential of mindfulness of the body. The point appears to be that this particular modality of mindfulness meditation offers such an all-encompassing perspective that it covers all that is needed for progress towards awakening.

On reviewing the exercises common to the two versions, the different yet complementary perspectives they present are remarkable. At one end of the spectrum there is the rather negative appraisal of the body as unclean with the contemplation of the anatomical parts, which has its counterbalance in the series of exercises concerned with the somatic experience of drenching and pervading the body with deep joy and happiness during absorption attainment. This contrast alone suffices to counter the impression that in early Buddhist meditation practice the body is unilaterally deprecated as something that is to be rejected.[55]

Another rather challenging exercise concerns directing mindfulness to a corpse in various stages of decay, vividly driving home the undeniable truth that the body is bound to fall apart. As a recollection of mortality, this exercise has a remarkable potential. A complement to this practice can be found in the contemplation of the body as composed of material elements, a deployment of mindfulness that can bring to light the similarity and even interrelatedness of the human body with the whole of the outer environment, all of it being similarly composed of these same elements.

A foundational practice of mindfulness of the body involves the bodily postures, the first in the above list of exercises. Such practice leads to a grounding in embodiment that can be further developed by cultivating clear knowing in relation

55 Anālayo 2017c: 43–63.

to various activities undertaken with mindful composure and circumspection. Embodied mindfulness cultivated in this way can serve as a stabilizing foundation for other meditation practices and thereby actualize the potential that the *Kāyagatāsati-sutta* and its *Madhyama-āgama* parallel mention after each contemplation, namely the gaining of concentration. In this way, the survey they offer fleshes out with various details how mindfulness can lead to concentration.

From the imagery of the great ocean, the two parallels proceed to a series of similes that illustrate how due to lacking mindfulness of the body one will fall prey to Māra, who in early Buddhist thought personifies various temptations or external threats that could obstruct one's progress on the path to liberation:[56]

> It is just like a pot empty of water that stands firmly upright on the ground, and a person were to come carrying water and pour it into the pot ...
>
> It is just like a strong person who were to throw a big heavy stone at a mass of wet mud ...
>
> It is just like a person searching for fire who were to use dry wood as a base and to drill it with a dry drill.

The *Kāyagatāsati-sutta* agrees in illustrating the predicament of one who has not cultivated mindfulness of the body with the same set of similes, although given in a different sequence. Just as water easily fills an empty pot, a heavy stone easily enters mud, and drilling dry wood easily produces fire, so Māra will easily get an opportunity to overpower the mind.

The situation changes, however, once mindfulness of the body has been cultivated. Such cultivation compares to a pot already full with water, which will not take in any more, to throwing a light object at a solid wall, which will not enter, and to drilling wet wood, which will not produce fire:[57]

---

56 The extracts are found between MĀ 81 at T I 556c16 and 557a23, parallel to MN 119 at MN III 95,3.

57 MĀ 81 at T I 556c29 to 557a3, parallel to MN 119 at MN III 95,20, which additionally has three more similes that describe tilting a full water jug, loosening the embankment of a pond full of water, and driving a chariot wherever one wishes.

> If any recluses and brahmins have properly established mindfulness of the body and dwell with a boundless mind, then Māra, the Bad One, on seeking an opportunity with them, will in the end not be able to get it. Why is that? Because those recluses and brahmins are not devoid of mindfulness of the body.

This goes beyond the role of mindfulness in leading to concentration. Here mindfulness of the body serves a "protective" role, by protecting the practitioner from becoming overwhelmed by unwholesome states.

The two versions conclude with a list of various attainments that can be reached by cultivating mindfulness of the body, which mention among others going beyond discontent and fear, being able to endure the vicissitudes of climate and hunger or thirst, attaining the four absorptions, and the gaining of awakening.[58] In other words, even just cultivating mindfulness by way of the first of the four *satipaṭṭhāna*s can already activate the "liberating" dimension of mindfulness and lead to a vast range of potential benefits.

MINDFULNESS OF BREATHING IN SIXTEEN STEPS (SĀ 803)

As the last passage in this chapter, I take up a *Saṃyukta-āgama* discourse that covers the whole meditative progression of mindfulness of breathing. Besides introducing a mode of practice that encompasses all four establishments of mindfulness and thereby serving as a transition to the next chapter, what follows is also meant to supplement the exposition of only the first four steps of mindfulness of breathing in the *Kāyagatāsati-sutta* and its *Madhyama-āgama* parallel. The full scheme covers sixteen distinct steps of meditative practice, preceded by a description of preliminaries:[59]

> One enters a forest or an empty hut, or [goes to] the root of a tree or vacant open ground. Seated properly with the body

58 Anālayo 2011: 678.

59 SĀ 803 at T II 206a22 to 206b11, parallel to SN 54.1 at SN V 311,11 (translated by Bodhi 2000: 1765).

kept straight and keeping mindfulness in front, one abandons lustful cravings in the world and becomes purified by removing sensuality, ill will, sloth-and-torpor, restlessness-and-worry, and by abandoning doubt, crossing over all perplexity. The mind gains certainty in wholesome states and is far removed from the five hindrances that afflict the mind, that cause a weakening of the power of wisdom, that partake of being obstructive, and that do not lead to Nirvāṇa.

One is mindful of the breath coming in, training well to keep being mindful of it, and one is mindful of the breath going out, training well to keep being mindful of it.

Breathing long ... breathing short ... experiencing the whole body when breathing in, one trains well [to experience] the whole body when breathing in; experiencing the whole body when breathing out, one trains well [to experience] the whole body when breathing out. Experiencing a calming of all bodily activity when breathing in, one trains well [to experience] a calming of all bodily activity when breathing in; experiencing a calming of all bodily activity when breathing out, one trains well [to experience] a calming of ⟨all⟩ bodily activity when breathing out.[60]

Experiencing joy ... experiencing happiness ... experiencing ⟨mental⟩ activity[61] ... experiencing a calming of mental activity when breathing in, one trains well to experience a calming of mental activity when breathing in; experiencing a calming of mental activity when breathing out, one trains well to experience a calming of mental activity when breathing out.

Experiencing the mind ... experiencing gladdening the mind ... experiencing concentrating the mind ... experiencing liberating the mind when breathing in, one trains well to experience liberating the mind when breathing in; experiencing liberating the mind when breathing out, one trains well to experience liberating the mind when breathing out.

Contemplating impermanence ... contemplating eradication ... contemplating dispassion ... contemplating cessation when

60 The translation "all" in the last sentence is based on an emendation of what must be a copyist's error.

61 The translation "mental activity" is based on an emendation; the text erroneously has "bodily activity" here.

> breathing in, one trains well to contemplate cessation when breathing in; contemplating cessation when breathing out, one trains well to contemplate cessation when breathing out.

The last three steps in the Pāli parallel are instead dispassion (*virāga*), cessation (*nirodha*), and letting go (*paṭinissagga*). Otherwise the instructions are fairly similar in the two versions, showing how, from an initial establishing of mindfulness on the breath as such, practice proceeds through sixteen distinct meditative steps.

For evaluating the role of mindfulness in relation to meditating on the breath, the whole progression of sixteen steps provides a significant perspective. Here it is particularly notable that the progression through these steps does not give the impression that an all-out focus on the breath is their main concern.[62] Instead, the chief modality of meditation on the breath appears to involve considerable breadth of mind, as it requires remaining aware of the breath alongside various other aspects of one's present experience. Such practice does begin with some degree of focus, when during the first two steps long and short breaths need to be discerned. But during the remainder of the practice, an exclusive focus is clearly not the main thrust of "mindfulness" of breathing.

Each of the four tetrads that emerge from this progression through the sixteen steps then corresponds to a particular establishment of mindfulness, namely body (from breathing long to calming bodily activity), feeling tone (from joy to calming mental activity), the mind (from experiencing to liberating the mind), and dharmas (from impermanence to cessation or else letting go). In this way, the above instructions show how all four establishments of mindfulness can be cultivated based on mindfulness of the breath. The overall purpose of such practice is to issue in a cultivation of the awakening factors and lead on to knowledge and liberation. From this perspective, the above instructions throw into relief the "liberating" dimension of mindfulness.

---

62 Anālayo 2019i.

SUMMARY

Mindfulness of the body can serve as a header for a variety of meditation practices, which range from examining the constitution of the body, via proprioceptive awareness and bodily circumspection, to the embodied bliss of deep concentration. Being mindful of the body can enable one to stay centred even amidst the most distracting activities, illustrated in the discourses with the examples of carrying a bowl of oil through a dancing spectacle and keeping six different animals reined in at a single place. Its cultivation can serve to remove sensuality and to lead to a boundless mental condition. A central point that emerges from the various passages surveyed in this chapter is the potential of cultivating an embodied form of mindfulness.

III

ESTABLISHING MINDFULNESS (1)

In what follows I explore discourses pertinent to the topic of the four establishments of mindfulness. The *Satipaṭṭhāna-sutta* (MN 10) and its *Madhyama-āgama* and *Ekottarika-āgama* parallels are, of course, of central relevance to this topic. However, as I have already dedicated three monographs to this discourse and its practical implications, one of which with a particular emphasis on the two Chinese parallels, in what follows I will take up other relevant material.[1] The passages surveyed below are in fact amply sufficient to cover topics relevant to the present book.

I begin with the Buddha's reflection, shortly after his awakening, on the potential of the four establishments of mindfulness (SĀ 1189), which became a central part of his teachings (DĀ 4). In the remainder of this chapter, I take up various discourses from the collected sayings on the four establishments of mindfulness in the *Saṃyukta-āgama*.[2] In my presentation, I follow the sequence of discourses as they appear in the original collection. As a result, my presentation is no longer as closely tied to a particular topic as in the preceding two chapters, simply because the collected sayings present the discourses in a sequence not entirely determined by concerns of topic interrelationship. Central dimensions of

1 Anālayo 2003b, 2013b, and 2018i; see also Anālayo 2011: 73–97.
2 Out of the discourses in this collection, translations of SĀ 605 to 615 can also be found in Hurvitz 1978.

mindfulness that emerge from the passages taken up in the present chapter can be found in its "liberating" and "receptive" dimensions, as well as in its "protective" quality that comes to the fore in some similes.

The collected sayings on the four establishments of mindfulness begin with injunctions to train in the establishments of mindfulness (SĀ 605 and SĀ 606). The next topic is the relation of the cultivation of mindfulness to the goal of liberation (SĀ 607 and SĀ 608). The collection then turns to the objects of the four establishments of mindfulness (SĀ 609), whose cultivation can have internal and external dimensions (SĀ 610). The four establishments of mindfulness are of a wholesome nature (SĀ 611), provide an inexhaustible topic for teachings (SĀ 612), and are the appropriate practice for a great person (SĀ 614).

At times meditation practice requires a shift from mindfulness to giving more emphasis to concentration (SĀ 615). In fact, one should mindfully adjust one's meditation practice, similar to a skilled cook who adjusts his dishes to the preferences of his master (SĀ 616). The relationship between mindfulness and sense restraint can be illustrated with a simile involving a quail caught by a hawk (SĀ 617). Mindfulness requires establishing balance, similar to two acrobats performing together (SĀ 619). Following the powerful imagery of this simile, the collected sayings on the four establishments of mindfulness in the *Saṃyukta-āgama* have still more material to offer, which I will explore in the next chapter.

THE BUDDHA'S AWAKENING AND THE DIRECT PATH (SĀ 1189)

The scheme of the four establishments of mindfulness and their potential benefits appears to be closely related to the Buddha's progress to, and eventual gaining of, awakening. For this reason, they form the topic of one of the reflections he had soon after having become a Buddha:[3]

3 SĀ 1189 at T II 322a28 to 322b3, parallel to SN 47.18 at SN V 167,5 and SN 47.43 at SN V 185,4 (translated by Bodhi 2000: 1647 and 1661), SĀ² 102 at T II 410b10, and SĀ³ 4 at T II 494a17.

> At one time the Buddha was dwelling at Uruvelā, by the side of the river Nerañjarā, below the tree of awakening, having just become a Buddha. At that time the Blessed One, being alone and reflecting in a quiet place, had the thought:
>
> "There is a single vehicle's path capable of purifying sentient beings, of transcending worry and sorrow, of extinguishing pain and affliction, and of attaining the truth according to the Dharma, namely the four establishments of mindfulness. What are the four? They are the establishment of mindfulness by contemplating the body [in regard to] the body ... feeling tones ... the mind ... the establishment of mindfulness by contemplating dharmas [in regard to] dharmas."

In agreement with its parallels, the *Saṃyukta-āgama* discourse continues by reporting that the celestial Brahmā came to express his approbation. In this way, on looking back over the path he had pursued, the recently awakened Buddha was apparently moved to express his appreciation of the "liberating" potential of the four establishments of mindfulness, an appreciation confirmed by Brahmā, a central figure in the ancient Indian pantheon. This liberating potential lies in their ability to bring about mental purification and to lead beyond various types of affliction.

According to the passage translated above, such practice can lead to the attainment of truth. The corresponding phrasing employed in the Pāli version speaks of the true method and the realization of Nirvāṇa. In spite of differing terminology, the basic implication would be similar.

The reference in the *Saṃyukta-āgama* version translated above to a "single vehicle's path" appears to be based on a misunderstanding or a textual error. As a result, what presumably would have been an equivalent to the Pāli version's *ekāyana*, a qualification of the path perhaps best understood as conveying the sense of being "direct",[4] became *ekayāna*, the path of "a single

4 The nuance of being a "direct path" is my preferred understanding among various possible explanations, for surveys of which see Gethin 1992: 59–66 and Klaus 2018.

vehicle".[5] Another two Chinese parallels contain translations that appear to reflect an Indic original similar to the Pāli phrase, thereby confirming the impression that the *Saṃyukta-āgama* version's reference to a "single vehicle's path" must be an error.[6]

The Pāli discourses tend to single out the establishments of mindfulness as the direct path for the purification of beings, etc., thereby throwing into relief the liberating power of mindfulness cultivated in this way. Discourses in the *Saṃyukta-āgama* differ insofar as they also apply the corresponding notion of a "single vehicle's path" to other practices, such as the three types of purification, the four bases of success, and the six recollections.[7] Pāli parallels to discourses expounding the three types of purification and the six recollections mention only the purification of beings, etc., without any reference to the direct path.[8] This makes it possible, although not certain, that the otherwise similar reference to the purification of beings, etc., attracted the reference to the direct path (understood as a single vehicle) during oral transmission. As a result, the *Saṃyukta-āgama* now has this reference not only for the establishments of mindfulness, but also in relation to other practices. From a practical viewpoint this seems less fitting, as the cultivation of mindfulness is indeed a direct path to liberation, whereas the same does not necessarily apply in the same way for the six recollections, for example.

---

5 A discussion of this translation error can be found in Nattier 2007. The apparent shift from *ekāyana* to *ekayāna* does not appear to be a problem of the Chinese translation of the *Saṃyukta-āgama* only, as another occurrence of the same rendering in SĀ 535 at T II 139a20 has a counterpart in a Tibetan parallel, Up 6029 at D 4094 *nya* 13a4 or Q 5595 *thu* 46a8, in *theg pa ni gcig*, the "single vehicle". However, a reference to the single vehicle in SĀ 550 at T II 143b22 has a counterpart in the "direct path" in a Sanskrit fragment parallel, MS 2380/1/1+2recto1, Harrison 2007: 202: *ekāyano mārgaḥ*. See also below note 16.

6 SĀ² 102 at T II 410b12 simply refers to "a single path". The relevant expression in SĀ³ 4 at T II 494a19 has been translated by Nattier 2007: 195 as "the way which is single-leading".

7 SĀ 563 at T II 147c14, SĀ 561 at T II 147b2, and SĀ 550 at T II 143b22.

8 AN 3.74 at AN I 221,7 (translated by Bodhi 2012: 307) and AN 6.26 at AN III 314,22 (translated by Bodhi 2012: 885). The parallel to SĀ 561, SN 51.15 at SN V 272,16 (translated by Bodhi 2000: 1733), simply introduces the four bases of success as the way to overcome desire, without any additional qualification.

Be that as it may, the key point to be taken from the passage translated above is that, soon after his awakening, the Buddha reflected on the "liberating" potential of the four establishments of mindfulness in leading to mental purification and realization.[9]

THE BUDDHA'S TEACHING OF THE FOUR ESTABLISHMENTS (DĀ 4)

In view of their liberating potential, it is hardly surprising to find instructions on the systematic cultivation of mindfulness, in the form of its four establishments, listed among various qualities and accomplishments of the Buddha. A passage in the *Dīrgha-āgama* parallel to the *Janavasabha-sutta* emphasizes this in the following manner:[10]

> The Tathāgata, the arahant, is well capable of analytically teaching the four establishments of mindfulness. What are the four? The first is contemplating the body internally with untiring energy and collected mindfulness that is not lost, removing greed and discontent in the world, and contemplating the body externally with untiring energy and collected mindfulness that is not lost, removing greed and discontent in the world. Contemplation of feeling tones ... mind ... dharmas is also like that, with untiring energy and collected mindfulness that is not lost, removing greed and discontent in the world.
>
> Having contemplated the body internally, one arouses knowledge of the bodies of others. Having contemplated feeling tones internally, one arouses knowledge of the feeling tones of others. Having contemplated the mind internally, one arouses knowledge of the minds of others. Having contemplated dharmas internally, one arouses knowledge of the dharmas of others.
>
> These are the four establishments of mindfulness which the Tathāgata is well capable of analytically teaching.

---

9 Gethin 1992: 66 concludes that "the four *satipaṭṭhāna*s provide a description of the path right from basics direct to the final goal ... deserving of the epithet *ekāyano maggo*."

10 DĀ 4 at T I 35c26 to 36a4.

The Pāli parallel also lists the four establishments of mindfulness, indicating that their cultivation requires combining mindfulness not only with diligence or energy, but also with clear knowing (a quality not mentioned in the extract translated above).[11] The *Janavasabha-sutta* offers additional information on how mindfulness cultivated internally in this way then leads over to knowledge of the bodies, feeling tones, minds, and dharmas of others, qualified as "externally". According to its presentation, with internal cultivation the mind becomes rightly concentrated, which then enables arousing knowledge and vision of the same phenomenon in others.

In evaluating this difference, it is worthy of note that the two versions continue by listing seven qualities that support concentration, one of which is right mindfulness.[12] Perhaps the wording of the earlier passage in the *Janavasabha-sutta* was influenced by the relationship between mindfulness and concentration drawn in this subsequent passage. If this should indeed have been the case, the reference to the mind becoming well concentrated would be a later addition to the *Janavasabha-sutta*. Although this is far from certain, it could be noted that the *Dīrgha-āgama* version shows no evident signs of a textual loss as an alternative possibility to explain the difference between the two.

The possibility of knowing the mind of another even without recourse to telepathic knowledge can be deduced from the *Dīrgha-āgama* parallel to the *Sampasādanīya-sutta*. The relevant passage proceeds as follows:[13]

> Having on one's own observed the body or heard the speech of another, one says to that person: "Your mind is like this, your mind is like this."

The *Sampasādanīya-sutta* does not explicitly mention the body and thus bases this type of knowledge only on what one has heard, together with subsequent reflection on that. The tone of voice and

11 DN 18 at DN II 216,10 (translated by Walshe 1987: 298).

12 DN 18 at DN II 217,1 and DĀ 4 at T I 36a6.

13 DĀ 18 at T I 78a3 to 78a4, parallel to DN 28 at DN III 104,1 (translated by Walshe 1987: 419); for a Sanskrit fragment parallel see Or. 15009/137r6, Kudo 2009: 189.

contents of what someone says do indeed allow a keen observer to discern what feeling tone or mental state that other person is probably experiencing, and the same holds even more if bodily posture and facial expression are also taken into account. The cultivation of the "receptive" dimension mindfulness in particular would strengthen such keen observational ability.

The need to progress from internal to external cultivation of mindfulness is a recurrent topic in the early discourses, as already mentioned in the previous chapter (see above p. 50). Otherwise the discourses do not expand on the implications of this distinction, and later tradition reflects a variety of perspectives on the matter.[14] Although this makes it difficult to take a definite stance on the import of these terms, the above passages and their Pāli parallels offer support for the suggestion made in the previous chapter that such references can be understood to refer to oneself (internally) and others (externally).[15]

At the same time, however, the description in the *Janavasabha-sutta* reads as if such knowledge is of a telepathic type, based on having first cultivated a considerable degree of concentration. In contrast, the passage from the *Dīrgha-āgama* could more easily be read as pointing to a knowledge that might not require any telepathic powers, in line with the indication in the *Sampasādanīya-sutta* and its *Dīrgha-āgama* parallel that one might assess the state of mind of another based on a more ordinary type of observation.[16] I will return to the topic of the

14 For a detailed survey of later exegesis on these terms in a range of different traditions see Schmithausen 2012.

15 See in more detail Anālayo 2003b: 94–102, 2013b: 17f, 2018f, 2018i: 35–40, 2020d, and below p. 232.

16 The relevant passage in another Chinese parallel, T 9 at T I 216a8, is fairly short and just mentions internal and external cultivation of the four establishments of mindfulness, without spelling out any further details and thus without a reference to the bodies, etc., of others and also without a reference to concentration. Of interest for an evaluation of T 9 at T I 216a11 is that it provides another instance of the "one vehicle" phrase being applied to the four establishments of mindfulness, discussed above in note 5; see also the discussion in Nattier 2007: 190. In this case, the "one vehicle" phrase is preceded by a reference to *bodhi* and followed by a reference to the right Dharma. This formulation does not give the impression of being particularly early, making it less probable that the remainder of the passage has preserved a more original version than DĀ 4 and DN 18.

implications of internal and external as key features of the "receptive" dimension of mindfulness towards the end of my survey in the last chapter (see below p. 232).

TRAINING IN THE FOUR ESTABLISHMENTS OF MINDFULNESS (SĀ 605 AND SĀ 606)

In the remainder of this chapter and the first part of the next chapter, I continue with passages from the *Saṃyukta-āgama* that occur in the collected sayings on the establishments of mindfulness (SĀ 605 to SĀ 639). My presentation follows the sequence of discourses as they occur in the Taishō edition. Whenever I do not translate a discourse, due to the absence of a Pāli parallel, I mention this explicitly. In this way I hope that the reader will be able to gain a first-hand impression of the character of the collected sayings on the establishments of mindfulness in the *Saṃyukta-āgama*.

The first two discourses in this part of the *Saṃyukta-āgama* have a single Pāli parallel, wherefore I take them up together:[17]

> There are four establishments of mindfulness. What are the four? They are reckoned to be the establishment of mindfulness by contemplating the body [in regard to] the body ... feeling tones ... the mind ... and the establishment of mindfulness by contemplating dharmas [in regard to] dharmas.

The second discourse among the collected sayings on the establishments of mindfulness differs from the preceding one only in so far as it instructs the listening monastics that they should train themselves in such practice:

> There are four establishments of mindfulness. What are the four? They are reckoned to be the establishment of mindfulness

17 SĀ 605 at T II 170c28 to 171a1 and SĀ 606 at T II 171a4 to 171a7, parallel to SN 47.24 at SN V 173,26 (translated by Bodhi 2000: 1652); SĀ 605 also has a parallel preserved in Tibetan translation, Up 6027 at D 4094 *nyu* 12b3 or Q 5595 *thu* 45b6 (translated by Dhammadinnā 2018: 23).

> by contemplating the body [in regard to] the body ... feeling tones ... the mind ... and the establishment of mindfulness by contemplating dharmas [in regard to] dharmas.
>
> In this way, monastics, with diligent effort, right mindfulness, and right knowing you should train in the full cultivation of these four establishments of mindfulness.

The Pāli counterpart does not have an injunction to the monastics that they should train and therefore in this respect is a closer parallel to the first of these two *Saṃyukta-āgama* discourses. It adds to each establishment of mindfulness that the respective contemplation should be "diligent, clearly knowing, and mindful, free from greedy desires and discontent in the world".[18] This has a counterpart only in the second discourse translated above, which also mentions that mindfulness collaborates with diligent effort and right knowing, although here this specification is found after the listing of the four establishments. The divergence in the position of these qualifications does not amount to a substantial difference in understanding; in fact other discourses in the *Saṃyukta-āgama* apply these qualifications to the actual listing of the four establishments, an example being SĀ 610 (see below p. 99). In general, there seems to be a tendency for more emphasis on these qualities in Pāli discourses.[19]

In sum, the overall presentation in the *Saṃyukta-āgama* can be seen to agree with the Pāli discourses that, in the cultivation of *satipaṭṭhāna*, mindfulness collaborates with the qualities of diligent effort and right or clear knowing. It is the combination of these qualities that engenders the "liberating" potential of *satipaṭṭhāna* meditation, which is precisely the topic of the next discourse in the collection.

---

18 SN 47.24 at SN V 173,29: *ātāpī samapajāno satimā vineyya loka abhijjhādomanassaṃ*.

19 See below p. 94n23, p. 107n45, p. 123n6, p. 227n59, and p. 227n61.

THE PATH OF MINDFULNESS (SĀ 607)

The four establishments of mindfulness can serve as a path to liberation from *dukkha*:[20]

> There is a single vehicle's path for the purification of sentient beings,[21] for causing the transcendence of worry and sorrow, for extinguishing affliction and pain, for attaining what accords with the truth of the Dharma,[22] that is, the four establishments of mindfulness. What are the four? [They are] the establishment of mindfulness by contemplating the body [in regard to] the body ... feeling tones ... the mind ... and the establishment of mindfulness by contemplating dharmas [in regard to] dharmas.[23]

The Pāli parallel, which is the first discourse in the *Satipaṭṭhāna-saṃyutta*, has the "true method" and the "realization of Nirvāṇa" as its counterpart to the "truth of the Dharma" mentioned in the passage translated above. The divergent terms employed in this way could be seen to complement each other in highlighting benefits to be achieved through cultivating the four establishments of mindfulness.

The main point made by this passage concurs with the earlier two discourses, by confirming that the overarching concern of *satipaṭṭhāna* meditation is to effect mental purification, to lead beyond being afflicted by worry, sorrow, and pain, and to bring about a realization of truth or Nirvāṇa. Cultivated in this way, mindfulness can become truly "liberating".

MINDFULNESS AND LIBERATION (SĀ 608)

The next discourse in a way builds on what has emerged so far by highlighting the necessity of cultivating the four

---

20 SĀ 607 at T II 171a10 to 171a13, parallel to SN 47.1 at SN V 141,10 (translated by Bodhi 2000: 1627).

21 On the reference to a "single vehicle's" path see above note 5.

22 The formulation here differs from SĀ 1189, taken up above p. 87, which had "the truth according to the Dharma".

23 SN 47.1 at SN V 141,15 adds that such mindfulness practice involves being "diligent, clearly knowing, and mindful, free from greedy desires and discontent in the world".

establishments of mindfulness in order to be able to progress to liberation:[24]

> If monastics are separated from the four establishments of mindfulness, they are separated from what accords with the truth of the noble Dharma. Being separated from what accords with the truth of the noble Dharma, they are separated from the noble path. Being separated from the noble path, they are separated from the Dharma of deathlessness. Being separated from the Dharma of deathlessness, they are unable to become free from birth, old age, disease, death, worry, sorrow, affliction, and pain. I say they are unable to attain liberation from [the mass of] *dukkha*.
>
> If monastics are not separated from the four establishments of mindfulness, they gain not being separated from what is noble and what accords with the truth of the Dharma.[25] Not being separated from what is noble and what accords with the truth of the Dharma, they are not separated from the noble path. Not being separated from the noble path, they are not separated from the Dharma of deathlessness. Not being separated from the Dharma of deathlessness, they are able to become free from birth, old age, disease, death, worry, sorrow, affliction, and pain. I say they are able to attain liberation from the mass of *dukkha*.

The Pāli parallel makes basically the same point in a simpler manner, as it equates neglecting the four establishments of mindfulness with neglect of the noble path leading to the complete destruction of *dukkha*. A relationship between the four establishments of mindfulness and the "deathless", *amata*, occurs in another discourse in the *Saṃyutta-nikāya*, which could be reckoned an additional, or more precisely a "partial", parallel to the above *Saṃyukta-āgama* discourse.[26]

---

24 SĀ 608 at T II 171a16 to 171a24, parallel to SN 47.33 at SN V 179,27 (translated by Bodhi 2000: 1656).

25 The phrasing here has changed from that of the preceding paragraph.

26 SN 47.41 at SN V 184,9 (translated by Bodhi 2000: 1660). Akanuma 1929/1990: 65 in fact lists SN 47.41 as the parallel to SĀ 608. Closer inspection, however, makes it preferable to consider SN 47.33 as the main parallel and SN 47.41 only as a partial parallel.

Looking back on the four discourses surveyed so far from the collected sayings on the establishments of mindfulness in the *Saṃyukta-āgama*, something of a crescendo effect can be noticed: the first discourse (SĀ 605) presents the four establishments, the second (SĀ 606) encourages training in them, the third (SĀ 607) shows their potential to lead to liberation, and the fourth (SĀ 608) clarifies that they are definitely required for that purpose. The resultant highlight on the "liberating" dimension of mindfulness shows that neglecting its cultivation is nothing other than neglecting the path to freedom.

THE IMPERMANENCE OF THE OBJECTS OF MINDFULNESS (SĀ 609)

Following on the crescendo effect created by the first four discourses, another perspective on the four establishments of mindfulness emerges from the next discourse, which concerns its objects. The discourse directs attention to the body, feeling tones, the mind, and dharmas as the four objects of *satipaṭṭhāna* meditation, with the question of what leads to their arising and their vanishing:[27]

> What is the arising of [the objects of] the four establishments of mindfulness? What is the vanishing of [the objects of] the four establishments of mindfulness? The arising of nutriment is the arising of the body; the cessation of nutriment is the vanishing of the body. In this way one is accordingly established in contemplating the [nature of] arising in the body, one is accordingly established in contemplating the [nature of] ceasing in the body, and one is accordingly established in contemplating the [nature of] arising and ceasing in the body. One is established in dwelling independently, without ever clinging to anything in the world.
>
> In the same way, the arising of contact is the arising of feeling tones; the cessation of contact is the vanishing of feeling tones.

27 SĀ 609 at T II 171a27 to 171b12, parallel to SN 47.42 at SN V 184,17 (translated by Bodhi 2000: 1660), Up 6031 at D 4094 *nyu* 15a5 or Q 5595 *thu* 48b5 (translated by Dhammadinnā 2018: 23), and an Uighur fragment, Zhang 2002: 109.

> In this way one is accordingly established in contemplating the nature of arising in feeling tones, one is accordingly established in contemplating the nature of ceasing in feeling tones, and one is accordingly established in contemplating the nature of arising and ceasing in feeling tones. One is established in dwelling independently, without [ever] clinging to anything in the world.
>
> The arising of name-and-form is the arising of the mind, the cessation of name-and-form is the vanishing of the mind. [In this way] one is accordingly established in contemplating the nature of arising in the mind, one is accordingly established in contemplating the nature of ceasing in the mind, and one is accordingly established in contemplating the nature of arising and ceasing in the mind. One is established in dwelling independently, without [ever] clinging to anything in the world.
>
> The arising of attention is the arising of dharmas, the cessation of attention is the vanishing of dharmas. [In this way] one is accordingly established in contemplating the nature of arising in dharmas, one is accordingly established in contemplating the nature of ceasing in dharmas, and one is accordingly established in contemplating the nature of arising and ceasing in dharmas. One is established in dwelling independently, without [ever] clinging to anything in the world.
>
> This is reckoned to be the arising of [the objects of] the four establishments of mindfulness and the vanishing of [the objects of] the four establishments of mindfulness.

The Pāli parallel also speaks of the arising and passing away of the four establishments of mindfulness, even though the exposition actually concerns their respective objects.[28] Hence the supplementation of "[the objects of]" in the above translation could similarly be employed in a translation of the Pāli version.

The first of these four objects is the body, which depends on nutriment, just as feeling tone depends on contact. Name-and-form usually serves as a condition for consciousness (*viññāṇa*),

---

28 Bodhi 2000: 1928n180 comments that "here *satipaṭṭhāna* obviously refers to the four objects of mindfulness"; see also Spk III 229,25: *imasmiṃ sutta sārammaṇasatipaṭṭhānā kathitā* and the discussion in Gethin 1992: 32ff.

whereas the term used in the present context is mind or mental state (*citta*).[29] The Pāli commentarial explanation relates this to the arising of the awakening factors, which results from the arising of wise or penetrative attention.[30]

The Chinese character couplet that I have translated as "attention" (*manasikāra*) can also render "mindful recollection". This range of possible meanings echoes observations made earlier regarding the memory nuances of mindfulness, as the usage by the Chinese translators (regardless of the term employed in the Indic original) agrees with a general impression of some fluidity in terminology.

The overall thrust of the presentation seems to be to highlight the conditionality of the objects of mindfulness meditation. A minor difference between the two versions is that the Pāli discourse just mentions the arising and passing away of each of these objects of mindfulness, without a reference to "contemplating" their arising and passing away and thereby also without a reference to dwelling independently without clinging to anything in the world.[31] Due to this difference, the *Saṃyukta-āgama* version comes with a bit more emphasis on relating this instruction to actual practice, thereby activating the "liberating" dimension of mindfulness in order to dwell independently and without clinging (mentioned regularly in the *Satipaṭṭhāna-sutta*).

Although not explicitly spelled out, the highlight placed here on the objects of mindfulness meditation could be taken to imply an encouragement to discern the conditionality of what is experienced during actual practice. Discerning conditionality is in fact an explicit part of instructions for contemplation of the hindrances and the awakening factors in

---

29 Bodhi 2000: 1928n181 explains that "in this passage *citta* is taken to be synonymous with *viññāṇa*; *nāmarūpa*, being the condition for the latter, is the condition for the former as well. For *citta* always arises based on the physical organism (*rūpa*) and in conjunction with contact, feeling, perception, volition, and attention, the constituents of *nāma*."

30 Spk III 229,23: *yonisomanasikārasamudayā bojjhaṅgadhammānaṃ samudayo*.

31 Anālayo 2013b: 15–17. The presentation in SĀ 609 thereby concurs with MN 10 and EĀ 12.1 against MĀ 98, which does not mention impermanence as an insight to be cultivated in relation to each exercise.

the *Satipaṭṭhāna-sutta* and its *Madhyama-āgama* parallel.[32] From this viewpoint, then, perhaps the present discourse could be taken to point to an application of the same procedure to the entire range of objects that can come within the purview of *satipaṭṭhāna* meditation.[33] Due to the different characteristics of each of these four domains, the main conditions to be discerned differ, ranging from nutriment via contact and name-and-form to attention. Such paying attention to discerning conditionality could then be related to the "attentive" dimension of mindfulness.

CULTIVATING THE ESTABLISHMENTS OF MINDFULNESS (SĀ 610)

According to the next discourse, a "cultivation" of the establishments of mindfulness requires directing mindfulness internally, externally, and both:[34]

> I will teach you the cultivation of the four establishments of mindfulness; listen carefully and pay proper attention. What is the cultivation of the four establishments of mindfulness? It is reckoned to be dwelling in contemplation of the body [in relation to] the body internally, with diligent effort, right knowing, and right mindfulness, overcoming worry and sorrow in the world; dwelling in contemplation of the body [in relation to the body] externally ... and internally and externally, with diligent effort, right mindfulness, and right knowing, overcoming worry and sorrow in the world.
>
> In the same way for dwelling in [contemplation of] feeling tones ... the mind ... and dharmas [in relation to] dharmas internally ... dharmas externally ... and dharmas internally and externally, with diligent effort, right mindfulness, and right knowing, overcoming worry and sorrow in the world.
>
> Monastics, this is called the cultivation of the four establishments of mindfulness.

---

32 Anālayo 2013b: 177–226.

33 See also Anālayo 2018i: 193–195.

34 SĀ 610 at T II 171b15 to 171b21, parallel to SN 47.3 at SN V 143,8 (translated by Bodhi 2000: 1629), MĀ 76 at T I 543c13, and Up 6028 at D 4094 *nyu* 12b4 or Q 5595 *thu* 45b8 (translated by Dhammadinnā 2018: 24).

The above discourse is followed by an indication that the cultivation of the four establishments of mindfulness in regard to the past and future should also be taught in this way. This type of reciter's instruction implies that another two discourses should be recited in the same way, with the only difference that the otherwise similar instructions should be related to the past and to the future. Since the cultivation itself is concerned with what is taking place in the present moment, this indication could be taken to convey that the way to practise the four establishments of mindfulness was the same in the past and will be the same in the future. In other words, the "receptive" dimension of mindfulness in relation to the internal and the external should be seen as a key feature of its cultivation in past, present, and future times.

The Pāli parallel stipulates the need to purify one's moral conduct and have straight view as a foundation for such mindfulness practice.[35] It expounds in a similar way the four establishments of mindfulness cultivated internally, externally, and both. With such practice (based on moral conduct), according to the Pāli report one can expect wholesome states to grow, day and night, and not decline.

The basic formulation describing the mindfulness practice itself is closely similar in the Pāli version, which also combines mindfulness with being diligent (*ātāpī*), clearly knowing (*sampajāna*), and overcoming greedy desire and discontent in the world (*vineyya loke abhijjhādomanassaṃ*). The same holds for parallels in the *Madhyama-āgama* and in Tibetan translation. The present discourse thereby affords a convenient opportunity for examining the qualities that collaborate with mindfulness in the context of *satipaṭṭhāna* meditation.

The term *ātāpī* can at times convey nuances of a rather strong effort, in the sense of strenuous or even ardent exertion. The Chinese original for the above translation combines characters

35 The introductory part in SN 47.3 at SN V 142,26 differs, as it starts off with a monastic asking for instruction in brief for the purpose of dwelling in seclusion and practising diligently. After some initial hesitation, the Buddha first stresses the importance of a foundation in virtuous conduct and straight view.

that render "effort" and "expedient", another Chinese parallel speaks of being "very energetic", and the Tibetan counterpart conveys the sense of being "diligent".[36] This is indeed the sense appropriate to the present context, namely ensuring a continuity of mindfulness in a balanced manner which avoids laxity just as much as overstrenuous exertion.

The Pāli counterpart to "right knowing" is *sampajañña* (noun) or *sampajāna* (adjective), a term related to the verb *pajānāti*, "one knows", which occurs repeatedly in the detailed instructions in the *Satipaṭṭhāna-sutta*. The corresponding noun is *paññā*, "wisdom". A definition given in the *Mahāvedalla-sutta* of one who has wisdom employs precisely the verb *pajānāti*.[37]

The similarity between the parallel versions in stipulating these qualities suggests that, in the context of the cultivation of the four establishments of mindfulness, the quality of clear or right knowing is in particular responsible for engendering wisdom. In some later traditions, however, mindfulness came to be seen as intrinsically a matter of wisdom, and at times was also equated to the quality of diligence. The basic formula describing the establishments of mindfulness shows that in early Buddhist thought mindfulness rather collaborates with clear knowing and with diligence. Hence for a proper appreciation of mindfulness as such, a distinction needs to be drawn between mindfulness on its own and its cultivation in conjunction with clear/right knowing and diligence as *satipaṭṭhāna*. This distinction is also of relevance for appreciating the ethical quality of mindfulness by itself as compared with *satipaṭṭhāna*.

THE WHOLESOME NATURE OF THE FOUR ESTABLISHMENTS (SĀ 611)

The ethical quality of *satipaṭṭhāna* meditation is the topic of the next discourse, which clarifies that the practice of the

36 MĀ 76 at T I 543c13 and Up 6028 at D 4094 *nyu* 12b6 or Q 5595 *thu* 46a1.

37 MN 43 at MN I 292,19: *pajānāti pajānātī ti kho, āvuso, tasmā paññavā ti vuccati* (translated by Ñāṇamoli 1995/2005: 387), with a counterpart in MĀ 211 at T I 790b29.

establishments of mindfulness is of a wholesome nature. This contrasts to the hindrances, which are rather unwholesome conditions of the mind:[38]

> There is a heap of wholesome states and a heap of unwholesome states.
>
> What is a heap of wholesome states? That is, it is the four establishments of mindfulness. These are rightly called such. Why is that? They are entirely and completely a pure heap, that is, the four establishments of mindfulness. What are the four? They are reckoned to be the establishment of mindfulness by contemplating the body [in regard to] the body ... feeling tones ... the mind ... and the establishment of mindfulness by contemplating dharmas [in regard to] dharmas.
>
> What is a heap of unwholesome [states]? The heap of unwholesome [states] is reckoned to be the five hindrances. These are rightly called such. Why is that? They are entirely [a matter of] negligence and completely a heap of what is unwholesome, that is, the five hindrances. What are the five? They are reckoned to be the hindrance of sensual desire, the hindrance of anger, the hindrance of sloth-and-torpor, the hindrance of restlessness-and-worry, and the hindrance of doubt.

The Pāli parallel takes the same position, with the minor sequential difference that it first takes up the five hindrances as a heap of what is unwholesome and only then the four establishments of mindfulness as a heap of what is wholesome; a procedure in line with a regular pattern of mentioning the negative first and then the positive.

The identification of the four establishments of mindfulness as a heap of what is wholesome could have provided a starting point for, or at least encouraged, the notion in some later traditions that mindfulness itself is invariably a wholesome quality.[39] This is not the case for early Buddhism, which

38 SĀ 611 at T II 171b25 to 171c4, parallel to SN 47.5 at SN V 145,26 (translated by Bodhi 2000: 1631); see also a Sanskrit fragment, SHT I 533 folio 106V7 to R2, Bechert and Wille 1989: 215, which has preserved part of the exposition of the hindrances as a heap of what is unwholesome.

39 Anālayo 2013b: 178–180.

recognizes wrong types of mindfulness. Wrong mindfulness clearly does not fit the category of being a wholesome quality. Hence in early Buddhist thought mindfulness itself is considered an ethically indeterminate quality. It could be wholesome, but could also fail to be so. However, when mindfulness features as part of a cultivation of the four establishments of mindfulness, then it definitely acquires a wholesome dimension.

Of further interest here is that such cultivation involves, among other things, directing mindfulness to the presence of the hindrances in one's own mind. Contrary to notions held in later tradition, this shows that mindfulness can be present at the time when an unwholesome quality is in the mind.[40]

THE INEXHAUSTIBILITY OF TEACHINGS ON MINDFULNESS (SĀ 612)

The preceding three discourses have defined some parameters of *satipaṭṭhāna* meditation. These concern observing the arising and passing away of the four objects of *satipaṭṭhāna* meditation so as to dwell independently and without clinging (SĀ 609) and the need for such cultivation to cover both what is internal and what is external (SĀ 610), followed by pointing to the intrinsically wholesome nature of such practice (SĀ 611). Although in itself this may seem already a rather comprehensive survey of the topic, as if to forestall the impression that all has by now been said, the next discourse clarifies that the establishments of mindfulness provide an inexhaustible topic for the Buddha (here referred to as the Tathāgata) to deliver teachings:[41]

> It is like [four] persons who hold in their hands [one of] four types of strong bow and with much strength and skill shoot [an arrow] through the shadow of a palm tree, which quickly passes through without obstruction.
>
> In the same way, [suppose] there are four types of disciple of the Tathāgata with supreme skills, sharp wisdom faculties

40 Anālayo 2017c: 22–24.
41 SĀ 612 at T II 171c7 to 171c17, parallel to MN 12 at MN I 82,32 (translated by Ñāṇamoli 1995/2005: 177).

> and a lifespan of a complete hundred years. In relation to the Tathāgata's teaching and instructing the Dharma for a hundred years, except for just having a rest to eat, for nourishment and defecation,[42] and for sleep, in between [these activities] they would constantly listen to what is constantly being taught by the Tathāgata, being spoken with wisdom and acuity, completely remembering it to the end without any obstruction, and without asking the Tathāgata any further questions, [yet] the Tathāgata's teaching of the Dharma would not have come to an end.
>
> Listening to the teachings for their complete lifespan of a hundred years, their life would have come to an end and still the Tathāgata would not have been able to complete his teaching of the Dharma.
>
> You should know that what is taught by the Tathāgata is immeasurable and boundless; the collection of his words, his phrases, and his expressions is also unlimited and without an end, namely on the four establishments of mindfulness. What are the four? They are reckoned to be the establishment of mindfulness on the body ... feeling tones ... the mind ... and the establishment of mindfulness on dharmas.

A Pāli parallel to the above discourse occurs in the final part of the *Mahāsīhanāda-sutta*, found in the *Majjhima-nikāya*. The context here is an assertion by the Buddha that his advanced age should not be considered to have had any impact on his wisdom. A minor difference is that in the *Mahāsīhanāda-sutta* the four disciples of a hundred-year lifespan continue to ask questions about the four establishments of mindfulness, whereas in the above passage the Buddha expounds the same topic on his own, without the disciples asking any questions.

Alongside such differences, the two passages agree in throwing into relief the inexhaustibility of the topic of the four establishments of mindfulness, such that even in a teaching marathon lasting a hundred years the Buddha would not have run short of material. This indication in a way puts into perspective my survey in this and other chapters as well as

42 The translation "nourishment" is based on a variant reading.

my attempt to summarize key aspects of mindfulness under the headings of being "protective", "embodied", "attentive", "receptive", and "liberating". The survey presented in this book can only be incomplete and the five qualities I have chosen only be inadequate in view of the inexhaustibility of the topic.

The above discourse is followed by an indication that all of the discourses so far on the topic of the four establishments of mindfulness should be repeated with a concluding injunction to the monastics that they should make a supreme effort and with diligence, right mindfulness, and right knowing train themselves in the cultivation of the four establishments of mindfulness. This strong call to put it all into practice confirms the impression that the highlight on the inexhaustibility of the topic of *satipaṭṭhāna* meditation in a way rounds off the preceding survey of different aspects of its cultivation.

The *Saṃyukta-āgama* continues with another discourse that takes up again the wholesome nature of the four establishments of mindfulness (SĀ 613), already broached in the preceding discourse (SĀ 611). Since this next discourse does not have a Pāli parallel, I do not provide a translation, in keeping with the approach I have adopted throughout of taking up only material that is found in one of the Chinese *Āgama*s and their parallels in the Pāli *Nikāya*s. The discourse differs from SĀ 611 in its definition of what is unwholesome, as instead of the five hindrances it mentions the three unwholesome roots.[43] Following this discourse, there are instructions to recite four additional discourses, which vary in what they contrast with the wholesome nature of the four establishments of mindfulness. Presented in summary form, the five modalities of unwholesomeness that emerge in this way are as follows:

- The three unwholesome roots: lust, anger, and delusion.
- The three bad conducts: bad bodily conduct, bad verbal conduct, and bad mental conduct.

43 SĀ 613 at T II 171c24.

- Three [unwholesome] perceptions: perceptions of sensuality, perceptions of anger, and perceptions of harming.
- Three [unwholesome] thoughts: thoughts of sensuality, thoughts of anger, and thoughts of harming.
- Three [unwholesome] elements: the element of sensuality, the element of anger, and the element of harming.

These permutations around the theme of what is unwholesome converge on accentuating the wholesome repercussions of the four establishments of mindfulness, which invariably provide a contrast to each of the items in the above list. Be it the five hindrances mentioned earlier or any of the unwholesome conditions listed above, the cultivation of *satipaṭṭhāna* serves as the wholesome counterpart.

A GREAT PERSON PRACTISES MINDFULNESS (SĀ 614)

The next discourse in a way reiterates what emerges from the above survey of unwholesome conditions to be overcome, differing in so far as it instead places more emphasis on the positive. It achieves this by clarifying that to become a great person (*mahāpurisa*) requires cultivating the four establishments of mindfulness in such a way that the mind becomes liberated:[44]

> If a monastic dwells mindfully contemplating the body [in regard to] the body and, having dwelled mindfully contemplating the body [in regard to] the body, the mind is not freed from [lust and] sensual desire and does not attain liberation by eradicating all the influxes, I say that such a one is not a great person. Why is that? Because the mind is not liberated.
>
> If a monastic dwells mindfully contemplating feeling tones ... the mind ... dharmas [in regard to] dharmas and the mind is not freed from [lust and] sensual desire and does not attain liberation

44 SĀ 614 at T II 172a13 to 172a23, parallel to SN 47.11 at SN V 158,15 (translated by Bodhi 2000: 1640).

> by eradicating all the influxes, I do not say that such a one is a great person. Why is that? Because the mind is not liberated.
>
> If a monastic dwells mindfully contemplating the body [in regard to] the body and the mind attains being freed from [lust and] sensual desire,[45] the mind attains liberation by eradicating all the influxes, I say that such a one is a great person. Why is that? Because the mind is liberated.
>
> If [a monastic] dwells mindfully contemplating feeling tones ... the mind ... dharmas [in regard to] dharmas and, having dwelled mindfully contemplating feeling tones ... the mind ... dharmas [in regard to] dharmas, the mind is freed from lust and sensual desire, it attains liberation by eradicating all the influxes, I say that such a one is a great person. Why is that? Because the mind is liberated.

The introductory narration to the above extract reports that an unnamed monastic had asked the Buddha about the significance of being called a great person. In the Pāli parallel, Sāriputta had asked the question.

Alongside such minor differences, the two versions agree in highlighting the importance of cultivating the establishments of mindfulness in such a way that they actualize the "liberating" potential of mindfulness. This is their central purpose and the way to become a great person. Together with the previous set of discourses, undertaking *satipaṭṭhāna* meditation can be summarized as enabling complete emergence from what is unwholesome and thereby becoming a truly great person.

SHIFTING BETWEEN CONCENTRATION AND MINDFULNESS (SĀ 615)

The next discourse gives more specific instructions for the actual cultivation of *satipaṭṭhāna*. When experiencing sluggishness during one's practice, it is commendable to shift from the

45 SN 47.11 at SN V 158,19 additionally stipulates that each of the four establishments of mindfulness should be undertaken being "diligent, clearly knowing, and mindful, free from greedy desires and discontent in the world."

cultivation of *satipaṭṭhāna* to another meditation practice in order to arouse joy and thereby in turn strengthen concentration. The relevant discourse is of additional interest, as its introductory narration features nuns as accomplished practitioners of mindfulness:[46]

> At that time, in the morning, the venerable Ānanda put on his robes and took his bowl to enter the town of Sāvatthī and beg for alms. On the way he thought: "Let me now first go to the monastic dwelling of the nuns." He went to the monastic dwelling of the nuns.[47]
>
> On seeing from afar that the venerable Ānanda was coming, the nuns swiftly prepared a seat and invited him to sit down. Then the nuns paid respect at the feet of the venerable Ānanda, withdrew to sit to one side, and said to the venerable Ānanda: "We nuns are established in cultivating the four establishments of mindfulness with a [well-]collected mind, of which we ourselves know successively whether it increases or decreases [in collectedness]."[48]
>
> The venerable Ānanda said to the nuns: "It is well, it is well, sisters, one should train as you have described. Anyone who is established in cultivating the four establishments of mindfulness with a well-collected mind should in this way know successively whether it increases or decreases [in collectedness]."
>
> Then the venerable Ānanda taught the Dharma in various ways to the nuns. Having taught the Dharma in various ways, he rose from his seat and left.
>
> At that time, after having returned from begging for alms in the town of Sāvatthī, having stored away his robe and bowl, and

---

46 SĀ 615 at T II 172a27 to 172b21, parallel to SN 47.10 at SN V 154,21 (translated by Bodhi 2000: 1638).

47 The introductory narration in SN 47.10 at SN V 154,21 is less detailed; it just reports that Ānanda, taking his robes and bowl, went to a certain monastic dwelling place of nuns and sat down on a prepared seat.

48 According to SN 47.10 at SN V 154,30, being well established in the four establishments of mindfulness, the nuns had reached higher stages of distinction. The corresponding phrase in the Chinese is cryptic and the translation offered here is only tentative.

having washed his feet, the venerable Ānanda approached the Blessed One. He paid respect with his head at the Buddha's feet, withdrew to sit to one side, and fully told the Blessed One what the nuns had said.

The Buddha said to Ānanda: "It is well, it is well. In this way one should train in being established in the four establishments of mindfulness with a mind that is well collected and know successively whether it increases or decreases [in collectedness]. Why is that? [Suppose] the mind pursues what is external. Yet, afterwards one controls that pursuing mind. A distracted mind does not become liberated, knowing everything as it really is.

"Suppose a monastic is established in mindfully contemplating the body as a body. Having become established in mindfully contemplating the body as a body, suppose the body is affected by drowsiness and the mental factors are sluggish.[49] That monastic should arouse inspired confidence by taking hold of an inspiring mark.

"Having aroused a mental state of inspired confidence by mindfully recollecting an inspiring mark, the mind becomes delighted. [The mind] having become delighted, joy arises. The mind having become joyous, the body becomes tranquil. The body having become tranquil, happiness is experienced with the whole being.[50] Having experienced happiness with the whole being, the mind becomes concentrated.

"The mind being concentrated, the noble disciple should undertake this training: 'It is for this purpose that I took hold of the mind that had been scattered externally. That has made it become quiet without giving rise to perceptions with [directed] awareness and has stopped perceptions of [sustained] contemplation. Being without [directed] awareness and [sustained] contemplation, I am

---

49 SN 47.10 at SN V 156,2 adds that the mind is distracted externally.

50 My translation assumes that a reference to the body here renders an instrumental *kāyena* in the Indic original, which in such contexts functions as an idiomatic expression to convey personal and direct experience; see Schmithausen 1981: 214 and 249 ad. note 50, Radich 2007: 263, Harvey 2009: 180 note 10, and Anālayo 2011: 379f note 203.

> equanimous and mindful, established in happiness. Being already established in happiness, I know it as it really is.'"

The discourse continues by indicating that the same holds for feeling tones, the mind, and dharmas. The Pāli parallel offers additional details that elucidate the point made with this instruction. When the practitioner realizes that the mind has become concentrated, whereby the purpose of directing the mind has been achieved, it becomes possible to withdraw it and to dwell without *vitakka* and *vicāra*. These two are factors of the mind that are present in stages of meditation leading up to and during the actual attainment of the first absorption. Their Chinese equivalents are "[directed] awareness" and "[sustained] contemplation".

The Pāli version also examines the case when bringing to mind an inspiring mark (*nimitta*) is not necessary and the practitioner is able to dwell happily in the establishment of mindfulness without needing to direct the mind, unlike what was necessary when the mind was distracted outwardly. These two modes of practice are presented under the headings of "directed meditation" and "undirected meditation", making it clear that there is a sufficient degree of difference to distinguish between these two modalities of practice.[51] At the same time, the purpose of the entire passage is of course to show how they can be skilfully interrelated.

The main problem thematized in both versions seems to be distraction that occurs while one is cultivating mindfulness. Realizing that this is the case, the advice is to arouse inspiration by temporarily taking up some meditation practice that leads to joy and tranquillity. Once the mind has become more settled and concentrated in this way, one returns to the practice of mindfulness. After having in this way delineated the interrelation between mindfulness and concentration as two distinct but complementary qualities, the collected sayings on *satipaṭṭhāna* in the *Saṃyukta-āgama* continue with several similes.

---

51 Anālayo 2007: 92 and 2019k.

THE SIMILE OF THE COOK (SĀ 616)

The instructions in the previous discourse imply that mindfulness meditation requires monitoring what is taking place and adjusting one's practice accordingly. This basic principle of cultivating "receptivity", essential for successful practice, finds illustration in a simile featuring a cook:[52]

> You should take hold of the marks of your own mind; do not let it be scattered externally. Why is that? Suppose those foolish monastics, who do not distinguish and are not skilful, do not take hold of the marks of their own mind but take hold of an external mark. Subsequently they decline and give rise to what obstructs themselves.[53]
>
> It is just like, for example, a foolish cook, who does not distinguish and is not skilful at combining various tastes, who waits upon his master with what is sour, salty, or bland in a way that does not suit his [master's] wishes, who is unable to grasp well his master's preferences properly in regard to what is sour, salty, or bland, in regard to combining these various tastes.[54]
>
> He is unable to wait on his master intimately [while standing by his] left and right sides, to serve him what is required, to be receptive to his desires, to grasp well his [master's] wishes. Following his own ideas, he combines the various tastes and presents them to his master. As these do not suit his [master's] wishes, the master is not pleased. Because of not pleasing [his master, the cook] will not receive a noble reward and will not be thought of fondly.
>
> Foolish monastics are also like that; they do not distinguish and are not skilful. When dwelling in contemplation of the body [in regard to] the body, they are unable to remove higher defilements, unable to collect their minds, and also unable to gain mental stillness within. They are unable to gain perfect right

52 SĀ 616 at T II 172b24 to 172c22, parallel to SN 47.8 at SN V 149,26 (translated by Bodhi 2000: 1634).

53 This first paragraph has no counterpart in SN 47.8, which begins immediately with the simile of the cook.

54 According to the parallel SN 47.8 at SN V 150,2, the cook failed to notice what the person he was serving took much of and what was praised.

mindfulness and right knowing, and they are also unable to attain the four types of higher state of mind, dwellings in happiness here and now, and [to attain] the previously not yet attained peace of Nirvāṇa.[55] These are called foolish monastics who do not distinguish,[56] are not skilful, are unable to take hold properly of the marks of the mind within, but take hold of an external mark, giving rise to obstructions for themselves.

Suppose there are monastics who are clever and capable, who have skilful means, who having taken hold of the mind within, after that take hold of an external mark. They will never subsequently decline or give rise to obstructions for themselves.[57]

It is just like, for example, a clever and capable cook who with skilful means waits upon his master, capable of combining various tastes,[58] what is sour, salty, or bland, and of well grasping the marks of his master's preferences in regard to combining various tastes so that they are agreeable to the mind, listening to his master's desires for what is tasty and frequently offering it. Having pleased the master, [the cook] will certainly gain high ranking and be thought of fondly, be trusted and revered. In this way, the clever cook well grasped his master's wishes.

[Clever] monastics are also like that. Mindfully dwelling in contemplation of the body [in regard to] the body, they remove higher defilements and well collect their minds, stilling the mind within. They have right mindfulness and right knowing, they attain the four higher states of mind, dwellings in happiness here and now, and they attain the previously not yet attained peace of Nirvāṇa. These are called monastics who are clever and capable, who have skilful means, who take hold of the marks of the mind within and [then] take hold of an external mark. They never fall back or give rise to obstructions for themselves.

55 In SN 47.8 at SN V 150,21 the foolish monastics do not become concentrated, do not abandon defilements, and do not take hold of the mark (*nimitta*). As a result, they do not gain a pleasant abiding in the here and now and do not gain mindfulness and clear knowing.

56 The translation "distinguish" is based on adopting an emendation in the CBETA edition of an obvious scribal error.

57 This paragraph has no counterpart in SN 47.8.

58 The translation "tastes" is based on adopting an emendation in the CBETA edition of an obvious scribal error.

The discourse continues by indicating that the same description should be applied to contemplation of feeling tones, the mind, and dharmas.

The Pāli version does not relate taking hold of the marks of one's own mind within to the ability not to fall back and give rise to obstructions when taking hold of an external mark. This description in the above passage could be taken as pointing to a need to bridge formal sitting meditation, during which one learns to take hold of the marks of one's own mind within, with daily-life situations, where in one way or another one has to handle external marks. On this understanding, the point would be that, by having familiarized oneself with the characteristics of one's own mind within, one increasingly learns to handle such external marks well.

The two versions agree in putting a spotlight on the potential of the four establishments to lead to deepening concentration. In both versions, the description of the cook points to the "receptive" dimension of mindfulness. Just as the cook needs to be receptive to how his food is being received, so mindfulness helps one to stay receptive to how the meditation is progressing. Not only in relation to meditation practice but in a range of different ways mindfulness can enhance one's receptivity and thereby help provide a better understanding of what is occurring so that one can adjust to it accordingly.

THE SIMILE OF THE QUAIL (SĀ 617)

The "protective" aspect of mindfulness comes to the fore in a simile that illustrates how even a quail can outwit a hawk:[59]

> In the distant past there was a bird, [of the species] called quail. It had been caught by a hawk, who flew up high into the sky. Up in the sky, [the quail] called out: "I was myself not alert and suddenly I met with this misfortune. Because I departed from my

59 SĀ 617 at T II 172c25 to 173a27, parallel to SN 47.6 at SN V 146,18 (translated by Bodhi 2000: 1632).

ancestral domain and journeyed to another's place, therefore I met with this misfortune. How else could I today be put in this difficulty by it, unable to be free!"

The hawk said to the quail: "What is the place of your own domain, where you are able to be free?"

The quail replied: "My own domain is in the midst of a ploughed furrow in a farm field. There I am fully free from misfortunes; that is my home and ancestral domain."

The hawk's pride was aroused. It said to the quail: "I set you free to leave, to return amidst ploughed furrows. Will you be able to escape me thereby?"[60]

Then the quail got out from the claws of the hawk and returned to the ploughed furrow, to a big clod below which there was a safe place to stay. Then it went on top of the clod, wanting to give battle to the hawk.[61]

The hawk was greatly enraged [thinking]: "That is [just] a little bird and it dares to give battle to me." Extremely angry, [the hawk] quickly flew straight down to fight. Then the quail entered beneath the clod. By the power of its flight, the hawk dashed with its breast against the solid clod, shattered its body, and died.[62]

Then the quail, being hidden deeply under the clod, faced upwards and spoke in verse:[63]

---

60 SN 47.6 at SN V 147,2 indicates that the hawk was confident of its strength but did not boast of it. The reading known to the commentary Spk III 200,14, however, appears to have rather been that the hawk was confident of its strength and boastful; see also Bodhi 2000: 1918n131. The wording in SĀ 617 supports the reading reflected in the commentary, which also fits the context better.

61 SN 47.6 does not mention a safe place to stay below the clod. According to its description at SN V 147,13, when the hawk had come close the quail got "inside" the clod. The idea of getting inside a clod is somewhat less straightforward, compared to the idea of getting into a small place below a big clod. Another version of this simile, T 212 at T IV 695a19, refers to a place between two clods or rocks, and indicates that the quail got "inside" of this space. After having reached the clod, according to SN 47.6 at SN V 147,7 the quail openly challenged the hawk to come and get it; the same is the case for T 212.

62 SN 47.6 does not describe the anger of the hawk and reports that the quail waited until the hawk had come close.

63 SN 46.7 does not report any verses spoken by the quail.

"The hawk came using its strength;
The quail relied on its own domain.[64]
Availing itself of anger and excessively ferocious strength
[The hawk] encountered misfortune and its body was
smashed.

"Endowed with penetration,
Relying on my own domain
I defeated [the hawk's] anger and my mind rejoices
Contemplating with joy my own strength.

"Suppose you are violent and stupid,
[Even] having the force of a hundred thousand elephants,
You are no match for my wisdom,
Even to a sixteenth part of it.
I contemplate my wisdom and superior distinction
In destroying and extinguishing the dark hawk."

In this way, monastics, foolish ones who give up their own ancestral domain and journey to another's place come to disaster like that hawk.[65] Monastics, you should also dwell in the area of you own domain, you should be well guarded and be apart from the domain of others, you should train in this way.[66]

Monastics, another's place and another's domain is reckoned to be the domain of the five sensual pleasures: seeing with the eye what is gratifying, likeable,[67] being aware of fine forms with a sensual mind that is defiled by attachment; being conscious with the ear of sounds ... being conscious with the nose of scents ... being conscious with the tongue of flavours ... being conscious with the body of touches that are gratifying, likeable, being aware

64 The first verse would presumably not be spoken by the quail itself, as in the remainder of the verses the quail uses the first person to refer to itself.
65 SN 46.7 does not compare the foolish ones to the hawk. In fact, the question of going out of one's ancestral domain appears to be relevant to the earlier behaviour of the quail and not the hawk.
66 SN 46.7 at SN V 146,17 adds that Māra will gain access to those who stray out of their own domain.
67 The translation here and below is based on adopting a variant reading.

of fine touches with a sensual mind that is defiled by attachment. Monastics, this is called another's place, another's domain.

Monastics, your own place and ancestral domain is reckoned to be the four establishments of mindfulness. What are the four? They are reckoned to be the establishment of mindfulness by contemplating the body [in regard to] the body ... feeling tones ... the mind ... and the establishment of mindfulness by contemplating dharmas [in regard to] dharmas. For this reason, monastics, you should train in dwelling in your own place, journeying in your own ancestral domain, stay far apart from another's place and another's domain.

The simile of the quail illustrates the "protective" dimension of mindfulness, particularly in relation to sensual distraction. If mindfulness is established, it becomes possible to withstand even strong forms of such distraction, comparable to the ability of a weak quail to outwit a much stronger hawk. In contrast, once mindfulness is lost, one is without protection. This in turn highlights the importance of training in continuity of mindfulness, making sure that, whenever the vantage point of mindfulness has been lost, it is regained as soon as possible.

The next discourse (SĀ 618) does not have a Pāli parallel properly speaking. It just states that one who cultivates the four establishments of mindfulness will attain one of the four levels of awakening.[68]

THE SIMILE OF THE ACROBATS (SĀ 619)

The foundational role that training in mindfulness serves for truly being able to help others comes to the fore in the simile of two acrobats performing together:[69]

In former times there was a teacher of acrobatics done in dependence on a pole. He placed the pole straight up on his

68 SĀ 618 at T II 173b1.

69 SĀ 619 at T II 173b7 to 173b18, parallel to SN 47.19 at SN V 168,19 (translated by Bodhi 2000: 1648) and a version in the Mūlasarvāstivāda *Vinaya*, T 1448 at T XXIV 32b10.

shoulder and told his disciple:[70] "Getting up and down on the pole,[71] you protect me and I will also protect you. Protecting each other we will put on a show and gain much wealth."

Then the disciple of acrobatics said to the teacher of acrobatics: "It will not do as you said. Instead, we should each take care to protect ourselves. [Like this] we will put on a show and gain much wealth. We will be physically at ease and yet I will get down safely."

The teacher of acrobatics said: "As you said, we will take care to protect ourselves, this is correct and is also the meaning of what I said."[72]

Having protected oneself,[73] one right away protects the other; when protecting the other and oneself as well, this is protection indeed.[74]

[How does protecting oneself protect others]?[75] Becoming

---

70 SN 47.19 does not mention where the pole was put, but T 1448 at T XXIV 32b11 also reports that it was placed on the shoulder.

71 SN 47.19 does not specify that the protecting of each other should be done while getting up and down on the pole; in fact in its account the teacher at first told the disciple to get up on his shoulders, which the latter then did, so that in SN 47.19 their discussion takes place with the disciple already standing on the shoulders of the teacher.

72 SN 47.19 does not have a reply by the teacher, continuing only with a brief remark: "that is the method here", *so tattha nāyo*. Whereas Woodward 1930/1979: 149 takes this to be still part of the disciple's speech, Bodhi 2000: 1648 translates it as part of the explanation subsequently given by the Buddha. The passage in question concludes the disciple's remark with the quotative *iti*, so the subsequent section should indeed be part of the Buddha's explanation. In T 1448 at T XXIV 32b19 no reply by the teacher is found, instead of which the Buddha comments that the indications made by the disciple are the correct method.

73 In SĀ 619 it is not clear at what point the speech of the teacher ends and the comment by the Buddha starts. My assumption that this occurs at the present juncture is based on the parallel versions. In SĀ 619 it could alternatively be the teacher who draws this general conclusion, in which case the Buddha's comment would only start with the remark on becoming familiar with one's own mind.

74 In SN 47.19 at SN V 169,11 the Buddha at first recommends the establishments of mindfulness to protect oneself and to protect another; he then indicates that protecting oneself one protects others and protecting others one protects oneself.

75 The supplementation of this query suggests itself from the context and the parallel versions, SN 47.19 at SN V 169,15 and T 1448 at T XXIV 32b22, where such a query serves as introduction to the corresponding explanation.

> familiar with one's own mind,[76] developing it, protecting it accordingly, and attaining realization; this is called "protecting oneself protects others."
>
> How does protecting others protect oneself? By the gift of fearlessness, the gift of non-violation, the gift of harmlessness,[77] by having a mind of *mettā* and empathy for others; this is called "protecting others protects oneself."
>
> For this reason, monastics, you should train yourself like this: "Protecting myself, I will develop the four establishments of mindfulness; protecting others, I will develop the four establishments of mindfulness."

For the two acrobats to perform their feat successfully, the teacher would have to keep the pole firmly straight and the disciple would have to maintain balance while on top of the pole. In view of this need for cooperation, the suggestion that they should protect each other is certainly meaningful, in that the teacher wishes to protect the disciple by keeping the pole firmly upright. At the same time, the teacher hopes that the disciple will protect him by avoiding any jerky movement that upsets the balance of the pole and makes it difficult to keep the pole straight. The teacher's concern would also be that, whether he makes a mistake or the disciple makes a mistake, in both cases the one who risks falling down is the disciple. Hence as the teacher and with a natural attitude of concern, he expresses himself in terms of protecting each other.

The additional perspective introduced by the disciple, according to which they should each take care to protect themselves, in a way brings a refinement to the basic principle

---

76 SN 47.19 at SN V 169,16 does not explicitly specify that the mind is the object of development, reading (in reply to the Buddha's question on how one protects oneself): "by practising, developing, and making much of it", which according to the commentarial explanation, Spk III 227,2, refers to one's meditation practice in particular. T 1448 at T XXIV 32b22 also does not mention becoming familiar with the mind.

77 Instead of these three, SN 47.19 at SN V 169,19 speaks only of patience and harmlessness. T 1448 at T XXIV 32b24 mentions not annoying, not angering, and not harming another. The three versions agree that one protects others through *mettā* and empathy.

of harmonious cooperation by indicating that neither of them should focus all their attention on protecting the other. This indication need not be seen as implying a rejection of a concern for each other. Rather, it can be understood to introduce the proper perspective for achieving smooth cooperation, namely being first of all centred oneself.

Learning to be first of all centred oneself then takes the form of cultivating the four establishments of mindfulness. It is in this sense that one first needs to take care to protect oneself, before being truly able to assist others.[78] For this reason, here *mettā* and empathy for others are the outcome of having first of all cultivated mindfulness, which provides the proper foundation for their flourishing.

From the viewpoint of mindfulness itself, the simile of the two acrobats can be seen to combine qualities mentioned in the previous two similes, namely "receptivity" and "protection". In order to protect each other and to protect themselves, the two acrobats need to be receptive not only to the needs of the other but also to their own needs. Out of this union of key qualities of mindfulness in receptivity and protection, *mettā* and compassion grow.

SUMMARY

The four establishments of mindfulness are a direct path to mental purification. They can be applied internally as well as externally, a distinction that seems to imply directing mindfulness to oneself as well as to others. Cultivation of the four establishments of mindfulness can lead to liberation from all *dukkha*. Their respective objects manifest due to conditions, as the body depends on nutriment, feeling tone on contact, mental states on name-and-form, and dharmas on attention.

In the context of the four establishments, mindfulness collaborates with diligent effort and clear or right knowing. Together these can lead to a mental condition free from

78 See in more detail Anālayo 2015b: 16–20 and 2019m.

greedy desire and discontent, thereby revealing the liberative potential of mindfulness meditation. Hence the establishments of mindfulness are of a wholesome nature, even though mindfulness itself is ethically undetermined. Teachings on their practice are an inexhaustible topic to such a degree that the Buddha could have given continuous lectures on them even for a hundred years.

The way to become a truly great person is the practice of mindfulness. When the mind is scattered during the cultivation of mindfulness, it can be helpful to shift to another meditation practice. Noticing the need for such a shift in meditation practice is a task of mindfulness, whose receptive monitoring compares to a skilful cook who observes how his or her dishes are received. Mindfulness can exert a protective function, as long as one remains within the domain of its presence. This is similar to the need for a quail to refrain from straying out of its proper domain in order to avoid being caught. Mindfulness also furnishes the proper foundation for being really able to assist others. This is comparable to two acrobats who, in order to perform a feat together, need first of all to establish their own balance and then are able to collaborate. The three similes of the cook, the quail, and the acrobats taken together point to two key qualities of mindfulness: receptivity and protection.

IV

ESTABLISHING MINDFULNESS (2)

In the first part of this chapter I continue with discourses from the collected sayings on the four establishments of mindfulness in the *Saṃyukta-āgama*.[1] I begin with another simile on the protective dimension of mindfulness, illustrated with the example of a monkey caught by a hunter (SĀ 620), and then turn to the cultivation of mindfulness as something relevant for newcomers and seasoned practitioners alike (SĀ 621). Mindfulness can protect one against the arising of sensual desire (SĀ 622). The intensive practice of mindfulness while in seclusion requires a firm moral foundation (SĀ 624). One who aspires to awakening should certainly dwell with mindfulness (SĀ 627). The whole purpose of moral training can be summarized as building the foundation for the cultivation of mindfulness (SĀ 628). Such cultivation has various benefits (SĀ 629) as well as an emancipating effect (SĀ 634). Mindfulness fulfils various functions in the gradual path to liberation (SĀ 637 and MĀ 144) and can become the way to rely on oneself (SĀ 638) and the means to face the passing away of close and dear ones (SĀ 639).

1 At one point I depart from the sequence of the collection when, between SĀ 637 and SĀ 638, I turn to a discourse from the *Madhyama-āgama*, MĀ 144, that is closely related to SĀ 637, after which I continue with the two remaining discourses in the collection.

In the remainder of the present chapter, I proceed from the collected sayings on the four establishments of mindfulness to other passages, where the cultivation of mindfulness serves as a form of taking refuge within oneself when one is worried about the health of a close and dear one (DĀ 2). Being with mindfulness is the proper approach to facing death (SĀ 1028). Anuruddha and the Buddha relied on mindfulness when experiencing physical pain (SĀ 541 and SĀ 1289). Another discourse even shows the Buddha recovering health through the power of the awakening factors, the first of which is mindfulness (SĀ 727).

THE SIMILE OF THE MONKEY (SĀ 620)

The "protective" dimension of mindfulness and the idea of staying in one's ancestral domain, which was the theme of the simile of the quail taken up towards the end of the last chapter, find another illustration in a simile that involves a monkey caught by a hunter:[2]

> Among the Himalayas there are icy and steep places, difficult to access even for monkeys, let alone humans. There are also mountains where monkeys dwell, but no humans. There are also mountains where people and animals dwell together.[3]
>
> A hunter takes sticky resin and puts it on top of some grass in a place where monkeys roam. Those monkeys who are clever keep far away from it and leave, but a foolish monkey is unable to avoid it. It touches it a little with a hand and the resin sticks to the hand. Using the second hand it then wishes to get it off again and tries to be free from it, so both hands stick to the resin. With the feet it tries to get it off again and the resin sticks to the feet.[4]

---

2 SĀ 620 at T II 173b21 to 173c10, parallel to SN 47.7 at SN V 148,8 (translated by Bodhi 2000: 1633) and a few lines in a Sanskrit fragment, SHT IV 162d8, Sander and Waldschmidt 1980: 106.

3 The description of the location in SN 47.7 at SN V 148,9 does not mention coldness, instead characterizing these areas as being difficult to reach and rugged.

4 In SN 47.7 at SN V 148,24 the monkey first uses only one foot. After that gets stuck, it uses the other foot.

> With the mouth it gnaws the grass and thereby the resin sticks to the mouth. The resin sticks to these five parts alike.
>
> [The monkey] lies on the ground, joined together as if it were rolled up. The hunter comes, spears [the monkey] on a stick and leaves, carrying it on his back.
>
> Monastics, you should know that the foolish monkey, who gave up its own ancestral domain and journeyed into another's domain, came to disaster. Monastics, in the same way some foolish ordinary person who dwells in dependence on a village puts on robes in the morning and takes the bowl to enter the village to beg alms without guarding well the body and without protecting the doors of the faculties.[5] Having seen a form with the eyes, the defilement of attachment arises. With the ears and sounds ... the nose and fragrances ... the tongue and flavours ... and the body and tangibles, with all of them the defilement of attachment arises. The foolish monastic, whose internal faculties and their external objects have become bound by a fivefold bondage, goes along with Māra's wishes.
>
> Monastics, for this reason you should train in such a way that you dwell in your own place, reside in your ancestral domain and stay in dependence on it. Do not go along to another's place and dwell in another's domain.
>
> Monastics, what is dwelling in your own place and your ancestral domain? It is reckoned to be the four establishments of mindfulness: dwelling mindfully contemplating the body [in regard to] the body ... feeling tones ... the mind ... dwelling mindfully contemplating dharmas [in regard to] dharmas.[6]

Whereas in the simile of the quail the emphasis was on how even a weak bird can overpower a strong bird by relying on its own domain, in the present simile the emphasis is more on the predicament of the monkey being caught. The detailed depiction of how the monkey gets more and more stuck to the bait, until all

5 SN 47.7 does not apply the teaching to the situation of going to beg alms; it only mentions the five types of sensual desires in general.

6 SN 47.7 at SN V 149,20 adds that these four establishments of mindfulness are cultivated while being "diligent, clearly knowing, and mindful, free from greedy desires and discontent in the world".

four limbs and even the mouth are bound, serves as a warning to illustrate the predicament of a loss of mindfulness and the resultant bondage. This is where mindfulness can provide vital protection against getting more and more stuck in the world of the senses.

NEWCOMERS AND SEASONED PRACTITIONERS (SĀ 621)

The four establishments of mindfulness are immediately relevant for newly ordained monastics and continue to be relevant to those who have completed the path to full awakening:[7]

> Together with a group of many monastics, the venerable Ānanda approached the Blessed One. They paid respect with their heads at [the Buddha's] feet and withdrew to sit to one side. The venerable Ānanda said to the Buddha: "Blessed One, how should these young monastics be instructed? What teaching should be taught to them?"
>
> The Buddha said to Ānanda: "These young monastics should be taught by way of the four establishments of mindfulness and be made to cultivate them. What are the four? That is, dwelling mindfully contemplating the body [in regard to] the body with diligent effort, dwelling without negligence, with right knowing and right mindfulness, stilling the mind ... *up to* ... to know the body; dwelling mindfully contemplating feeling tones ... the mind ... dharmas [in regard to] dharmas with diligent effort, dwelling without negligence, with right mindfulness and right knowing, stilling the mind ... *up to* ... to know dharmas.
>
> "Why is that? Suppose monastics dwell at the stage of trainees and have not yet attained entry into the supreme. At the time of being intent on seeking the peace of Nirvāṇa, they dwell mindfully contemplating the body [in regard to] the body with diligent effort, dwelling without negligence, with right mindfulness and right knowing, stilling the mind ... *up to* ... [to not be attached to the body]; they dwell mindfully contemplating feeling tones

---

7 SĀ 621 at T II 173c13 to 173c29, parallel to SN 47.4 at SN V 144,16 (translated by Bodhi 2000: 1630).

> ... the mind ... dharmas [in regard to] dharmas with diligent effort, dwelling without negligence, with right mindfulness and right knowing, stilling the mind ... *up to* ... to not be attached to dharmas.[8]
>
> "Suppose there are arahants who have already eradicated the influxes, done what had to be done, given up the heavy burden, eradicated all fetters, being well liberated through right knowing, at that time they will also cultivate and dwell mindfully contemplating the body [in regard to] the body with diligent effort, dwelling without negligence, with right mindfulness and right knowing, stilling the mind ... *up to* ... [having gained not being attached to the body]; they dwell mindfully contemplating feeling tones ... the mind ... dharmas [in regard to] dharmas ... *up to* ... [having] gained not being attached to dharmas."

The Pāli parallel does not report that Ānanda approached the Buddha with a group of young monastics, so that here the Buddha gives the instruction of his own accord. The Pāli discourse also has a somewhat stronger emphasis on the cultivation of concentration, as in its presentation the purpose of the four establishments of mindfulness, cultivated by these three different types of practitioners, is to become mentally unified, have a bright mind, and become concentrated and single-minded. Given that some of the newly ordained monastics might just be starting meditation practice, it would seem reasonable to recommend that they try to collect their mind, without expecting them to become fully concentrated and single-minded right away. Such could more reasonably be expected at a later time, when sufficient grounding in mindfulness training has been established and it becomes indeed feasible and commendable for them to proceed from such training to deeper degrees of concentration. Hence in this respect the *Saṃyukta-āgama* version seems to be more to the point.

Although mindfulness clearly serves to build a foundation for concentration, the main concern of the cultivation of the

---

8 In SN 47.4 at SNV 145,5 the task of the trainees is to develop full understanding (*pariññā*).

establishments of mindfulness is gradual progress towards awakening and the removal of defilements (as well as serving as the appropriate modality of practice once this has been achieved). This is the case to such an extent that the "direct path" statement, discussed earlier (see above p. 94), mentions a range of benefits of mindfulness meditation but not the gaining of concentration. Although such absence of explicit reference needs to be considered alongside the indubitable contribution that mindfulness makes to deeper experiences of concentration, it nevertheless clearly shows what the early discourses consider to be chief purposes of *satipaṭṭhāna* meditation. First and foremost, mindfulness serves as a chief quality for progress towards awakening, hence its "liberating" function is not confined to freeing the mind from distractions in order to enable a deepening of concentration. Instead, its liberating function covers the whole range of the path to awakening.[9]

MINDFUL PROTECTION AGAINST LUSTFUL DESIRES (SĀ 622)

The next passage points to the "protective" potential of mindfulness, especially when cultivated in conjunction with effort and right knowing, to forestall the arising of sensual desire. The narrative context is a visit paid by the courtesan Ambapālī, famed for her beauty, to the Buddha and his monastic disciples:[10]

9 The emphasis on liberating insight here and in the next discourses to be taken up stands in contrast to the proposal by Sujato 2005: 113 that "in the early teachings satipatthana was primarily associated not with vipassana but with samatha"; see also Anālayo 2019l. This is not to deny the substantial contribution *satipaṭṭhāna* can make to the cultivation of tranquillity (*samatha*), but only to point out that the chief purpose of such practice, in the way described in the early discourses, is the cultivation of liberating insight (*vipassanā*).

10 SĀ 622 at T II 174a3 to 174a21, parallel to DN 16 at DN II 94,28 (translated by Walshe 1987: 242), see also SN 47.2 at SN V 142,5, which has only the instructions and does not mention Ambapālī's arrival (translated by Bodhi 2000: 1628), a Sanskrit fragment version, Waldschmidt 1951: 172, DĀ 2 at T I 13b19, T 5 at T I 163c3, T 6 at T I 178c26, and T 7 at T I 194c5; for a comparative study of this episode see Waldschmidt 1944: 76–78.

At that time Ambapālī heard that the Blessed One, who was journeying among the Vajjian people, had reached Ambapālī's Grove and was staying in it. She adorned herself and, riding a chariot, went out of Vesālī to approach the Blessed One to pay her respects and make offerings. Arriving at the entry of Ambapālī's Grove, she descended from the chariot to proceed on foot. From afar she saw that the Blessed One was giving a teaching surrounded by a large community.

Seeing from afar that Ambapālī was coming, the Blessed One said to the monastics: "Monastics, make an effort to dwell with a collected mind, with right mindfulness and right knowing. Ambapālī is coming now; for this reason I am warning you.

"How does a monastic make an effort to dwell with a collected mind? Suppose a monastic gives rise to desire, effort, energy, and collectedness of the mind so that already arisen bad and unwholesome mental states will be abandoned ... not yet arisen bad and unwholesome mental states are not made to arise ... not yet arisen wholesome mental states are made to arise ... and gives rise to desire, effort, energy, and collectedness of the mind so that already arisen wholesome mental states are made to be established without loss, by cultivating their increase and fulfilment. This is reckoned [how] a monastic makes an effort to dwell with a collected mind.

"What is reckoned to be right knowing for a monastic? Suppose a monastic has dignified manners and constantly is in accordance with right knowing when going and coming, when looking backward or forward, when bending or stretching, when taking hold of robes and bowl, when walking, standing, sitting, or lying down, when sleeping or waking up, when speaking or being silent, and dwells in relation to all these in accordance with right knowing. This is right knowing.

"What is right mindfulness? Suppose a monastic dwells mindfully contemplating the body [in regard to] the body internally with diligent effort, with right knowing and right mindfulness, overcoming greed and discontent in the world. In the same way feeling tones ... the mind ... [the monastic] dwells mindfully contemplating dharmas [in regard to] dharmas with diligent effort, with right knowing and right mindfulness, overcoming greed and discontent in the world. This is reckoned right mindfulness for a monastic.

"For this reason, you should make an effort [to dwell] with a collected mind, with right mindfulness and right knowing. Ambapālī is coming now; for this reason I am warning you."

The discourse continues by reporting that the Buddha gave Ambapālī a teaching and then accepted her invitation for a meal the next day. After the meal, the Buddha spoke a set of verses in praise of generosity.[11]

The Pāli parallel in the *Dīgha-nikāya* reports her visit after the above instructions (another Pāli parallel does not cover her visit). Here the *Saṃyukta-āgama* version offers a more meaningful presentation, in that the Buddha would have given instructions on the appropriate meditative attitude to prepare some of the less advanced male monastics in the assembly for the arrival of the beautiful Ambapālī. Both Pāli parallels also lack a reference to the four right efforts, which in the passage translated above come under the heading of "dwelling with a collected mind".

The next discourse in the collected sayings on the establishments of mindfulness presents the simile of carrying a bowl of oil through a crowd that watches a beautiful girl singing and dancing (SĀ 623), which I have already taken up in chapter 2 (see above p. 57). This simile conveys basically the same message as the Ambapālī episode, in that both point to the protective dimension of mindfulness in relation to potential sensual distraction. As long as mindfulness is established, it will be possible to avoid getting snared by such a type of distraction. The simile of the bowl of oil adds to this the potential of "embodied" mindfulness. Such anchoring in whole-body awareness will strengthen one's ability to avoid getting carried away by sensually alluring objects.

---

11 A comparable set of verses, addressed to the general Sīha, can be found in AN 5.34 at AN III 40,13 (translated by Bodhi 2012: 660).

THE MORAL FOUNDATION FOR INTENSIVE PRACTICE (SĀ 624)

The next topic in the collected sayings on mindfulness is the need for a firm foundation in morality as a basis for cultivating mindfulness. This necessity is part of an instruction given to a monastic who wishes to withdraw into seclusion for intensive practice:[12]

> At that time the venerable Uttiya approached the Buddha, paid respect with his head at the Buddha's feet, and withdrew to sit to one side. He said to the Buddha: "It would be well if the Blessed One were to give me a teaching so that, on having heard the teaching, I shall alone in a quiet place give focused attention to it and dwell without negligence, reflecting on that for whose sake a clansman's son shaves off beard and hair, [puts on monastic robes,] and goes forth out of right faith into homelessness to train in the path ... *as spoken above up to* ... [realizing] there will be no receiving of any further existence."
>
> The Buddha said to Uttiya: "It is like this, it is like this, as said by you. Yet, one who in relation to the teachings spoken by me does not please my mind, who has not accomplished the conduct that is to be undertaken, will not get benefits in spite of following me and instead will give rise to obstructions."[13]
>
> Uttiya said to the Buddha: "In relation to what the Blessed One teaches, I am able to make the Blessed One's mind be pleased and I shall accomplish my own conduct without giving rise to obstructions. May the Blessed One give me a teaching so that I shall alone in a quiet place give focused attention to it and dwell without negligence ... *as spoken above up to* ... [realizing] there will be no receiving of any further existence."
>
> In the same way he requested it a second and a third time.[14]

---

12 SĀ 624 at T II 174c22 to 175a11, parallel to SN 47.16 at SN V 166,14 (translated by Bodhi 2000: 1646); both the original Pāli and the translation are abbreviated and require supplementation from the previous discourse SN 47.15.

13 Such a warning is not found in SN 47.16.

14 As in SN 47.16 the Buddha teaches right after being asked the first time, the Pāli version does not have a counterpart to Uttiya repeating his request three times.

> At that time the Blessed One said to Uttiya: "You should first purify your preliminary conduct and after that your cultivation of the celibate life."
>
> Uttiya said to the Buddha: "How should I now purify my preliminary conduct and my cultivation of the celibate life?"
>
> The Buddha said to Uttiya: "You should first purify your morality and straighten up your view. Be endowed with the three [types of virtuous] deeds [by body, speech, and mind]. After that you cultivate the four establishments of mindfulness. What are the four? One dwells mindfully contemplating the body [in regard to] the body internally with diligent effort, with right knowing and right mindfulness, overcoming greed and discontent in the world. In the same way one dwells mindfully contemplating the body externally ... the body internally and externally ... feeling tones ... the mind ... one dwells mindfully contemplating dharmas [in regard to] dharmas, *which should also be fully recited in this way*."

In the Pāli version, the Buddha teaches right after being requested the first time, without any hesitation. However, this part of the Pāli discourse is given in abbreviation and therefore just follows the pattern of the previous discourse in the *Saṃyutta-nikāya*. Whether with or without hesitation, in both versions the Buddha stresses the need for a moral foundation for mindfulness practice undertaken in an intense manner in a secluded setting. The parallels agree that Uttiya was able to put the instruction to good use, as he eventually became a fully awakened one, an arahant. This confirms the potential of dedicating attention to laying the proper moral foundation for intensive mindfulness practice aimed at reaching liberation. The firmer such foundation has been made, the better intensive mindfulness practice can take off and unfold its "liberating" potential.

The *Saṃyukta-āgama* continues with a brief indication that the same discourse should be repeated, with the difference of being addressed to an unnamed monastic.[15] The next discourse

15 This would then correspond to SN 47.3 at SN V 142,23 (translated by Bodhi 2000: 1628), already taken up in the previous chapter as a parallel to SĀ 610, see above p. 99.

in the collection (SĀ 625) is again closely similar but addressed to another monastic by the name of Bāhika.[16] A difference is that here the four establishments of mindfulness, based on purification of morality, lead to going beyond Māra, a celestial being that at times functions as a personification of death. A comparable relationship can be seen in the *Saṃyutta-nikāya* account of the teaching given to Uttiya, where the Buddha relates the practice of the four establishments of mindfulness to going beyond the realm of death.[17] The *Saṃyukta-āgama* adds still another variation, as it indicates that the same discourse should be repeated with the difference that, instead of going beyond Māra, the same practice leads to going beyond birth and death (SĀ 626).

All of these passages converge in putting a spotlight on the importance of a sound ethical foundation for the cultivation of mindfulness to lead to liberating insight. In a way, the very building of such a foundation can already be a potential field for the cultivation of mindfulness. Understood in this way, a moral life becomes a life with mindfulness.

THE MINDFUL DWELLING OF A TRAINEE (SĀ 627)

In addition to its role in building a moral foundation, mindfulness continues to be relevant to those who have already made substantial progress on the path to freedom. Hence a trainee, one who has reached a lower level of awakening and aspires to full liberation, should keep cultivating the four establishments of mindfulness:[18]

16 The Pāli parallel, SN 47.15 at SN V 165,6 (translated by Bodhi 2000: 1645), gives the monastic's name as Bāhiya and notes Bāhika as a variant reading (also noted in the Ceylonese edition); a Sanskrit fragment parallel has preserved the name as Bāhika; see SHT X 3911V2, Wille 2008: 215. This seems to be also the Indic original underlying the Chinese transcription of the name, as the character used for the last syllable reflects Sanskrit *ka* or *kā*; see Pulleyblank 1991: 143. Besides the famous protagonist of Ud 1.10 at Ud 6,26, Bāhiya Dāruciriya, the name Bāhiya (variant reading Bāhīriya) also occurs in SN 35.89 at SN IV 63,20, a discourse for which no parallel appears to be known.

17 SN 47.16 at SN V 166,15.

18 SĀ 627 at T II 175a29 to 175b10, parallel to SN 47.26 at SN V 174,28 (translated by Bodhi 2000: 1653).

> At that time the venerable Anuruddha approached the Buddha, paid respect with his head at [the Buddha's] feet, and withdrew to sit to one side. He said to the Buddha: "Blessed One, suppose a monastic dwells in the stage of a trainee who has not yet attained the supreme entry into the peace of Nirvāṇa, yet is seeking it with diligence. What should such a noble disciple in this right teaching and discipline cultivate, cultivate much, so as to attain the eradication of the influxes ... *up to* ... knowing for oneself that there will be no receiving of any further existence?
>
> The Buddha said to Anuruddha: "If a noble disciple dwells in the stage of a trainee who has not yet attained the supreme entry into the peace of Nirvāṇa, yet is seeking it with diligence, at such a time one should dwell mindfully contemplating the body [in regard to] the body internally with diligent effort, with right knowing and right mindfulness, overcoming greed and discontent in the world.
>
> In the same way one dwells mindfully contemplating feeling tones ... the mind ... dharmas [in regard to] dharmas with diligent effort, with right knowing and right mindfulness, overcoming greed and discontent in the world. On having cultivated them much in this way, a noble disciple attains the eradication of the influxes ... *up to* ... knowing for oneself that there will be no receiving of any further existence."

In the Pāli parallel, Anuruddha is the speaker instead of the questioner. He replies to Sāriputta and Mahāmoggallāna, who have asked him to define a trainee. In his reply, Anuruddha explains that a trainee is one who has cultivated the four establishments of mindfulness "in part".[19] The next *Saṃyutta-nikāya* discourse then has the corresponding enquiry about how to define one who is no longer in training, that is, an arahant. Anuruddha clarifies that such a one has "completely" cultivated the four establishments of mindfulness.[20]

The overall point that emerges in this way is the continuous relevance of mindfulness. This relevance ranges from building

19 SN 47.26 at SN V 175,6.
20 SN 47.27 at SN V 175,19 (translated by Bodhi 2000: 1653).

a foundation in morality via advanced stages on the path all the way up to its final consummation.

MORALITY IS FOR THE PURPOSE OF MINDFULNESS (SĀ 628)

The next discourse returns to the relationship between morality and the cultivation of mindfulness. This relationship is such that, in a way, the teachings given to monastics on ethical conduct are precisely for the purpose of cultivating the four establishments of mindfulness:[21]

> At that time the venerable Udāyin approached the venerable Ānanda and, after they had exchanged cordial greetings with each other, he withdrew to sit to one side.[22] He said to the venerable Ānanda: "The Tathāgata, the arahant, the Fully Awakened One, who has knowledge and vision, has declared noble morality for all monastics to be kept without breach, without deficiency, without discrimination, without separation; a morality that is not clung to, that is well consummated, well upheld, praised by the wise, and free from reproach. For the sake of what has the Tathāgata, the arahant, the Fully Awakened One, who has [knowledge and] vision, declared noble morality for all monastics [to be made] without breach, without deficiency ... *up to* ... praised by the wise, and free from reproach?"
>
> The venerable Ānanda said to Udāyin:[23] "It is for the sake of cultivating the four establishments of mindfulness. What are the four? They are reckoned to be dwelling mindfully contemplating the body [in regard to] the body ... feeling tones ... the mind ... dwelling mindfully contemplating dharmas [in regard to] dharmas.

In the Pāli parallel the enquiry is simply about the purpose of "wholesome moralities", without drawing out in detail that these should be without breach, etc. (although the same

21 SĀ 628 at T II 175b14 to 175b22, parallel to SN 47.21 at SN V 171,9 (translated by Bodhi 2000: 1650).
22 In SN 47.21 at SN V 171,9 Ānanda's visitor is instead Bhadda.
23 In SN 47.21 at SN V 171,16 Ānanda first praises his visitor for the good question he has asked.

can safely be assumed to be implied). Alongside such minor differences in formulation, the parallels agree in presenting the training in ethical conduct as having as its overarching purpose the facilitation of the practice of mindfulness. This is where it all comes together, in a way.

Taking the cultivation of mindfulness as an orientation point invests moral conduct with a clear-cut pragmatic function. This can effect a shift from guilt-driven submission to taking responsibility for oneself, motivated by the wish to ensure that the ground is prepared for the practice of mindfulness. Understood in this way, ethical restraint becomes indeed a fertile soil for the growth of mindfulness, both during its implementation and by building up the foundation for deeper meditative practice.

THE POTENTIAL OF THE FOUR ESTABLISHMENTS (SĀ 629)

The motivation for strengthening ethical conduct can be further enhanced by keeping in mind the potential fruits of mindfulness practice. The next discourses in the *Saṃyukta-āgama* provide precisely such an incentive by relating the cultivation of the four establishments of mindfulness to various benefits. The first of these discourses proceeds as follows:[24]

> Then the venerable Bhadda asked the venerable Ānanda: "Is there a teaching on cultivating of which, cultivating it much, one gains non-retrogression?"
>
> The venerable Ānanda said to the venerable Bhadda: "There is a teaching on cultivating of which, cultivating it much, one is able to bring about the gaining of non-retrogression. It is reckoned to be the four establishments of mindfulness. What are the four? They are [reckoned to be] dwelling mindfully contemplating the body [in regard to] the body ... feeling tones ... the mind ... dwelling mindfully contemplating dharmas [in regard to] dharmas.

24 SĀ 629 at T II 175b26 to 175c1, parallel to SN 47.23 at SN V 173,3 (translated by Bodhi 2000: 1651).

In the Pāli parallel, Bhadda enquires instead about the decline and the non-decline of the true Dharma.[25] The preceding discourse in the *Saṃyutta-nikāya* reports another similar exchange between these two monastics, with the difference that Bhadda asks why the true Dharma does not endure after the passing away of the Tathāgata.[26]

The *Saṃyukta-āgama* instead has another three exchanges between Bhadda and Ānanda, which do not have parallels in the *Saṃyutta-nikāya*. These involve enquiries by Bhadda about teachings to be cultivated for different aims. In reply to each, Ānanda points to the cultivation of the four establishments of mindfulness. The different aims that can be achieved in this way are as follows:

- make not-purified sentient beings gain purification and increasing splendour (SĀ 630),
- make sentient beings who have not yet crossed over to the other shore gain a crossing over to the other shore (SĀ 631),
- [make one] become an arahant (SĀ 632).

The next discourse in the *Saṃyukta-āgama* (SĀ 633) also does not have a Pāli parallel. It reports a brief explanation by the Buddha which equates "all teachings" with the four establishments of mindfulness.[27]

EMANCIPATION THROUGH MINDFULNESS (SĀ 634)

The cultivation of the four establishments of mindfulness can have an emancipating effect:[28]

> Suppose a monastic cultivates the four establishments of mindfulness, cultivating them much, then this is said to be ennobling and emancipating. What are the four? They are

25 SN 47.23 at SN V 173,4: *saddhammaparihānaṃ hoti*.
26 SN 47.22 at SN V 173,8: *saddhammo na ciraṭṭhitiko hoti*.
27 SĀ 633 at T II 175c27.
28 SĀ 634 at T II 176a3 to 176a5, parallel to SN 47.17 at SN V 166,21 (translated by Bodhi 2000: 1646).

> reckoned to be dwelling mindfully contemplating the body [in regard to] the body ... feeling tones ... the mind ... dwelling mindfully contemplating dharmas [in regard to] dharmas.

The Pāli parallel adds that the ennobling and emancipating cultivation of the four establishments of mindfulness leads to the complete destruction of *dukkha*. This explains in what sense they can be ennobling and emancipating, confirming that the main point is the "liberating" dimension of the four establishments of mindfulness.

The *Saṃyukta-āgama* continues with an instruction according to which several additional discourses should be recited similar to the present one, with the difference that "emancipating" should be replaced with these terms:

- the right eradication of *dukkha*,
- the unsurpassed transcendence of *dukkha*,
- the attainment of great fruit,
- the attainment of great benefit,
- the attainment of the state of deathlessness,
- the unsurpassed deathlessness,
- the realization of the state of deathlessness.

All of these alternatives seem to be related, in one way or another, to the "liberating" potential of mindfulness cultivated by way of its four establishments.

The next discourse in the *Saṃyukta-āgama* (SĀ 635) does not have a Pāli parallel. It reports the Buddha announcing that the cultivation of the four establishments of mindfulness "makes not-purified sentient beings gain purification and makes sentient beings that are already purified increase their splendour".[29] The *Saṃyukta-āgama* continues with instructions for further discourses, achieved by replacing "the purification of beings" with the following:

- makes those who have not yet crossed over to the other shore cross over,

29 SĀ 635 at T II 176a12.

- attain arahantship,
- attain [the awakening of] a Paccekabuddha,
- attain the supreme and perfect awakening [of a Buddha].

The last three reflect a distinction in types of awakening that is more prominent in later texts. It seems fair to conclude that this threefold distinction is a later addition to a description that would originally only have been concerned with arahantship.

The various perspectives that emerge from these discourses converge on throwing into relief the "liberating" function of mindfulness. As already noted above, progress towards awakening and the removal of defilements is clearly the chief concern of mindfulness practice in early Buddhist thought.

MINDFULNESS IN THE GRADUAL PATH (SĀ 637)

For progress to liberation, mindfulness can be employed in a variety of ways. These can be examined from the viewpoint of descriptions of the gradual path of training, which bring together various aspects of conduct and practice to be undertaken from the moment someone decides to go forth up to the attainment of awakening.

An account of the gradual path can be found in a *Saṃyukta-āgama* discourse (SĀ 636) that does not have a parallel in the *Saṃyutta-nikāya*. The same account recurs in abbreviated form in the next *Saṃyukta-āgama* discourse (SĀ 637), which does have a partial Pāli parallel. Hence in what follows I take up both *Saṃyukta-āgama* discourses together, one after the other, on the understanding that the first of the two serves to supplement what the second abbreviates. The first of the two discourses introduces its presentation as a teaching on the cultivation of the four establishments of mindfulness. This sets the context for the following exposition:[30]

> A Tathāgata who is an arahant, a Fully Awakened One, endowed with knowledge and conduct, a Well-gone One, a knower of the worlds, an unsurpassable person, a leader of persons to be tamed,

30 SĀ 636 at T II 176a21 to 176b18.

a teacher of celestials and humans, a Buddha, a Blessed One, has emerged in the world. He delivers teachings on the true Dharma that are spoken well in the beginning, also spoken well in the middle, and also spoken well in the end, with good meaning and good purpose, entirely and fully pure, disclosing the celibate life.

Suppose a clansman's son or a clansman's daughter hears the Dharma from the Buddha and gains serene faith in their minds to train themselves in such a way as to see that being in the home life is conjoined with the fault of sensual delights and the bondage of affliction. They delight in dwelling out in the open, in homelessness to train in the path, they do not delight in the home life [but] in going to dwell in homelessness. They desire solely purification, for their whole life to be in entire and full purity, to be in the pure celibate life: "I shall shave off hair and beard, don the yellow robes and, out of right faith, go forth into homelessness to train in the path." Having had this reflection, they in turn give up wealth and relatives, shave off hair and beard, don the yellow robes, and out of right faith go forth into homelessness to train in the path.

With right bodily comportment they guard themselves against the four verbal transgressions and with purified right livelihood they cultivate the morality of noble ones.

They guard the doors of the faculties and protect the mind with right mindfulness. When seeing a form with the eye, they do not grasp at its appearance. If they were to dwell without restraining the eye faculty, greed and discontent in the world, bad and unwholesome states, would frequently flow into the mind. Thus they now arouse right restraint in relation to the eye. Rightly arousing restraint in relation to the ear, nose, tongue, body, and mind is also like this.

Based on being accomplished in the moral conduct of noble ones and on guarding well the doors of the faculties, when coming and going in daily activities, when looking back or forward, when bending or stretching, when sitting or lying down, when sleeping or waking up, when speaking or being silent, they dwell knowingly, with right knowing.

Being accomplished like this in noble morality, in guarding the doors of the faculties, and in right knowing and right mindfulness, they sit down in a quiet, secluded, and empty place, at the root of a tree or in an empty hut, with straight body and right mindfulness. Collecting the mind to dwell in peace, they abandon greed and discontent in the world. Being separated from sensual desires, they purify themselves from sensual desires. They abandon aversion, sloth-and-torpor, restlessness-and-worry, and the hindrance of doubt in the world. Being separated from aversion, sloth-and-torpor, restlessness-and-worry, and the hindrance of doubt, they purify themselves from aversion, sloth-and-torpor, restlessness-and-worry, and the hindrance of doubt.

They abandon the five hindrances which afflict the mind and weaken the power of wisdom, which pertain to what obstructs and do not lead to Nirvāṇa. For this reason, they dwell mindfully contemplating the body [in regard to] the body internally with diligent effort, with right knowing and right mindfulness, overcoming greed and discontent in the world. In the same way they dwell mindfully contemplating the body externally ... the body internally and externally ... feeling tones ... the mind ... and contemplating dharmas [in regard to] dharmas, *these should also be recited in this way*. This is reckoned how a monastic cultivates the four establishments of mindfulness.

The description of the gradual path in the above extract is similar to gradual-path accounts in other discourses, with the exception that these usually mention the attainment of the four absorptions instead of the cultivation of the four establishments of mindfulness.

As already mentioned, the next *Saṃyukta-āgama* discourse (SĀ 637) repeats the above description of the gradual path in abbreviated form. It differs in so far as it gives a more detailed account of moral restraint:[31]

Having gone forth in this way, dwelling in a quiet place, one upholds restraint by the code of rules, accomplishing it in conduct and abiding, upholding the training in morality, giving rise to great fear in relation to minor transgressions. Abstaining from

31 SĀ 637 at T II 176b22 to 176b26, partial parallel to SN 47.46 at SN V 187,16 (translated by Bodhi 2000: 1662).

> killing one has abandoned killing and does not delight in killing sentient beings ... *all the pathways of action should be recited as above up to* ... one takes along with the body one's robes and bowl, like a bird [takes along] its two wings. Being accomplished in this way in the training in morality, one cultivates the four establishments of mindfulness.

The pathways of action, mentioned in this passage, are altogether ten; they cover refraining from unwholesome conduct in body, speech, and mind. The bodily dimension covers killing, stealing, and sexual misconduct. The verbal dimension includes false speech, malicious speech, harsh speech, and gossiping. The mental dimension comprises covetousness, ill will, and wrong view.

The ten pathways of action are not mentioned in the partial Pāli parallel, which starts with an unnamed monastic requesting a teaching in brief. In reply to this request, the Buddha recommends dwelling restrained by the code of rules, seeing danger in the slightest faults. Based on that foundation in moral conduct, the four establishments of mindfulness should be cultivated.

The same basic relationship between the building of an ethical foundation and mindfulness practice emerges with more detail in the *Saṃyukta-āgama* presentation, as it clarifies in what way the transition from the former to the latter takes place. This transition involves sense restraint, right knowing with various bodily activities, and then withdrawing to a secluded place for formal meditation, which commences by overcoming the hindrances. All of these practices involve mindfulness in one way or another. In the above *Saṃyukta-āgama* discourse, their combination leads up to none other than mindfulness again, now cultivated by way of its four establishments.

Following the present discourse, the collected sayings on the four establishments of mindfulness in the *Saṃyukta-āgama* have another two discourses on the four establishments of mindfulness, which relate to the theme of how to face death. Before continuing with these two discourses, however, I briefly depart from the sequence of discourses in the *Saṃyukta-āgama* in order to take up another account of the gradual path, found in the *Madhyama-āgama*. Comparable to the two *Saṃyukta-āgama* discourses just examined, this *Madhyama-āgama* discourse also gives prominence to the four establishments of mindfulness, although these are already introduced at an earlier stage in the description of the gradual path.

THE GRADUAL PATH AND MINDFULNESS (MĀ 144)

The *Gaṇakamoggallāna-sutta* and its *Madhyama-āgama* parallel illustrate the gradual nature of the early Buddhist path to liberation with the examples of walking up a staircase or training someone step by step in archery or accountancy. In both versions the first part of this gradual path requires establishing oneself in purity of conduct.[32]

> Come, monastics, guard the purity of your livelihood with your body, [guard the purity of your livelihood] with your speech, and guard the purity of your livelihood with your mind.

The above injunction in the *Madhyama-āgama* discourse, found similarly in another parallel extant in Chinese, in a way summarizes different dimensions of ethical conduct as converging on livelihood. From the viewpoint of the mendicant life of monastics in ancient India, involving a complete dependence on the support provided by others, this offers a meaningful perspective on the foundation building in moral conduct that is required to be indeed worthy of the offerings received. The Pāli parallel is more specific, mentioning restraint by the monastic code of rules and perfection in conduct, seeing fear in the slighted transgression when training in the precepts.

The *Madhyama-āgama* version next brings in the four establishments of mindfulness, followed by the same practice carried out in the absence of unwholesome thoughts:[33]

---

32 MĀ 144 at T I 652b1 to 652b2, parallel to MN 107 at MN III 2,7 (translated by Ñāṇamoli 1995/2005: 874) and T 70 at T I 875b6.

33 MĀ 144 at T I 652b3 to 652b4 and 652b6 to 652b8, parallel to MN 107 at MN III 2,13 and T 70 at T I 875b8 (which does not have the second stage of cultivating the four establishments of mindfulness without thoughts); see also Anālayo 2011: 620.

> Come, monastics, contemplate the body as a body internally ... *up to* ... contemplate feeling tones, the mind, dharmas as dharmas ...
>
> Come, monastics, contemplate the body as a body internally and do not think thoughts associated with sensuality ... *up to* ... contemplate feeling tones, the mind, dharmas as dharmas and do not think thoughts associated with what is contrary to the Dharma.

The four establishments of mindfulness are also mentioned in the other parallel extant in Chinese, but not in the *Gaṇakamoggallāna-sutta*. A progression from the four establishments of mindfulness to the same practice free from unwholesome thought is found in another *Madhyama-āgama* discourse, which I will take up at the outset of chapter 6 on mindfulness and liberation (see below p. 200), and in this case a similar presentation also occurs in the respective Pāli parallel.

The next topic in the present *Madhyama-āgama* discourse is sense restraint, also covered in its Pāli parallel:[34]

> Come, monastics, guard the sense faculties, be always mindful of stopping thoughts of sensuality and have a clear understanding. Mindfully guard the mind and become accomplished in that, constantly giving rise to right knowing.

Whereas the other Chinese parallel agrees with the above passage in mentioning mindfulness,[35] the description of sense restraint in the *Gaṇakamoggallāna-sutta* does not explicitly refer to mindfulness.[36] Nevertheless, the same can be assumed to be implicit. Without mindfulness, it would hardly be possible to guard the senses and ensure that what is experienced does not provoke unwholesome reactions in the mind. An otherwise unrelated discourse in the *Aṅguttara-nikāya* in fact explicitly mentions mindfulness in relation to sense restraint, with the additional indication that such mindfulness performs a "protective" role.[37] As one of the chief qualities of mindfulness,

34 MĀ 144 at T I 652b10 to 652b12.
35 T 70 at T I 875b12.
36 MN 107 at MN III 2,13.
37 AN 5.114 at AN III 138,20 (translated by Bodhi 2012: 737); no parallel to this discourse appears to be known.

this protective dimension is indeed of considerable relevance to sense restraint.

The *Gaṇakamoggallāna-sutta* continues at this juncture with the need for moderation with food and the practice of wakefulness. Neither of these is covered in the two Chinese parallels. The practice of wakefulness requires one to meditate in the first and last parts of the night. When taking a rest during the middle portion of the night, one should do so with mindfulness and clear knowing, keeping in mind the idea of getting up again. In the ancient Indian setting, without recourse to an alarm clock, there was naturally a need to ensure that one did not oversleep. In the next chapter, I will return to the topic of mindful eating and the practice of wakefulness (see below pp. 175 and 183).

The variations that emerge in this way between the *Gaṇakamoggallāna-sutta* and its *Madhyama-āgama* parallel are in line with a recurrent feature of accounts of the gradual path in various discourses. Such accounts differ not only from one reciter tradition to the other, but even within the same discourse collection of the same reciter tradition.[38]

In the present case, several other discourses in the same *Majjhima-nikāya* collection provide a description of the gradual path without mentioning moderation with food or wakefulness, thereby diverging from the *Gaṇakamoggallāna-sutta*.[39] Such variations need not be seen as implying substantially different views of the relevance of such practices to progress to liberation. Instead, they appear to reflect variations due to the context of the particular teaching situation.

Here it can be helpful to keep in mind the difficulties of putting into fixed sequence what in actual practice are interrelated aspects of the training, in the sense that they can be undertaken simultaneously. As a result, accounts of the gradual path naturally vary, dependent on what particular perspective is taken or what practices are given emphasis in the particular setting in which the discourse was spoken.

---

38 See in more detail Anālayo 2017c: 65–90.
39 Anālayo 2011: 621n177.

The *Gaṇakamoggallāna-sutta* and its parallels agree in covering clear knowing in relation to various activities, which in the *Madhyama-āgama* version takes the following form:[40]

> Come, monastics, be with right knowing when going out and coming in, properly contemplate and distinguish when bending, stretching, lowering, or raising [a limb]; with appropriate deportment properly wear the double robe, [other] robes, and the bowl; always be with right knowing when going, standing, sitting down, lying down, [falling] asleep, waking up, speaking, and being silent.

The present passage is similar to one of the exercises mentioned in the *Madhyama-āgama* parallel to the *Kāyagatāsati-sutta*, discussed above (see p. 69). In both cases, the respective Pāli version additionally mentions eating, drinking, consuming food, tasting, defecating, and urinating as activities to be done with clear knowing.[41] From a practical perspective, such variations are probably of little significance, as both descriptions are not meant to be exhaustive. Instead, they just single out some activities as examples for the cultivation of right knowing, based on what would be an "embodied" form of mindfulness.

The next task in the *Gaṇakamoggallāna-sutta* and its parallels is the removal of the hindrances:[42]

> Come, monastics, dwell alone and in seclusion ... being already in a secluded place or having gone to the base of a tree or an empty peaceful place, put down the sitting mat and sit on it cross-legged with straight body, right aspiration, and mindfulness that is undivided.

Of particular interest here is the reference to "undivided mindfulness", which has its counterpart in the Pāli version in the idea of establishing mindfulness "to the fore" (*parimukha*), a

---

40 MĀ 144 at T I 652b25 to 652b28.
41 These activities are also not mentioned in T 70 at T I 875b24.
42 MĀ 144 at T I 652c2 to 652c6.

sense that also appears to underlie the other Chinese parallel.[43] The Pāli expression as such is open to different interpretations.[44] One of these interpretations, according to which mindfulness is to be made predominant in the mind, would concur with the notion of it being "undivided" in the above extract.

A temporary removal of the hindrances then leads to the attainment of the four absorptions. Such removal would involve mindfulness, which according to the *Satipaṭṭhāna-sutta* and its *Madhyama-āgama* parallel facilitates recognition of the presence or absence of a hindrance and of the conditions responsible for such presence or absence.[45] The *Gaṇakamoggallāna-sutta* in fact explicitly mentions mindfulness (and clear knowing) in relation to overcoming the hindrance of sloth-and-torpor.[46]

Mindfulness is of continuous relevance to the attainment of the four absorptions and is mentioned explicitly in the standard accounts of the third and fourth absorptions. Here is the *Madhyama-āgama* description of these two:[47]

> Separated from joy and desire, dwelling in equanimity and without seeking anything, with right mindfulness and right knowing, experiencing happiness with the body, one dwells having attained and accomplished the third absorption, which noble ones reckon an ⟨abiding⟩ in a happy abode with ennobling equanimity and mindfulness,[48] ...

---

43 T 70 at T I 875c2 actually speaks of the "mind" being fully in front, employing a character that, besides its more common tendency to render *manas* or *citta*, can also translate *smṛti*; see also the discussion below p. 170n16).

44 Anālayo 2003b: 128f and 2019j: 16f.

45 Anālayo 2013b: 177–194.

46 MN 107 at MN III 3,32.

47 MĀ 144 at T I 652c11, parallel to MN 107 at MN III 4,7+8 and MN III 4,12 and T 70 at T I 875c6. MĀ 144 and T 70 abbreviate, wherefore the translation given above is supplemented from an earlier occurrence of the full description in the *Madhyama-āgama*, found in MĀ 3 at T I 423b10 to 423b15 (parallel to AN 7.63 at AN IV 112,11; translated by Bodhi 2012: 1079, given as number 67).

48 The emendation involves replacing a reference to "emptiness" with "abode", two characters frequently confused with each other in descriptions of the third absorption.

> With the cessation of happiness and the cessation of pain, and with the earlier cessation of joy and displeasure, with neither-pain-nor-pleasure, with purity of equanimity and mindfulness, one dwells having attained and accomplished the fourth absorption.

In evaluating this explicit reference, it needs to be kept in mind that such descriptions are not meant to provide exhaustive accounts of all mental factors present in a particular experience, unlike what is often found in later exegesis. Hence it would hardly do justice to the usual descriptions of the first two absorptions to assume that mindfulness is not present in these experiences, just because it is not mentioned explicitly. Such an interpretation would imply that mindfulness has been cultivated in various ways during preceding forms of practice but then is to be abandoned for the first two absorptions only to be taken up again with the higher two. Obviously, this does not work. Instead, a more compelling interpretation of the standard way of presentation is that with the third and fourth absorptions mindfulness becomes particularly prominent and is more easily noticed, and it is for this reason that it is mentioned explicitly.[49]

The *Gaṇakamoggallāna-sutta* and its parallels conclude with the delighted approval of the brahmin who had received this exposition of the gradual path, contrasting those who have bad qualities, such as a lack of mindfulness, to those who have good qualities, such as being with mindfulness.[50] It is clearly the latter type who will be able to make the most of the gradual path.

In this way, the *Gaṇakamoggallāna-sutta* and its parallels draw the same relationship between a firm foundation in morality and the four establishments of mindfulness, and in one way or another show how mindfulness offers support to a range of different aspects of the gradual path of training. It would be difficult to think of another quality that has such a wide-ranging field of application in the early Buddhist path to deliverance.

---

49 Anālayo 2017c: 150 and 2019l.

50 MĀ 144 at T I 653b24 and MN 107 at MN III 6,24; see also T 70 at T I 876b4.

MINDFUL RELIANCE ON ONESELF (SĀ 638)

In addition to the multifaceted contributions made by mindfulness to progress to liberation, it can unfold its "protective" and "liberating" potential in relation to a range of challenging situations. One of these is grief. When faced with the death of dear ones, mindfulness can fortify and provide a refuge within:[51]

> [Ānanda] said to the Buddha: "Blessed One, now my whole body is [as if it were] falling apart, the four directions are [as if] they had changed their order, the teachings I learned are [as if they were] blocked off, as the novice Cunda has come and told me: 'My preceptor, the venerable Sāriputta, has [attained final] Nirvāṇa. I have come bringing his bodily remains and his robes and bowl.'"
>
> The Buddha said: "How is it, Ānanda, has Sāriputta [attained final] Nirvāṇa and taken [along] the receiving of the aggregate of precepts? Has he [attained final] Nirvāṇa [and taken along] the aggregate of concentration ... the aggregate of wisdom ... the aggregate of liberation ... the aggregate of knowledge and vision of liberation?" Ānanda said to the Buddha: "No, Blessed One."
>
> The Buddha said to Ānanda: "The teachings I declare, having myself known them on attaining full awakening, that is, the four establishments of mindfulness, the four right efforts, the four bases for success, the five faculties, the five powers, the seven factors of awakening, and the eightfold path, has he [attained final] Nirvāṇa [and taken along these]?"
>
> Ānanda said to the Buddha: "No, Blessed One. Although he has not [attained final] Nirvāṇa and taken [along] the receiving of the aggregate of precepts ... *up to* ... [he has not attained final] Nirvāṇa [and taken along] the teachings on the path, yet the venerable Sāriputta was virtuous and learned. He had few wishes and was contented. He continually practised seclusion, with diligent effort and collected mindfulness, dwelling at peace with a unified and concentrated mind. He had swift wisdom, penetratingly sharp wisdom, transcending wisdom, discriminative wisdom, great

51 SĀ 638 at T II 176c8 to 177a13, parallel to SN 47.13 at SN V 162,12 (translated by Bodhi 2000: 1643).

wisdom, pervasive wisdom, profound wisdom, and incomparable wisdom. He was endowed with the treasure of knowledge and was able to instruct, able to teach, able to illuminate, able to delight, and well able to extol when teaching the Dharma to assemblies. For this reason, Blessed One, because of the Dharma and because of those who receive the Dharma, I am sad and distressed."[52]

The Buddha said to Ānanda: "Do not be sad and distressed. Why do [I say] that? What arises,[53] what occurs, what is constructed, is of a nature to become destroyed. How could it not become destroyed? Wishing for it not to become destroyed is [wishing] for what is impossible. I have earlier told you, various kinds of things and agreeable matters, everything for which one has thoughts of affection, all of it is entirely of a nature to become separated from one. One cannot keep it forever.

"It is just like a great tree with luxuriant roots, trunk, branches, leaves, flowers, and fruits, whose great branches break first. It is like a great treasure mountain, whose great peak collapses first.[54] In the same way, in the large community of the followers of the Tathāgata the great disciples [attain] Nirvāṇa first.

"In the direction in which Sāriputta dwelled, in that direction I had no concerns. Because of the presence of Sāriputta, that direction was certainly not empty for me."[55]

"Now, Ānanda, earlier I purposely told you that whatever there is of various agreeable matters for which one has thoughts of affection, all of this is of a nature to become separated from one; it is as I said earlier. Therefore do not be so very sad, Ānanda.

---

52 Ānanda's eulogy of Sāriputta in SN 47.13 at SN V 162,25 is shorter and emphasizes more the assistance Ānanda had received from him.

53 The translation "arises" is based on adopting a variant reading.

54 SN 47.13 does not have the simile of the mountain.

55 The present reference is without a counterpart in SN 47.13. A to some extent comparable statement can be found in the next discourse, SN 47.14 at SN V 164,1, where the Buddha notes that the assembly seems empty to him after Sāriputta and Mahāmoggallāna have passed away, and that he earlier had no concerns in relation to the direction in which the two were dwelling. The parallel to SN 47.14, SĀ 639 at T II 177a19 (to be taken up next), also reports the assembly being empty because Sāriputta and Mahāmoggallāna have passed away; it has no counterpart to the Buddha having no concerns in relation to the direction where the two had been living.

You should know that soon the Tathāgata will also be of the past. Therefore, Ānanda, you should make yourself an island by relying on yourself, you should make the Dharma your island by relying on the Dharma; you should make yourself no other island, no other reliance."

Ānanda said to the Buddha: "Blessed One, how does one have oneself as an island by relying on oneself? How does one have the Dharma as an island by relying on the Dharma? How does one have no other island, no other reliance?"[56]

The Buddha said to Ānanda: "[This takes place] if a monastic establishes mindfulness by contemplating the body [in regard to] the body [internally], with diligent effort, right knowing, and right mindfulness, overcoming greed and discontent in the world, and in the same way the body externally and the body internally and externally ... feeling tones ... the mind ... and establishes mindfulness by contemplating dharmas [in regard to] dharmas, *which should also be recited in this way*.[57]

Ānanda, this is called having oneself as an island by relying on oneself, having the Dharma as an island by relying on the Dharma, having no other island, no other reliance."[58]

In the Pāli parallel, the Buddha similarly points Ānanda back to the practice of mindfulness as the means to find a refuge within that will enable him to overcome his sorrow. The two parallel versions thereby bring out another aspect of the protective dimension of mindfulness by becoming self-reliant.

---

56 SN 47.13 does not report a query by Ānanda at this point, so that in its presentation the Buddha continues on his own to expound the meaning of his statement regarding having oneself and the Dharma as an island and a refuge.

57 SN 47.13 at SN V 163,14 does not explicitly mention practice undertaken internally, externally, and both. In fact, even SĀ 638 does not qualify the first instance of body contemplation as being internal, but it then does use the qualifications external as well as internal and external. Perhaps the first instance reflects an earlier reading, in line with the Pāli version, in which case the references to "external" and "internal and external" would be later additions. Alternatively, the reference to "internal" contemplation could also have been lost.

58 In SN 47.13 at SN V 163,20 the Buddha adds that those who follow his instruction on dwelling with themselves and the Dharma as a refuge will be foremost among those keen on training.

MINDFULLY FACING THE DEATH OF OTHERS (SĀ 639)

The next discourse continues on the same topic of facing the death of others, this time in the form of instructions on mindfulness in the face of the passing away of both Sāriputta and Mahāmoggallāna:[59]

> At that time, the venerable Sāriputta and Mahāmoggallāna had recently attained final Nirvāṇa. It was the time of the observance day on the fifteenth day of the month and the Blessed One was seated on a seat prepared in front of a large community. At that time the Blessed One, having surveyed the community, said to the monastics: "Surveying the large community, I have seen it to be void, because Sāriputta and Mahāmoggallāna have [entered] final Nirvāṇa.
>
> "Of my disciples only these two were fully and well able to teach, admonish, instruct, and eloquently explain the Dharma.[60] There are two types of wealth, monetary wealth and the wealth of Dharma. Monetary wealth is sought from people of the world and the wealth of Dharma from Sāriputta and Mahāmoggallāna. [Of course], the Tathāgata is already free from [seeking for] worldly wealth and the wealth of Dharma.[61]
>
> "Do not have sorrow and affliction because of the final Nirvāṇa of Sāriputta and Mahāmoggallāna.[62] It is just like a great tree that has flourishing roots, trunk, branches, leaves, flowers, and fruits, whose great branches break first. It is also like a [great] treasure mountain, whose great peak collapses first. In the same way, from among the large community of the Tathāgata, the two

59 SĀ 639 at T II 177a16 to 177b7, parallel to SN 47.14 at SN V 163,27 (translated by Bodhi 2000: 1644).

60 SN 47.14 at SN V 164,12 instead highlights their compliance with the teacher and their dearness to the four assemblies.

61 The translation "worldly" is based on adopting a variant reading. The whole phrase is cryptic in the original and my rendering is only tentative. The two types of wealth are not mentioned in SN 47.14, where at SN V 164,5 the Buddha instead announces that past and future Buddhas also had and will have two such disciples.

62 Instead of enjoining that the monastics should not feel sorrow, in SN 47.14 at SN V 164,15 the Buddha draws attention to his own freedom from sorrow.

> great disciples Sāriputta and Mahāmoggallāna have first entered Nirvāṇa.[63]
>
> "Therefore, monastics, do not give rise to sorrow and affliction. How could it be that what is of a nature to be born, of a nature to arise, of a nature to be constructed, of a nature to be conditioned, of a nature to change, will not be obliterated? The wish to make it not become destroyed is for something that is impossible. Earlier I already told you: 'From every one of the things that one can have affection towards, one will again come to be separated from them all.' Now I myself will soon also pass away.
>
> "For this reason, you should know that by relying on yourself you have yourself as an island, by relying on the Dharma you have the Dharma as an island, having no other island and no other reliance. That is, dwell mindfully contemplating the body [in regard to] the body internally, with diligent effort, right knowing, and right mindfulness, overcoming greed and discontent in the world, *in the same way for* the body externally ... the body internally and externally ... feeling tones ... the mind ... dwell mindfully contemplating dharmas [in regard to] dharmas with diligent effort, right knowing, and right mindfulness, overcoming greed and discontent in the world.
>
> "This is called having yourself as an island by relying on yourself, having the Dharma as an island by relying on the Dharma, having no other island and no other reliance."

The Pāli parallel similarly presents the cultivation of the four establishments of mindfulness as the means to become self-reliant. By finding a refuge within through mindfulness practice, undertaken in accordance with the Dharma, one becomes empowered to face the vicissitudes of life, even the death of those who are close and dear.

With the above discourse the collected sayings on the four establishments of mindfulness in the *Saṃyukta-āgama* come to an end. In the remainder of this chapter, I continue with a few other passages that touch on the related theme of facing death or pain with mindfulness.

---

63 SN 47.14 at SN V 164,21 has only the simile of the great tree whose largest branches break off; it has no counterpart to the simile of the mountain.

FINDING A MINDFUL REFUGE IN ONESELF (DĀ 2)

The power of mindfulness as one's refuge when one is worried about the health of others also features in the *Dīrgha-āgama* parallel to the *Mahāparinibbāna-sutta*. Both versions report a situation where the Buddha had just recovered from being seriously ill and his attendant Ānanda expresses how worried he had been about the Buddha's condition. In reply, the Buddha recommends that Ānanda should find a refuge in himself:[64]

> Ānanda, you should be a light to yourself,[65] having a light in the Dharma, without another light; you should be a refuge to yourself, having a refuge in the Dharma, without another refuge. How can you be a light to yourself, a light in the Dharma, without another light, a refuge to yourself, a refuge in the Dharma, without another refuge?
>
> Ānanda, a monastic contemplates the body internally, diligently without laxity, with recollective mindfulness that is not lost, removing greed and discontent in the world. One contemplates the body externally ... contemplates the body internally and externally, diligently without laxity, with recollective mindfulness that is not lost, removing greed and discontent in the world. One contemplates feeling tones ... the mind ... dharmas ... *also again in this way*.

The corresponding passage in the *Mahāparinibbāna-sutta* does not explicitly refer to internal and external practice of the four establishments of mindfulness. Alongside such minor differences, the parallels agree in highlighting the grounding potential of mindfulness practice such that one will be able to

---

64 DĀ 2 at T I 15b5 to 15b12, parallel to DN 16 at DN II 100,20 (translated by Walshe 1987: 245), also found in SN 47.9 at SN V 154,5 (translated by Bodhi 2000: 1637), and parallel to Sanskrit fragments, Waldschmidt 1951: 200, and T 6 at T I 180b2.

65 The translation "light" reflects an alternative understanding of what would be the same Indic term that in the previously translated passages from the *Saṃyukta-āgama* was instead rendered as "island". Norman 1990/1993: 87 comments on the corresponding Pāli term that it "could mean either 'a lamp for oneself' or 'an island, i.e., refuge, for oneself' ... either *ātma-dīpa* or *ātma-dvīpa*"; see also the discussion in, e.g., Bapat 1957, Brough 1962/2001: 210, Nakamura 2000: 95, and Wright 2000.

face even the serious illness and impending death of very close and dear ones with balance, having found a refuge in oneself and the teachings.

FACING DEATH WITH MINDFULNESS (SĀ 1028)

In combination with right knowing, mindfulness also serves to face one's own death:[66]

> You should be with right mindfulness and right knowing when awaiting your time.

The injunction in the Pāli parallel is similarly about awaiting one's time with mindfulness and clear knowing. The idiom of awaiting one's time refers to being on the verge of death.[67] Both versions add an explanation to the two qualities appropriate for such an occasion. The explanation clarifies that the reference to mindfulness relates to the four establishments of mindfulness, and the mention of clear (or right) knowing refers to acting with circumspection. These are the practices to rely on when death draws close.

FACING PAIN WITH MINDFULNESS (SĀ 541)

Anuruddha is on record for his ability to face physical pain by relying on the same practice of the four establishments of mindfulness:[68]

> Dwelling in the four establishments of mindfulness, my bodily pains have been gradually appeased. What are the four? That is, the establishment of mindfulness by contemplating the body as a body internally ... *up to* ... the establishment of mindfulness by

---

66 SĀ 1028 at T II 268c1, parallel to SN 36.7 at SN IV 211,1 (translated by Bodhi 2000: 1266).

67 Elsewhere in Pāli discourses, the actual event of death is referred to as "doing one's time", *kālaṃ karoti* or *kāla(ṅ)kiriyā*, and those who are dead have "done their time", *kāla(ṅ)kata*; see also Rhys Davids and Stede 1921/1993: 211 and Anālayo 2019n.

68 SĀ 541 at T II 140c19 to 140c22, parallel to SN 52.10 at SN V 302,19 (translated by Bodhi 2000: 1757); see also SĀ 540 (translated by Anālayo 2016c: 54).

> contemplating dharmas as dharmas. These are called the four establishments of mindfulness. Because of dwelling in these four establishments of mindfulness, my bodily pains have gradually calmed down.

In the Pāli parallel, Anuruddha specifies that, due to his dwelling in the four establishments of mindfulness, bodily pains were unable to overwhelm his mind. This provides a helpful clarification. It is not the case that bodily pains just disappear when one is with mindfulness. However, when one is established in mindfulness, an experience of bodily pain is no longer as overwhelming as it would have been otherwise. The bodily pain no longer afflicts the mind in the way it would have done if one had not been with mindfulness. It is in this sense that one can speak of bodily pains being gradually appeased or calmed down.

THE BUDDHA BEARS PAIN WITH MINDFULNESS (SĀ 1289)

Comparable to the case of Anuruddha above, the Buddha is also on record for facing bodily pain with mindfulness:[69]

> At that time the Blessed One's foot had been pierced by a hard splinter, giving rise to painful feeling tones in his body that he had never before experienced, no matter how long ago. He was able to gain a mental state of equanimity with right knowing and right mindfulness, enduring it and being himself at peace, without withdrawing from or decreasing his perception.

The Pāli parallel similarly reports that the Buddha faced his pain with mindfulness and clear knowing, although without specifying that these pains were of a type he had never before experienced. The Pāli version also does not have a counterpart to the reference to withdrawing from or decreasing perception. This reference is somewhat cryptic, but perhaps the idea could be that he just faced the pain squarely, without attempting to

69 SĀ 1289 at T II 355a20 to 355a22, parallel to SN 1.38 at SN I 27,15 (translated by Bodhi 2000: 116) and SĀ² 287 at T II 473c28 (translated by Anālayo 2016c: 60f).

evade it in any way. Given his meditative expertise, it can be assumed that he would have been able to enter some meditative attainment enabling him to withdraw from the pain or at least substantially decreasing the perception of bodily pain.[70]

This would then imply that even a highly accomplished meditator might opt for mindfulness in such a challenging situation. In the end, it seems that what really counts is mindfulness, whose "receptive" presence enables staying open to what happens, at the same time being "protected", through that same presence, from being overwhelmed by it.

HEALING THROUGH THE AWAKENING FACTORS (SĀ 727)

In addition to offering a powerful tool to face pain and thereby reduce its impact on the mind, mindfulness cultivated in conjunction with the other awakening factors can also have a positive influence on bodily health:[71]

> At one time the Buddha, who was travelling among the villages of the Malla people, was staying between the city of Kusinārā and the Hīraññavatī River.[72] By the side of a village he said to the venerable Ānanda: "Arrange the Blessed One's outer robe by folding it four times, I now have back pain and wish to lie down to rest a little."[73]
>
> Having received the instruction and arranged the outer robe by folding it four times, the venerable Ānanda said to the Buddha:

---

70 See also the discussion in Anālayo 2016c: 64.

71 SĀ 727 at T II 195b29 to 196a11, parallel to SN 46.16 at SN V 81,1 (translated by Bodhi 2000: 1581); see also the discussion in Anālayo 2013b: 212–214.

72 The parallel SN 46.16 at SN V 81,2 has instead the Squirrels' Feeding Place in the Bamboo Grove at Rājagaha as its venue.

73 SN 46.16 at SN V 81,4 only briefly reports that the Buddha was sick and therefore has no counterpart to the narration in SĀ 727 that precedes the recitation of the awakening factors. This narration, together with the subsequent verses, is part of the Sanskrit fragment version of the *Mahāparnirvāṇa-sūtra*, Waldschmidt 1951: 286–292, and of the Chinese and Tibetan translations of the corresponding section in the Mūlasarvāstivāda *Vinaya*, Waldschmidt 1951: 287–293 and T 1451 at T XXIV 391c26 to 392b9. Parallels to the verses have been preserved in Sanskrit and Uighur fragments, von Gabain 1954: 13 and Waldschmidt 1967: 244.

"Blessed One, the outer robe has been arranged by being folded four times, may the Blessed One know the time [has come to lie down]."

At that time the Blessed One, using a thick fold of the outer robe as a pillow for the head, placing one foot on the other, with collected mindfulness and clarity of perception lay down on the right side.[74] With right mindfulness and right knowing he was aware of the idea of rising up again. He said to Ānanda: "Proclaim the seven factors of awakening."[75]

Then the venerable Ānanda said to the Buddha: "Blessed One, they are reckoned to be the mindfulness awakening factor, which the Blessed One realized himself through full awakening and taught as being supported by seclusion, supported by dispassion, and supported by cessation, leading to letting go. The investigation-of-dharmas ... energy ... joy ... tranquillity ... concentration ... and equipoise awakening factor, which the Blessed One realized himself through full awakening and taught as being supported by seclusion, supported by dispassion, and supported by cessation, leading to letting go."

The Buddha said to Ānanda: "Did you say: energy?" Ānanda said to the Buddha: "I said energy, Blessed One, I said energy, Well-gone One."

The Buddha said to Ānanda: "Energy indeed, which I cultivated, cultivated much, to reach supreme and full awakening."[76] Having said this, he sat up with a straight body and with mindfulness established.[77]

Then another monastic spoke these verses:

"Delighting in hearing the wonderful Dharma,
Enduring a disease, [the Buddha] told someone to proclaim it.
A monastic proclaimed the Dharma,
The unfolding of the seven awakening factors.

74 The translation "perception" is based on adopting a variant reading.

75 In SN 46.16 at SN V 81,9 the monastic whom the Buddha requests to recite the awakening factors is Mahācunda.

76 SN 46.16 at SN V 81,22 does not single out energy in particular, but only reports that the Buddha confirmed that these are the factors of awakening.

77 SN 46.16 at SN V 81,24 indicates that the Buddha recovered from the disease, after which the discourse concludes.

"Well done, venerable Ānanda,
Skilfully you proclaimed
A teaching that is superbly pure.
Stainless and sublime is what you proclaimed:

"Mindfulness, investigation-of-dharmas, energy,
Joy, tranquillity, concentration, and the awakening [factor]
of equipoise,
These are indeed the seven awakening factors,
They are sublime and well taught.

"Hearing the seven awakening factors being proclaimed
Thoroughly experiencing the flavour of full awakening,
[Although] the body had been afflicted by great pain
[The Buddha] sat up straight to listen, enduring the illness.

"See the master of the true Dharma,[78]
Who always teaches it widely to people,
How he delighted in hearing what was being proclaimed,
How much more do those who have not yet heard it.

"[Sāriputta], the one foremost in great wisdom,[79]
Esteemed by the One with the ten powers,[80]
He, too, on being afflicted by disease,
Came to hear the right Dharma being proclaimed.

"Those who are well learned and have clear understanding
Of the discourses and the higher teachings,[81]
Capable at reciting the teachings and the discipline
Should listen to it, let alone others.

---

78 The translation is based on adopting a variant reading.

79 According to the Sanskrit fragment parallel, this is a reference to Sāriputta.

80 The "One with the ten powers" would refer to the Buddha, who according to tradition was endowed with the ten powers of a Tathāgata; see, e.g., MN 12 at MN I 69,31 (translated by Ñāṇamoli 1995/2005: 165) and its parallel T 757 at T XVII 592c3 (a survey of other references to the ten powers can be found in Anālayo 2011: 110–112).

81 SĀ 727 at T II 195c29 here speaks of the Abhidharma, which I have rendered as "higher teachings"; for a survey of references to the Abhidharma in the early discourses see Anālayo 2014: 69–79. The Sanskrit fragment parallel instead refers to the bearers of the *mātṛkā*s, Waldschmidt 1967: 245 (§7): *(sūtra)dharā mātṛk(ā)dharāś caiva*; on the *mātṛkā*s and their possible relationship to the Abhidharma see Anālayo 2014: 21–53.

"Hearing the Dharma being proclaimed, as it really is,
Listening with a collected mind, intelligently and wisely,
To the Dharma proclaimed by the Buddha
One attains delight and joy free from sensuality.

"With delight and joy the body becomes tranquil,
The mind also becomes happy by itself,
The happy mind gains attainments,
And proper insight into becoming, realms, and formations.

"Those who are disenchanted with the three destinations
Abandon desire and liberate the mind,
Being disenchanted with all becoming and destinations,
They do not arise among humans or celestials,
Without remainder, like an extinguished lamp,
They [enter] final Nirvāṇa.

"It is very beneficial to hear the Dharma
That has been proclaimed by the supreme victor.
Therefore, with unified attention, one should
Listen to what the great teacher has proclaimed."

Having spoken these verses, that other monastic rose from his seat and left.

The *Saṃyutta-nikāya* has another two discourses that describe two accomplished disciples of the Buddha also recovering their health following a recitation of the awakening factors.[82] A discourse in the *Ekottarika-āgama* reports that another sick monastic similarly recovered, with the difference that, instead of hearing a recitation of the awakening factors, he had been told by the Buddha to recite them himself.[83] In each of these instances, it can safely be assumed that the recitation served as an aid for meditative recollection. In this way, based on mindfulness as the

82 SN 46.14 at SN V 79,19 (translated by Bodhi 2000: 1580) and SN 46.15 at SN V 80,20 (translated by Bodhi 2000: 1581). SN 46.14 has a discourse parallel preserved in Tibetan, D 40 *ka* 281b1 or Q 756 *tsi* 298a8 (translated by Anālayo 2017d: 14f), whose rendering into Tibetan was apparently based on a Pāli original; see Skilling 1993.

83 EĀ 39.6 at T II 731a26.

foundation for the other awakening factors, a mental condition can be reached that, according to these discourses, can have a substantial impact on the physical body.

SUMMARY

The protective function of mindfulness can be compared to the need of a monkey to refrain from straying out of its proper domain in order to avoid being caught. Mindfulness is beneficial for those who have just started to practise, those who are already trained in it, and those who are highly accomplished meditators. In line with the potential protection afforded by mindfulness, broached in the previous chapter, being with mindfulness established can forestall the arising of sensual desire. Just as its cultivation can strengthen one's ethical conduct, so too ethical conduct in turn supports mindfulness by providing its cultivation with a firm foundation. Mindfulness needs to be supported by morality to lead to purification of the mind and to have a liberating effect.

In some accounts of the gradual path to awakening, the four establishments of mindfulness occupy the position usually taken by the four absorptions. In fact the presence of mindfulness is part of the standard description of the two higher absorptions and therefore even relevant to those accounts that instead describe absorption attainment. The protective and liberating dimensions of mindfulness provide a refuge within when having to face death or pain, one's own or that of others. The cultivation of the awakening factors, of which mindfulness is the first, can even bring about healing on the physical level.

V

DIMENSIONS OF MINDFULNESS

In this chapter and the next, I survey various passages on mindfulness not yet taken into account so far, covering a miscellany of aspects of mindfulness. Whereas in the first two chapters I was able to group together material under an overarching topic and in the third and fourth chapters the collected sayings on the establishments of mindfulness provided some inner coherence and structure, what follows now is somewhat unsystematic. This in a way reflects the nature of the early discourses as testimonies of individual discussions and teachings in an oral setting, which differs from the systematization found in later exegesis. Hence, although I have tried to achieve at least some collation of similar passages, the extent to which this is possible with the type of material left for exploration is limited.

I begin with passages that show how mindfulness relates to other factors of the eightfold path (MĀ 189 and SĀ 305). This role finds illustration in a simile of a charioteer (SĀ 769). The role of right mindfulness in relation to the Buddhist path has its foundation in the basic distinction between the right and the wrong path (SĀ 271). Although this distinction between what is "right" and what is "wrong" is central in much of the early Buddhist teachings, it appears to be less relevant in the case of two other passages related to mindfulness. One of these describes celestial beings who excessively indulge in merriment, and the other depicts a cowherd watching his cows with mindfulness (DĀ 21 and MĀ 102).

A Buddha has mindfulness already at his conception (DĀ 1 and MĀ 32). Mindfulness can also be relevant to partaking of food, as evident in instructions on eating mindfully given by the Buddha to King Pasenadi (SĀ 1150). The presence of mindfulness is similarly relevant to the topic of sleeping (SĀ 1087) and its complement in wakefulness (EĀ 21.6). The need for the same quality when living alone in a forest (MĀ 26) also extends to sense restraint when going into the next village or town to get food (EĀ 33.4, SĀ 1191, and SĀ 1260). Throughout, one should give priority to mindfulness (MĀ 107).

Wishing to teach mindfulness to others, one first of all needs to cultivate it oneself (MĀ 91). Those who cultivate this quality tend to keep company with each other (SĀ 450). Mindfulness is a path of Dharma (DĀ 9), it serves as an authority (MĀ 113), and functions in a way comparable to a ford or the proper pasture ground for cattle (EĀ 49.1). A specific modality of mindfulness can be seen in the cultivation of "bare awareness" (SĀ 312).

MINDFULNESS IN THE NOBLE EIGHTFOLD PATH (MĀ 189)

The role of mindfulness as the seventh factor in the noble eightfold path can be explored with the help of the *Mahācattārīsaka-sutta* and its *Madhyama-āgama* parallel. In agreement with another parallel extant in Tibetan translation, the Pāli and Chinese versions describe how right effort and right mindfulness relate to the first factor of the noble eightfold path, right view:[1]

> To see that wrong view is wrong view, this is reckoned right view. To see that right view is right view, this is also reckoned right view. Having understood it like this, one then seeks to train with the wish to abandon wrong view and to accomplish right

1 MĀ 189 at T I 735c22 to 735c27, parallel to MN 117 at MN III 72,22 (translated by Ñāṇamoli 1995/2005: 935) and Up 6080 at D 4094 *nyu* 44b4 or Q 5595 *thu* 84a5; see also Anālayo 2011: 658.

> view; this is reckoned right effort. With mindfulness a monastic abandons wrong view and accomplishes right view; this is reckoned right mindfulness. These three factors go along with right view.

The three parallels agree in applying the same principle to the path factors of right intention, right speech, right action, and right livelihood. In the case of right intention, for example, right view stands for the distinction between right and wrong types of intention. The effort made to implement the former and overcome the latter is right effort. Mindfulness in turn has the function of monitoring what is taking place. Through its "receptive" potential, mindfulness is able to supervise the effort to leave behind wrong types of intention and to oversee the cultivation of right types of intention.

This implies that mindfulness can be present at the time when a quality manifests that is detrimental for progress on the path, by way of noticing this and providing the required information to right view. This is just one example in a general pattern, also evident in the instructions given in the *Satipaṭṭhāna-sutta* and its parallels, in which mindfulness can be present in the mind at the very time when a defilement manifests.[2]

Based on the presence of mindfulness, right view then brings in the aspect of clear recognition of a wrong path factor as "wrong". This clear recognition in turn leads to a deployment of right effort in order to emerge from the wrong path factor. The whole procedure is continuously monitored by right mindfulness.

For an understanding of mindfulness, it is telling that the same procedure is also applied to wrong action, which comprises killing, stealing, and sexual misconduct. These three wrong actions involve serious breaches of the basic conduct expected from a Buddhist lay disciple (let alone monastics), who take unto themselves the observance of five precepts. Three of these

2 On the position in some later traditions, according to which mindfulness cannot coexist in the same state of mind with something that is unwholesome, see Anālayo 2017c: 22–24.

precepts require precisely abstaining from killing, stealing, and sexual misconduct. Even in regard to wrong action, involving such fundamental ethical breaches, the task of mindfulness remains one of monitoring without directly interfering. The actual effort to keep the respective precepts is the domain of right effort, for whose deployment mindfulness provides the required information. But mindfulness itself just monitors.

In addition to showing the interrelation of the path factors in this way, the three parallels also depict their sequential build-up:[3]

> Right view gives rise to right intention, right intention gives rise to right speech, right speech gives rise to right action, right action gives rise to right livelihood, right livelihood gives rise to right effort, right effort gives rise to right mindfulness, and right mindfulness gives rise to right concentration.

This sequential presentation could hardly imply that each factor should only be developed once the preceding ones are fully established. Such an interpretation would conflict with the previous description of their interrelation. Instead, the point appears to be that, in a general sense, the path factors build on each other. Here right view is the indispensable foundation, informing intention that then leads to aligning speech, action, and livelihood accordingly. These support the deployment of right effort in order to remove what is unwholesome. The less the mind is in the grip of defilements, the easier it is to cultivate mindfulness, and with mindfulness well established the mind naturally becomes collected in concentration.

To appreciate this sequential building up, it would be of relevance that an equation of right concentration with the

---

3 MĀ 189 at T I 735c8 to 735c10, an exposition which here precedes the depiction of the interrelation of right view with right effort and right mindfulness, etc. The corresponding sequential build-up of the path factors in the parallels, MN 117 at MN III 76,1 and Up 6080 at D 4094 *nyu* 46b2 or Q 5595 *thu* 86a6, occurs only after the detailed exposition of the path factors. A similar progression can be found in MĀ 179 at T I 721c4 (translated by Anālayo 2012: 131), which in this case is absent from the Pāli parallel MN 78; see Anālayo 2011: 429.

four absorptions might not be the earliest formulation of right concentration in the discourses. Instead, the original idea appears to have been that concentration, whatever its depth, needs to be cultivated in conjunction with the other path factors.[4]

Yet another perspective, offered in the *Mahācattārīsaka-sutta* and its parallels, concerns the difference between the path of someone who is training to reach full awakening and one who has reached the final goal. An arahant is endowed not only with superior manifestations of the factors of the noble eightfold path, but also with the two additional factors of right knowledge and right liberation:[5]

> What are the eight factors with which one in training is endowed? The right view of one in training ... *up to* ... the right concentration of one in training; these are the eight factors with which one in training is endowed.
>
> What are the ten factors with which an arahant, who has destroyed the influxes, is endowed? The right view of one beyond training ... *up to* ... the right knowledge of one beyond training; these are reckoned the ten factors with which an arahant, who has destroyed the influxes, is endowed.

The Pāli version has the two additional path factors of an arahant in the opposite sequence, with right knowledge followed by right liberation (the last is abbreviated in the Chinese parallel).[6] Both together mark the perfection of the path, reached with full awakening. Nevertheless, the other factors are not relinquished and their perfection is characteristic of the conduct and practice of one who has taken the path to its final completion. In other words, the path is an integral dimension of the goal and the goal is in turn a perfection of the path.

In the case of mindfulness, the successful attainment of the goal then finds its expression in the right mindfulness of one

4 See in more detail Anālayo 2019c.
5 MĀ 189 at T I 736b21 to 736b24. The ten path factors of an arahant, one who is beyond training, are also found, e.g., in MN 65 at MN I 446,32 (translated by Ñāṇamoli 1995/2005: 550) and its parallel MĀ 194 at T I 749b20; see also Anālayo 2011: 362.
6 See in more detail Anālayo 2011: 663.

beyond training. This ties in with passages to be taken up in the next chapter, according to which arahants are superbly mindful (see below p. 227).

All in all, the first of the above three perspectives on the noble eightfold path shows the monitoring role of right mindfulness in relation to other path factors. The second reveals the degree to which mindfulness relies on previous path factors (in particular the establishment of an ethical foundation) and in turn supports concentration. The third discloses its continuous relevance not only for those who practise the path, but also for those who have reached the final goal. Each of these three perspectives throws a light on the functions of mindfulness in relation to the path and thereby reveals the degree to which the cultivation of mindfulness is integral to the path to awakening.

THE EIGHTFOLD PATH IN MEDITATION (SĀ 305)

With the next passage I turn to another perspective on how the factors of the eightfold path relate to actual meditation practice, complementing the discourse just taken up. The relevant passage occurs after a description of the cultivation of knowledge and vision in relation to the six senses. This requires that one knows, in accordance with reality, each sense, its corresponding object, consciousness, contact, and the three types of feeling tone arisen in dependence on such contact. Through such knowing, one is no longer attached, one's clinging to the five aggregates diminishes, one's craving is abandoned, and one is mentally and physically at ease:[7]

> One who has knowledge in this way and vision in this way is called one who cultivates the fulfilment of right view, right intention, right effort, right mindfulness, and right concentration; previously, what are designated as right speech, right action, and right livelihood have been purified and fulfilled by cultivation.

7 SĀ 305 at T II 87b29 to 87c3, parallel to MN 149 at MN III 289,2 (translated by Ñāṇamoli 1995/2005: 1138) and Up 4006 at D 4094 *ju* 205a2 or Q 5595 *tu* 234a1; see also Anālayo 2011: 842.

> This is reckoned to be the purification and fulfilment of a cultivation of the noble eightfold path.

The Pāli version agrees that, based on earlier purification of right speech, right action, and right livelihood, the other path factors can be cultivated through the practice of insight meditation in relation to the senses.[8] This complements the perspective that emerged in the previous discourse on the collaboration of right view, right effort, and right mindfulness in relation to the implementation of other path factors. In this way, a dynamic perspective emerges regarding a cultivation of the noble eightfold path as an implicit dimension of insight meditation.

Yet another dimension emerges from an indication in the parallels that the above depicted cultivation of the noble eightfold path then issues in the cultivation of the four establishments of mindfulness (and the four right efforts, four bases of success, five faculties, etc.). In this way, mindfulness has been aroused during meditation on the six senses and comes fully into bloom by way of its four establishments. This shows how a flexible deployment of mindfulness in different ways can evolve under the overarching concern of ensuring progress to awakening.

THE CHARIOTEER SIMILE (SĀ 769)

In a comparison of the noble eightfold path to a chariot, the role of mindfulness finds illustration in a good charioteer:[9]

> Being well protected by right mindfulness is like being a good charioteer.

The Pāli parallel similarly considers mindfulness to be comparable to a watchful charioteer. The task to be performed by such a charioteer would require combining present-moment awareness with an overview of the whole traffic situation and keeping in mind the right direction. Understood in this

---

8 The Tibetan parallel includes right speech among the factors developed during insight meditation.

9 SĀ 769 at T II 201a4, parallel to SN 45.4 at SN V 6,10 (translated by Bodhi 2000: 1526) and an Uighur fragment, von Gabain 1954: 16.

way, the simile can be understood to bring out in particular the "receptivity" of mindfulness in its monitoring function in relation to the other path factors and its resultant potential to provide an overview as well as a sense of direction.

In another simile, mindfulness occurs in a comparison of various mental qualities to aspects of agriculture:[10]

> Right mindfulness is one's own guard.

The Pāli parallel instead compares mindfulness to the ploughshare and goad used by a farmer in agriculture, and a Sanskrit fragment parallel speaks rather of mindfulness as a watchful charioteer.[11] The reference to a "guard" in the passage translated above might go back to an original expressing the same idea of "watchfulness" as found in relation to the charioteer.[12]

The Pāli parallel stands alone in relating mindfulness to the ploughshare and goad of a farmer. The somewhat more active connotations of this illustration are thus not supported by the parallels. The idea behind this imagery could perhaps be that mindfulness can help to reveal things and thereby make them ready for being worked on just as a ploughshare turns over the earth and makes it ready for being worked on, and that it provides guidance just as the goad guides the oxen who are pulling the plough.

THE WRONG AND THE RIGHT PATH (SĀ 271)

The notion of right mindfulness as a path factor is based on the general distinction between right and wrong path factors. A simile relevant to this distinction describes someone knowledgeable about a particular path to be taken. The knowledgeable person provides directions to another person

10 SĀ 98 at T II 27a28, parallel to SN 7.11 at SN I 172,32 (translated by Bodhi 2000: 267), Sn 77 (translated by Bodhi 2017: 168), Enomoto 1997: 98, SĀ² 264 at T II 466c1, and SĀ³ 1 at T II 493a20.

11 Enomoto 1997: 98.

12 The term *ārakkha* / *ārakṣa* used in the previous charioteer simile (and in the present Sanskrit parallel) to convey the sense of a "watchful" charioteer can also carry the sense of a "guard" or "protection".

who does not know the path. Such directions take the form of recommending that the left path should be avoided and the right path should be taken, etc. The image of the left and the right path then receives the following explanation:[13]

> The left path is the three unwholesome states: thoughts of lust, hatred, and harming. The right path is the three wholesome thoughts: thoughts of renunciation and dispassion, thoughts without hatred, and thoughts of not harming.
>
> Going forward on the left path is reckoned to be wrong view, wrong intention, wrong speech, wrong action, wrong livelihood, wrong effort, wrong mindfulness, and wrong concentration. Going forward on the right path is reckoned to be right view, right intention, right speech, right action, right livelihood, right effort, right mindfulness, and right concentration.

In both versions, taking the right path eventually leads to Nirvāṇa. A difference is that the Pāli parallel does not have a counterpart to the first of the two paragraphs translated above. As a result, it simply identifies the left path with the wrong eightfold path and the right path with its right counterpart. The additional distinction drawn in the first paragraph from the above *Saṃyukta-āgama* discourse, although perhaps a later addition, helps to flesh out the implications of the distinction between the wrong and the right paths. It shows that what makes a path wrong is the presence of thoughts of lust, hatred, and harming. In contrast, the right path involves dispassion, as well as the absence of hatred and of harming. The same can safely be assumed to be implicit in the Pāli version, in particular in the contrast between right and wrong intentions, given that right intention is precisely intention of renunciation, non-hatred, and non-harming. Such intentions must inform mindfulness if it is to be reckoned as "right".[14] The present passage thereby reinforces the importance of an ethics of the mind in relation to mindfulness.

---

13 SĀ 271 at T II 71c1 to 71c6, parallel to SN 22.84 at SN III 109,1 (translated by Bodhi 2000: 930).

14 On right mindfulness see also below p. 185.

THE DIRE EFFECTS OF A LOSS OF MINDFULNESS (DĀ 21)

The next passage to be taken up, with which my survey moves to mindfulness in a celestial realm, does not seem to be easily amenable to the distinction between right and wrong types of mindfulness. The passage in question, found in the *Dīrgha-āgama* parallel to the *Brahmajāla-sutta*, describes a particular type of celestial beings fond of excessive amusement:[15]

> Some [celestial] sentient beings are corrupted by pleasure, in manifold ways they play, laugh, and amuse themselves. At the time of playing, laughing, and amusing themselves, their body becomes very tired and they in turn lose their mindfulness.[16] On losing mindfulness, their life in turn comes to an end.

The Pāli description refers just to a loss of mindfulness as what led to the passing away of these celestial beings, without bringing in a tiredness of their bodies.[17] Alongside this difference, the parallel versions agree that, in the case of this particular type of celestial beings, loss of mindfulness is actually a matter of life and death.

The loss of mindfulness of these celestial beings has a counterpart in the passage from the *Sakkapañha-sutta* and its parallels, discussed in a previous chapter (see above p. 20), where celestial beings in an inferior realm were able to ascend

15 DĀ 21 at T I 90c15 to 90c17, parallel to DN 1 at DN I 19,14 (translated by Walshe 1987: 77), two Tibetan parallels, Weller 1934: 28,23 and Up 3050 at D 4094 *ju* 146a4 or Q 5595 *tu* 168a4, T 21 at T I 266c9, and T 1548 at T XXVIII 657b12.

16 DĀ 21 at T I 90c16 (see also T 1548 at T XXVIII 657b14) speaks literally of a loss of "mind", using a Chinese character that usually renders *manas*, but which at times can also translate "mindfulness" (*smṛti*); see Hirakawa 1997: 491. This seems to be the meaning appropriate to the present context, as confirmed by a reference to "mindfulness" in the other parallels. Further confirmation can be found in a quote in the **Mahāvibhāṣā* (which parallels another description of these particular celestial beings in DN 24 at DN III 31,5 and its parallel DĀ 15 at T I 69b28), where the relevant passage in T 1545 at T XXVII 190c19 also speaks of a loss of mindfulness.

17 DN 1 at DN I 19,14 reads *satiyā sammosā te devā tamhā kāyā cavanti*. The formulation leaves open the possibility that a reference comparable to the term *kāya* in DN 1, where it stands for the "realm" or "state" of these celestial beings, might have led to a misunderstanding by the Chinese translators and became a reference to the "body" of these beings.

to a higher realm by regaining mindfulness. This took the form of recollecting the Buddha's teachings, with which they had been familiar in their previous lives as Buddhist monastics. In the present case the nuance of remembering the teachings is not of relevance, as there is no indication that the celestial beings, who excessively amuse themselves, had any previous exposure to instructions by the Buddha.

An intriguing aspect of the description is that these celestial beings must possess some degree of mindfulness while living in their celestial realm, otherwise loss of mindfulness could hardly have such dramatic consequences for them. Such mindfulness is not easily classed as "right" or else "wrong", in so far as it does not have a direct relationship to the practice of the path to liberation nor does it seem to run counter to it. In addition, it is also not quite clear how far such mindfulness is the result of intentional cultivation.

A COWHERD'S MINDFULNESS (MĀ 102)

The next passage is also relevant to the question of how thoroughly the distinction between right and wrong forms of mindfulness applies to the various manifestations of mindfulness recognized in early Buddhist thought. It involves a simile, found in the *Dvedhāvitakka-sutta* and its *Madhyama-āgama* parallel. The simile begins by describing a cowherd who has to watch closely over the cows and at times hit them in order to prevent them from straying into the ripened fields.[18] The situation changes, however, once the crop has been harvested:[19]

> It is just like in the last month of autumn, when the entire harvest has been collected, and a cowherd boy, when setting the cows free in the uncultivated fields, is mindful of them with the thought: "My cows are there in the herd." Why is that? Because the cowherd boy does not see that he would be scolded, beaten, or imprisoned for any trespassing. For this reason, he

---

18 See Anālayo 2013b: 147.

19 MĀ 102 at T I 589b27 to 589c2, parallel to MN 19 at MN I 116,36 (translated by Ñāṇamoli 1995/2005: 209); see also Anālayo 2011: 139.

is mindful of them with the thought: "My cows are there in the herd."

The *Dvedhāvitakka-sutta* uses the term *sati* in describing the cowherd just being aware of the cows without any need to control them. The Chinese counterpart is ambivalent, due to the fact that the character used to render *sati* can also translate "thought". In my translation, I have tried to convey both nuances by rendering the same term twice as "mindful" and "with the thought". Although, when taken on its own, one might opt for understanding the passage just as a referent to thought, in view of the Pāli parallel it seems more probable that the underlying Indic original would rather have had a reference to mindfulness at the present juncture.

The situation described in this simile, which at least in the Pāli version definitely involves the term "mindfulness", does not seem to lend itself naturally to the distinction between right and wrong forms of this quality. The cowherd's awareness of the cattle grazing in the fields, where the crop has already been harvested, will not lead to awakening. But neither does it lead in the opposite direction. In conjunction with the other example, involving celestial beings who excessively amuse themselves, it seems fair to conclude that early Buddhist thought recognizes forms of mindfulness that, although falling short of being "right", nevertheless do not for that reason automatically fall into the opposite category of being completely "wrong".

Moreover, the cowherd's mindfulness of the cows does not appear to be the result of intentional meditative cultivation. The same would hold for the celestial beings in the preceding passage. This in turn is relevant to the question of whether mindfulness in early Buddhist thought was considered a state or a trait. In other words, is mindfulness something that only manifests as a result of meditative cultivation or is it rather a quality that, to some degree at least, is inherent in human and celestial beings?[20]

20 Brown and Ryan 2004: 246 argue that "mindfulness is not merely a product of meditation ... mindfulness is an inherent, natural capacity of the human organism." Here it may also be of relevance to note that AN 10.77 at AN V 149,19 (translated by Bodhi 2012: 1439) lists loss of

A PAST BUDDHA'S ENTRY INTO HIS MOTHER'S WOMB (DĀ 1)

A form of mindfulness that also does not seem to be the result of intentional meditative training occurs in a description of various qualities or accomplishments of a past Buddha by the name of Vipassin. The relevant discourse accompanies each of these qualities or accomplishments with a statement indicating that these are characteristic of all Buddhas. The description relevant to the topic of mindfulness concerns how Vipassin, who at that time had not yet become a Buddha and therefore is referred to as a "bodhisattva", was conceived:[21]

> This is an unchanging law for all Buddhas: [when] the bodhisattva Vipassin descended from Tusita Heaven into his mother's womb, he entered it from the right side, being with right mindfulness and without confusion.

The Pāli parallel, the *Mahāpadāna-sutta*, also reports that Vipassin entered into his mother's womb while being in the possession of mindfulness (and clear knowing).[22] Another two parallels extant in Sanskrit fragments and in an individual Chinese translation, however, do not refer at all to Vipassin's mental condition at his conception. This leaves open the

---

mindfulness among ten bad qualities of a crow. This gives the impression that perhaps some animals were seen as having mindfulness. Such seems to be the case for a tale involving two parrot chicks in the *Divyāvadāna*, Cowell and Neil 1886: 199,19, which are described as having mindfully recollected the Buddha, the Dharma, and the community when passing away. However, Ohnuma 2017: 195n41 comments that "in all ways – from their use of human language to their taking of the three refuges and the five moral precepts – these chicks seem to function more like human laypeople than like animals. And – correspondingly – they win rebirth in heaven through their mindfulness ... the story thus seems like an anomaly and is not characteristic of animals in general." In other words, an interpretation of such descriptions needs to keep in mind that the relationship established to mindfulness might just be a by-product of fable-telling and need not reflect a well-reasoned doctrinal position on the mental abilities or disabilities of animals.

21 DĀ 1 at T I 3c14 to 3c16, parallel to DN 14 at DN II 12,4 (translated by Walshe 1987: 203), a Sanskrit fragment version, Waldschmidt 1956: 82 or Fukita 2003: 54, and T 2 at T I 152b14.

22 DN 14 at DN II 12,4: *sato sampajāno mātukucchiṃ okkami*, a description that does not refer to the mother's right side.

possibility that the reference to mindfulness, or even right mindfulness in the passage translated above, could be a later addition.

Nevertheless, the existence of this reference in the *Dīrgha-āgama* discourse and its Pāli parallel implies that, at the time of such an addition, mindfulness was considered a quality already possessed by a Buddha-to-be at the time of his conception. In agreement with its Pāli parallel, the *Dīrgha-āgama* version in fact continues emphasizing mindfulness, reporting that Vipassin was endowed with mindfulness during his stay in his mother's womb and at the time of his birth, a continuous presence of mindfulness shared by all those who are going to become Buddhas in that same life.[23]

THE BUDDHA'S MINDFULNESS AT CONCEPTION (MĀ 32)

The notion that all Buddhas have mindfulness already at the time of conception in their mother's womb recurs in relation to the present Buddha in the *Acchariyabbhutadhamma-sutta*.[24] Whereas the Pāli version speaks of mindfulness and clear knowing, the *Madhyama-āgama* parallel only mentions the second of these two qualities:[25]

> When his life in Tusita Heaven came to an end, the Blessed One entered his mother's womb knowingly.

The Chinese character employed in this context can also render "mindfulness",[26] although in the *Madhyama-āgama* it usually

23 DĀ 1 at T I 4a1 and 4b15. The next discourse in the collection, DĀ 2 at T I 16a5 and 16a7, reports possession of mindfulness during entry into the womb and during birth for bodhisattvas in general (as part of an enumeration of occasions for an earthquake to occur). A similar presence of mindfulness on these two occasions is mentioned in the Pāli parallel DN 16 at DN II 108,10 and 108,14 (translated by Walshe 1987: 248), but not in the Sanskrit fragment parallel, Waldschmidt 1951: 214 and 216, or in the parallels T 5 at T I 165b4, T 6 at T I 180c19, and T 7 at T I 191c28.

24 MN 123 at MN III 119,35 (translated by Ñāṇamoli 1995/2005: 980); see also AN 4.127 at AN II 130,20 (translated by Bodhi 2012: 510).

25 MĀ 32 at T I 470a14; see also Anālayo 2011: 702.

26 Hirakawa 1997: 885.

stands for "knowing". This makes it doubtful whether the original used for translation had a reference to mindfulness at this juncture.[27] Nevertheless, even a reference to knowing (*sampajañña*) on its own would imply the presence of some degree of mindfulness. When considered from this perspective, although not beyond doubt, it seems still fair to propose that the basic idea conveyed by the parallels is similar. On this understanding, the present passage reinforces the point made above, in that mindfulness was considered a quality possessed by a Buddha-to-be already at the time of his conception. Keeping in mind that the early discourses reflect a period when the fully fledged bodhisattva ideal had not yet come into existence,[28] such mindfulness does not seem to be the result of intentional meditative cultivation.

OVEREATING AND MINDFULNESS (SĀ 1150)

Already in the early discourses, mindfulness finds employment for the decidedly this-worldly purpose of weight loss through mindful eating. The instructions given in this respect to a king named Pasenadi are of considerable importance for relating mindfulness in early Buddhism to its current applications in healthcare and related areas. By way of introduction, I briefly survey information found in other discourses regarding this particular king, before taking up the actual instructions he received on mindful eating.

King Pasenadi apparently performed a major sacrifice at which hundreds of animals were slaughtered.[29] On other occasions he had a large number of people arrested,[30] presumably arbitrarily, or else is found employing spies to gather intelligence from

---

27 A description of the same entry into the mother's womb in the *Mahāsaṃvartanīkathā*, Okano 1998: 113, does mention mindfulness: *viveśa tasyāḥ smṛta eva kukṣau*, "mindful indeed he entered her womb".

28 On the beginnings of the bodhisattva ideal see Anālayo 2010 and 2017a.

29 SN 3.9 at SN I 75,31 (translated by Bodhi 2000: 171), parallel to SĀ 1234 T II 338a23 and SĀ[2] 61 at T II 394c27.

30 SN 3.10 at SN I 76,31 (translated by Bodhi 2000: 172), parallel to SĀ 1235 at T II 338b13 and SĀ[2] 62 at T II 395b5.

other countries.[31] Two discourses report him engaging in battle in defence against another king's attack.[32] In apparent recognition of his warrior activities, in another discourse the Buddha employs the example of having to go to battle as an expedient means for illustrating to the king a teaching on charity.[33]

These passages do not occur in chronological order, making it uncertain to what degree they reflect his behaviour before or after he had come to consider himself a disciple of the Buddha. In the case of one Pāli discourse and its Chinese parallel, however, the conversation between the Buddha and King Pasenadi makes it unmistakeably clear that this must have been their last meeting. This becomes evident from the circumstance that Pasenadi, as part of a series of expressions of his affection and respect for the Buddha, refers to the fact that they are both eighty,[34] which is the age at which the Buddha appears to have passed away.

The relevant Pāli discourse and its Chinese parallel report an unusual detail in their introductory narrations, namely that King Pasenadi had handed the royal insignia over to his commander-in-chief before approaching the Buddha. According to the Pāli commentary on this discourse and a passage in the Mūlasarvāstivāda *Vinaya*,[35] the commander-in-chief seized the opportunity to bring the insignia to Pasenadi's son and crown him king. After his conversation with the Buddha, King Pasenadi discovered what had happened and rushed to secure the support of another king in regaining his throne by force.

---

31 SN 3.11 at SN I 79,8 (translated by Bodhi 2000: 174) and Ud 6.2 at Ud 66,5 (translated by Ireland 1990: 90), parallels to SĀ 1148 at T I 306a9 and SĀ² 71 at T II 399b11.

32 SN 3.14 at SN I 82,30 (translated by Bodhi 2000: 177), parallel to SĀ 1236 at T II 338c5 and SĀ² 63 at T II 395c8. SN 3.15 at SN I 84,6 (translated by Bodhi 2000: 178), parallel to SĀ 1237 at T II 338c24, SĀ² 64 at T II 395c21, Speyer 1906/1970: 54,10, and T 212 at T IV 716a3.

33 SN 3.24 at SN I 98,31 (translated by Bodhi 2000: 190), parallel to SĀ 1145 at T II 304a8 and SĀ² 68 at T II 397b8.

34 MN 89 at MN II 124,17 (translated by Ñāṇamoli 1995/2005: 733), MĀ 213 at T I 797b13, and a version of the discourse in the Mūlasarvāstivāda *Vinaya*, T 1451 at T XXIV 238b17, with a Tibetan parallel in D 6 *tha* 86a2 or Q *de* 82b6.

35 Anālayo 2011: 518n368.

Due to his age and the haste with which he tried to reach the other king, he overstrained himself and died. This story implies that, even at the end of his long-standing relationship with the Buddha, who was quite explicit on the dire repercussions of warfare,[36] the king was ready to give battle in order to defend his rule.

Taken together, the above surveyed instances convey the impression that King Pasenadi, in spite of being a devoted disciple of the Buddha, was not necessarily a paragon of Buddhist lay virtue. Nevertheless, the Buddha had no qualms about giving him instructions on mindfulness. These relate to his apparent habit of overeating:[37]

> Then King Pasenadi, whose body was very bulky, with his whole body perspiring, approached the Buddha, paid respect with his head at the Buddha's feet, and withdrew to sit to one side. He was gasping heavily for breath. At that time the Blessed One said to King Pasenadi: "Great King, your body has become rather bulky."
>
> The Great King said to the Buddha. "It is like this, Blessed One, I am worried by the bulkiness of my body. Because my body is so bulky, I am often ashamed, disgusted, and afflicted."
>
> Then the Blessed One spoke in verse:
>
> "People should collect themselves with mindfulness,
> Knowing their measure with each meal.
> This then decreases their feeling tones;
> They digest easily and guard their longevity."[38]
>
> A youngster, called Uttara, was then seated in the assembly. Then King Pasenadi said to Uttara: "Are you able to learn this verse from the Blessed One and recite it for me, every time I take a meal?

36 See, e.g., Anālayo 2009a.

37 SĀ 1150 at T II 306c3 to 306c25, parallel to SN 3.13 at SN I 81,21 (translated by Bodhi 2000: 176) and SĀ² 73 at T II 400a1; see also Anālayo 2018b and 2018e.

38 A minor difference is that the otherwise closely corresponding verse in SN 3.13 at SN I 81,33 speaks of "aging slowly", *saṇikaṃ jīrati*. Given that the verb *jīrati* can also convey the sense of digesting, it is probable that the Indic original of the verse in SĀ 1150 was similar to SN 3.13 in this respect (the same holds for SĀ² 73 at T II 400a8, which also refers to digestion).

If you are able to do that, I will grant you a hundred thousand coins and also give you food regularly."

Uttara said to the king: "I received your instruction and will recite it."

Then King Pasenadi, having heard what the Buddha had said, rejoiced and was delighted. He paid respect and left.

Then Uttara, knowing that the king had left, went in front of the Blessed One to learn the verse to be spoken.[39] At the time of the king's meals, he recited it when the food was being eaten, saying to the Great King: "As said in verse by the Buddha, the Blessed One, who is a Tathāgata, an arahant, rightly and fully awakened, with knowledge and vision:[40]

"People should collect themselves with mindfulness,
Knowing their measure with each meal.
This then decreases their feeling tones;
They digest easily and guard their longevity."

In this way, at a later time, the body of King Pasenadi gradually became slim and his appearance graceful. Being atop of his storied mansion, he held his hands together respectfully towards the direction where the Buddha was dwelling, knelt with his right knee on the ground, and said three times:[41] "Homage to the Blessed One, the Tathāgata, the arahant, rightly and fully awakened, homage to the Blessed One, the Tathāgata, the arahant, rightly and fully awakened, who has benefited me in the present, benefited me in the future, benefited me in the present and the future, because of whom I know my measure with food and drink."

The Pāli version is shorter. It precedes its version of the verse only by reporting that the Buddha had noted that the king

39 SN 3.13 does not describe how the youngster, here called Sudassana, actually learned the verse.
40 His recitation in SN 3.13 at SN I 82,11 just concerns the verse itself, without a comparable introductory remark on its original speaker.
41 SN 3.13 does not report him expressing homage to the Buddha, instead of which he just strokes his limbs with his hands, in apparent satisfaction with his slim bodily condition, and formulates an inspired utterance that relates his personal well-being in present and future times to the Buddha's compassion.

was replete and panting, without referring to his overweight condition. In line with not broaching the topic of bulkiness, it also does not contain a reply by Pasenadi in which the king describes his sense of shame at his own bodily condition. Another Chinese parallel, however, reports such an exchange.[42]

Another difference concerns the payment the king promised to Uttara. The reference to a hundred thousand coins in the discourse translated above is clearly an instance of exaggeration; the Pāli version and the other Chinese parallel agree that he was to receive just a hundred coins.[43] After all, he had been asked to perform a relatively simple task. Even a payment of a hundred coins seems rather generous, let alone a hundred thousand coins.

A tendency to exaggerate some of the features of this story can also be found in later Pāli tradition. A version of the present event in the commentary on the *Dhammapada* reports that Pasenadi used to eat a whole bucketful of food.[44] A Burmese inscription from the twelfth century then gives a detailed list of his daily food intake as comprising one buffalo, eight pigs, sixteen fowls, thirty quails, etc.[45]

Alongside such exaggerations, however, the three discourses agree fairly closely on the main import of the instruction on mindful eating. These instructions point to the "receptive" dimension of mindfulness, which enables clear recognition of one's proper measure with food. The final result of such practice is also relevant to the "liberating" aspect of mindfulness, as it eventually frees the king from his compulsion to overeat.

42 SĀ^2 73 at T II 400a5.

43 SN 3.13 at SN I 82,6 and SĀ^2 73 at T II 400a11. Notably, SN 3.13 has the reference to a hundred coins twice: *kahāpaṇasataṃ kahāpaṇasataṃ* (the second instance is given in brackets in the Burmese edition and not found in the Ceylonese and Siamese editions). Should a comparable doubling have been found also in the Indic original of SĀ 1150, it might have given rise to the misunderstanding that this refers to a hundred times a hundred coins, i.e. ten thousand coins, which then eventually might have led to the idea of a hundred thousand coins.

44 Dhp-a III 264,14 (translated by Burlingame 1921: 206).

45 Luce and Shin 1961: 383 (I am indebted to Lilian Handlin for drawing my attention to this inscription).

The significance of this instruction can be further evaluated by surveying other discourses that involve King Pasenadi, in order to determine if these show him getting instructions on mindfulness or other forms of meditation on other occasions.

Only two Pāli discourses, together with their Chinese parallels, report Pasenadi receiving teachings even distantly related to cultivation of the mind. In one of these two instances the Buddha repeats to the king a conversation he had earlier had with Ānanda on spiritual friendship, concluding with a verse in praise of heedfulness (*appamāda*).[46] In the other instance, the Buddha gives the king a teaching in praise of such heedfulness.[47]

Although the quality of heedfulness is of considerable relevance to the practice of mindfulness, it is not exclusively related to it. One example is the depiction of a small child putting something into its mouth that needs to be extracted, even at the cost of pain, to prevent choking. Once the child has grown up, however, there is no longer any need to have any such apprehensions, as by then the child will no longer act in such a "heedless" manner.[48] The acquisition of heedfulness by the child simply reflects maturity of age and has no necessary relationship to mindfulness.

The same holds for two other passages, according to which the heedlessness of certain deities is responsible for a lack of rain and the heedlessness of people for a loss of wealth.[49] This does not imply that the deities must be practising mindfulness every time it rains, or else that everyone who gains wealth must have been mindful.[50]

---

46 SN 3.18 at SN I 89,21 (translated by Bodhi 2000: 182), parallel to SĀ 1238 at T II 339b9 and SĀ² 65 at T II 396b1.

47 SN 3.17 at SN I 86,29 (translated by Bodhi 2000: 179), parallel to SĀ 1239 at T II 339b22 and SĀ² 66 at T II 396b14.

48 AN 5.7 at AN III 6,14 (translated by Bodhi 2012: 633).

49 AN 5.197 at AN III 243,16 and AN 5.213 at AN III 252,23 (translated by Bodhi 2012: 815 and 823). The first discourse lists five obstacles to the manifestation of rain and the second contrasts loss of wealth incurred by an immoral person through heedlessness to gain of wealth by a moral person through heedfulness.

50 It seems to be only in later commentarial texts that heedfulness becomes a synonym for mindfulness. For example, It-a 80,14 explains that

On this understanding of the implications of heedfulness, it follows that the two discourses related to this quality would not fall into the category of instructions on mindfulness, at least from the viewpoint of the early Buddhist usage of the term "heedfulness". Given that the substantial number of discourses that involve King Pasenadi do not report any other meditation instructions, it seems as if the verse translated above on being mindful while eating is the only recorded occasion in which he received explicit instructions on mindfulness.

The relevant instructions are clearly meant to address his tendency to overeat and they are successful in achieving weight reduction. Moreover, the narrative involves someone who receives regular payment for delivering instructions in mindfulness practice. In this way, this episode provides a remarkable precedent for the current employment of mindfulness in healthcare-related programmes.

GOING TO SLEEP WITH MINDFULNESS (SĀ 1087)

Not only when eating, but even when just going to sleep, mindfulness is commendable. The extract below from a *Saṃyukta-āgama* discourse reports the Buddha going to sleep with mindfulness:[51]

> At that time the Blessed One did walking meditation from the early night until the late time of the night, when he washed his feet, entered his hut, and lay down on his right side with collected mindfulness and clarity of perception,[52] with right mindfulness

heedfulness stands for the non-absence of mindfulness, in the sense of its continuous establishment. Such an understanding does not seem to reflect fully the canonical usage of this term. In fact the historically earlier *Mahāniddesa*, Nidd I 59,17, presents an understanding of heedfulness that fits the canonical usage better. This confirms the impression of a development in understanding of this quality over time that eventually turned *appamāda* into a synonym for *sati*.

51 SĀ 1087 at T II 285a17 to 285a19, parallel to SN 4.7 at SN I 107,12 (translated by Bodhi 2000: 199) and SĀ² 26 at T II 381c17 (translated by Bingenheimer 2011: 131); see also Anālayo 2017f: 204.

52 The rendering "perception" is based on adopting a variant reading.

> and right knowing, forming the thought and perception of rising up [again].

The Pāli parallel similarly reports that the Buddha went to sleep with mindfulness and clear knowing, paying attention to the perception of rising up again. In the ancient Indian setting, such setting up of a perception of rising up would have fulfilled the purpose that nowadays is served by an alarm clock.

Another description of the Buddha going to sleep, found in a different *Saṃyukta-āgama* discourse, indicates that he "connected mindfulness to the perception of clarity" and then gave attention to the perception of rising up again.[53] This formulation seems to relate mindfulness directly to the type of clarity of mind that in turn would enable getting up in time, instead of continuing to sleep. In terms of the different dimensions of mindfulness, this appears to relate to "attentiveness", by way of attending to the time to get up again.

The same form of mindfulness practice forms part of the training for monastics in general and is not confined to the case of the Buddha only. A discourse in the *Aṅguttara-nikāya*, of which no parallel is known, lists a range of advantages to be expected from going to sleep with mindfulness.[54] These include sleeping well and waking up well, as well as absence of both bad dreams and nocturnal emissions.[55] Although this is not stated explicitly, the description seems to imply that, due to having established mindfulness when going to sleep, the mind is in a more balanced state and therefore less prone to get carried away by bad dreams or the type of sexual fantasies that could lead to nocturnal emissions. Moreover, the quality of sleep improves, and consequently one wakes up well, perhaps able to pick up mindfulness practice right away again.

53 SĀ 1176 at T II 316b10 (as in the case of the previously translated SĀ 1087, the rendering "perception" is based on adopting a variant reading), parallel to SN 35 202 at SN IV 184,13 (translated by Bodhi 2000: 1245).

54 AN 5.210 at AN III 251,16 (translated by Bodhi 2012: 822).

55 A fifth benefit is being protected by celestials.

WAKEFULNESS (EĀ 21.6)

Continuity of mindfulness throughout the night could be related to the cultivation of "wakefulness", which stands in particular for meditating during the first and last parts of the night, instead of sleeping. A description of such wakefulness can be found in the following passage from the *Ekottarika-āgama*:[56]

> How are monastics not remiss in walking meditation? Here monastics in the early [part] of the night and the late [part] of the night are continually mindful during walking meditation, they are not remiss in regard to the opportunity to be constantly mindful, being with the mind collected in the qualities conducive to awakening.
>
> Suppose it is daytime, whether walking or sitting, they give attention to the sublime teachings and eliminate the hindrances. Again, in the first watch of the night, whether walking or sitting, they give attention to the sublime teachings and eliminate the hindrances. Again, in the middle watch of the night they lie down on their right sides with attention given to collecting the mind in clarity. Again, in the last watch of the night they rise up and, whether walking or sitting,[57] they give attention to the profound teachings and eliminate the hindrances.

The Pāli parallel does not explicitly mention mindfulness when introducing the practice of wakefulness. Here, mindfulness only occurs in relation to going to rest in the middle watch of the night. In fact, the *Ekottarika-āgama* version translated above also does not explicitly mention mindfulness in its description of walking and sitting undertaken before or after sleeping. Yet, its introductory statement makes it clear that these involve a continuous cultivation of mindfulness. The desirability of such continuity of mindfulness can safely be assumed to be also in the background of the Pāli version. In this way, an "attentive"

---

56 EĀ 21.6 at T II 604a13 to 604a19, parallel to AN 3.16 at AN I 114,9 (translated by Bodhi 2012: 212).

57 The translation is based on adopting a variant reading in line with the same formulation found earlier.

form of mindfulness can become one's constant companion throughout the night.

DWELLING IN A FOREST WITH MINDFULNESS (MĀ 26)

In the traditional setting, a commendable way of life for those wholeheartedly dedicated to progress to liberation is to dwell alone in a forest. Here mindfulness features as one among various qualities that one who lives in a forest should cultivate, failing which censure can be expected when the forest dweller encounters other monastics:[58]

> Forest-dwelling monastics who practise forest dwelling should train in right mindfulness and right knowing. Venerable friends, suppose forest-dwelling monastics who practise forest dwelling are often without right mindfulness and without right knowing, they will incur criticism and censure from [other] monastics: "These venerable forest dwellers, for what purpose are they practising forest dwelling? Why is it that these venerable forest dwellers, who practise forest dwelling, are [nevertheless] often without right mindfulness and without right knowing?"

The Pāli parallel reports similar criticism, which here concerns the contrast between mindfulness being established or lost. It does not qualify such mindfulness as "right" and does not refer to right or clear knowing.

Alongside such differences in formulation, the basic message remains the same. The commendable secluded lifestyle of dwelling in a forest is not an end in itself. The good repute a monastic may gain through such dwelling needs to be sustained by making an effort at being mindful. It is the actual cultivation of mindfulness (and other commendable qualities) that really counts.

The same could be applied to modern-day meditation practice in retreat. The commendable lifestyle of regularly

---

58 MĀ 26 at T I 455b20 to 455b25, parallel to MN 69 at MN I 471,22 (translated by Ñāṇamoli 1995/2005: 575); see also Anālayo 2011: 374.

going on retreat needs to be combined with an effort to sustain mindfulness, both during the retreat itself and when being out of it and facing daily life again. Otherwise one might incur deserved censure, as others might query what purpose the regular going on retreat serves if one is still frequently without mindfulness and clear knowing.

MINDFUL BEGGING FOR FOOD (EĀ 33.4, SĀ 1191, AND SĀ 1260)

Whether living alone in a forest or in a village or town, in the traditional setting a monastic needed to go out regularly to beg for food, during which time mindfulness should be properly established. This topic comes up in a survey of how some male monastics begged for food, found in a discourse in the *Ekottarika-āgama*. Some of these monastics had become overpowered by sensual lust on seeing a woman or speaking to her, with the result that they eventually disrobed. Through undertaking proper restraint of the senses, however, this can be avoided – an avoidance that relates to the "protective" dimension of mindfulness:[59]

> When the time has come, that monastic puts on the robes and takes the bowl to enter the village and beg for alms with body, speech, and mind protected. Even though he sees a woman, he does not give rise to sensual perceptions and is without wrong mindfulness. Suppose he exchanges words together with the woman, he still does not give rise to sensual perceptions and is still without wrong mindfulness.

Instead of mentioning wrong mindfulness, the Pāli version speaks of mindfulness that is either not established (in the case of those who succumb to lust) or else established (in the counterpart to the above passage). In addition to protection of body, speech, and mind, the Pāli version also mentions sense restraint. The same comes up in a discourse in the *Saṃyukta-*

59 EĀ 33.4 at T II 688a8 to 688a11, parallel to AN 5.76 at AN III 99,20 (translated by Bodhi 2012: 708).

āgama, which enjoins that a monastic should go to beg for food in the following manner:[60]

> With the faculties restrained and mindfulness collected in the mind.

In this way, combining an establishing of mindfulness with sense restraint can prevent unwholesome reactions from occurring during the daily begging tour. A description of mindful begging in a different discourse in the same *Saṃyukta-āgama* also brings in the notion of protecting the body (which had been mentioned in the *Ekottarika-āgama* discourse and its Pāli parallel together with protection of speech and mind):[61]

> You should train like this: "We will enter the village to beg for food with the body well protected, the doors of the faculties guarded, and the mind collected in right mindfulness."

The idea of protecting the body could refer to the cultivation of circumspect behaviour, in the sense of being with clear knowing in relation to what happens with one's bodily actions. Notably, just as the *Ekottarika-āgama* passage mentioned above brought in the nuance of being without "wrong" mindfulness, the present passage makes a similar point by qualifying one who guards body and sense faculties as having "right" mindfulness.

Although the passages surveyed here come with an emphasis on a male monastic seeing a woman, another Pāli discourse, of which no parallel in the Chinese *Āgama*s is known, describes the alternative possibility of a male monastic who goes begging without mindfulness and then sees a layman enjoying himself with sensual pleasures.[62] This has the same result of motivating the monastic to disrobe. Yet another Pāli discourse, of which also no parallel is known, mentions that a female monastic can

---

60 SĀ 1191 at T II 322c27, parallel to SN 6.13 at SN I 154,21 (translated by Bodhi 2000: 248) and SĀ² 104 at T II 411a13.

61 SĀ 1260 at T II 345c21 to 345c22, parallel to SN 20.10 at SN II 271,18 (translated by Bodhi 2000: 712).

62 AN 4.122 at AN II 125,15 (translated by Bodhi 2012: 504), which has a Pāli counterpart in a description found in MN 67 at MN I 461,26 (translated by Ñāṇamoli 1995/2005: 564); see also Anālayo 2011: 369.

also have wrong mindfulness, although the implications of such wrong mindfulness are not spelled out in a manner comparable to the passage from the *Ekottarika-āgama* above.[63]

Even though the above passages are formulated from the viewpoint of monastics, the same need for mindfulness could be applied to laypeople going shopping for their household supplies, for example. In any daily-life situation, mindfulness can be of substantial help in avoiding the arising of defilements. All of this revolves around the "protective" quality of mindfulness.

GIVING PRIORITY TO MINDFULNESS (MĀ 107)

The need to give priority to mindfulness over other concerns, already evident from the passages surveyed above, receives a highlight in a *Madhyama-āgama* discourse that depicts the conditions under which a monastic should stay in the same place or else better leave and go elsewhere. Living a mendicant life in the ancient Indian setting, Buddhist monastics were dependent on others for their basic requisites, such as food, robes, medicine, and shelter. Hence it might seem natural to leave a place where these are difficult to obtain and to go where they are easily acquired. Yet, the recommendation given in the present discourse is to give priority instead to one's meditative practice. If one finds that mindfulness, concentration, and liberation of the mind from defilements do not improve, one should leave. But if they improve, one should stay even if requisites are difficult to obtain, based on the following reflection:[64]

> I went forth to train in the path not for the sake of robes, nor for the sake of food, drink, bedding, and medicine, and also not for the sake of any [other] necessities of life. Yet, dwelling in dependence on this forest and having lacked right mindfulness, I am in turn gaining right mindfulness; having had a mind that

63 AN 5.120 at AN III 141,29 (translated by Bodhi 2012: 740).

64 MĀ 107 at T I 597a26 to 597b1, parallel to MN 17 at MN I 106,1 (translated by Ñāṇamoli 1995/2005: 199); see also Anālayo 2011: 133.

> lacks concentration, I am in turn gaining a concentrated mind; not having become liberated, I am in turn attaining liberation.

On realizing this, the monastic should determine to stay in that very place. The clear-cut priority accorded to cultivation of the mind that emerges in this way could also be applied to the situation of lay practitioners who have not gone forth, but nevertheless are training in the path. It could then be taken to convey that one should give overall importance to training oneself in mindfulness, over the wish to have everything as nice and cosy as it could possibly be.

CULTIVATING MINDFULNESS BEFORE TEACHING OTHERS (MĀ 91)

The next passage highlights the need to be established in mindfulness oneself when wanting to teach it to others. The passage in question comprises a whole list of qualities, one of which is the presence or absence of mindfulness. Lacking mindfulness (or any of the other qualities mentioned) finds the following illustration:[65]

> If one is not tamed oneself, to want to tame another who is not tamed is [wanting] what is certainly impossible. [If] one is drowning oneself, to want to pull out another who is drowning is [wanting] what is certainly impossible.

In other words, one who has no mindfulness is not able to train another in mindfulness. The reverse then holds for those who have themselves cultivated what they wish to inculcate in others:

> If one is tamed oneself, to want to tame another who is not tamed is [wanting] what is certainly possible. [If] one is not drowning oneself, to want to pull out another who is drowning is [wanting] what is certainly possible.

---

65 The two extracts occur in MĀ 91 between T I 574b2 and 574b7, parallel to MN 8 at MN I 45,3 (translated by Ñāṇamoli 1995/2005: 130) and EĀ 47.9 at T II 784a20; see also Anālayo 2011: 65.

The imagery used illustrates why it is preferable not to set oneself up prematurely as a teacher of what one has not really cultivated oneself. The same discourse offers several indications on how to build up one's practice, which will eventually enable one to guide and inspire others. One of these involves the image of two types of path:[66]

> It is just like a wrong path which has a proper path as its opposite, and it is just like a bad ford which has a proper ford as its opposite; in the same way ... lack of mindfulness [has the establishing of mindfulness as its opposite].

In the end it is simply a matter of re-establishing mindfulness whenever it has been lost. The discourse provides yet another injunction, according to which one should train oneself with the thought that, even if others are without mindfulness, one will be with mindfulness oneself.[67]

MINDFUL COMPANY (SĀ 450)

Training oneself to cultivate mindfulness when others are without it can be quite challenging. In fact people of similar inclinations and interests tend to seek each other's company. This applies also to the case of either having or else lacking mindfulness:[68]

> Those who lack mindfulness regularly congregate with those who lack mindfulness ... those who do not lack mindfulness regularly congregate with those who do not lack mindfulness.

The Pāli parallel presents the same contrast. In this way, associating whenever possible with others who are dedicated to the cultivation of mindfulness becomes a natural way of

---

66 MĀ 91 at T I 574a8 to 574a18, parallel to MN 8 at MN I 43,35 and EĀ 47.9 at T II 784a19 (although here this is not applied to mindfulness).

67 MĀ 91 at T I 573c20, parallel to MN 8 at MN I 43,20.

68 SĀ 450 at T II 115c23 (the passage is given in abbreviation), parallel to SN 14.17 at SN II 159,8 (translated by Bodhi 2000: 641); another two parallels, SĀ[3] 20 at T II 497c14 and T 111 at T II 504c1, do not include the contrast between possession and lack of mindfulness in their presentation.

expressing and supporting one's own cultivation of the same quality. The passage can also be taken to point to a shift in interests and even lifestyle once one begins to dedicate oneself wholeheartedly to mindfulness practice, in that one will tend to prefer activities that do not foster distraction and loss of mental balance.

MINDFULNESS AS A PATH OF DHARMA (DĀ 9)

Mindfulness features among four "paths of Dharma" listed in the *Dīrgha-āgama* parallel to the *Saṅgīti-sutta*:[69]

> There are four paths of Dharma: Being without lust is a path of Dharma, being without anger is a path of Dharma, right mindfulness is a path of Dharma, and right concentration is a path of Dharma.

The Pāli commentary explains that the expression "path" in the present context stands for a "division" of the Dharma.[70] The four paths or divisions of the Dharma point to central dimensions of the practice. These are avoiding desire and aversion as well as cultivating mindfulness and concentration.

MINDFULNESS AS A FORM OF AUTHORITY (MĀ 113)

A series of brief statements, found in a discourse in the *Madhyama-āgama*, provides a spotlight on the prominence of mindfulness. The basic theme of the discourse is "all things". A first perspective on this theme emerges with the question "what is the root of all things?", which receives the reply "desire is the root of all things."[71] This sets the pattern for the remainder of the discourse, in that any metaphysical speculations or ontological claims regarding "all things" are implicitly dismissed and

69 DĀ 9 at T I 50c29 to 51a1, parallel to DN 33 at DN III 229,3 (translated by Walshe 1987: 492) and Sanskrit fragments, Stache-Rosen 1968: 103.
70 Sv III 1022,1.
71 This particular statement, unlike the statement to be taken up below, is also preserved in a Gāndhārī fragment; see Jantrasrisalai et al. 2016: 57.

replaced with a pointer to some aspect of subjective experience. The question relevant to the topic of mindfulness is: what has authority over all things? This receives the following reply:[72]

> Mindfulness has the foremost authority over all things.

The Pāli parallel similarly states that mindfulness has authority (*ādhipateyya*) over all things. The idea of mindfulness as a form of authority recurs in another discourse in the *Aṅguttara-nikāya* with further explanations.[73] These explanations relate mindfulness to other aspects of the practice, which are the training in morality and the celibate life, the cultivation of wisdom, and the reaching of liberation. Here mindfulness well established internally enables one to purify the training in morality and the celibate life and to sustain it wisely where it has already been purified. Again, mindfulness enables one to scrutinize with wisdom what has not been scrutinized and to sustain wisely what one has already scrutinized. Mindfulness facilitates realizing liberation and sustaining wisely what has been realized. Understood in this way, mindfulness can provide authority over all things, an eminent role it probably acquires through its ability to monitor and hence supervise.

THE FORD OR PASTURE OF MINDFULNESS (EĀ 49.1)

As part of an *Ekottarika-āgama* version of a simile that illustrates various commendable qualities with activities and qualities of a cowherd, the four establishments of mindfulness compare to knowing the proper ford to take the cattle across water:[74]

---

72 MĀ 113 at T I 602c15, parallel to AN 8.83 at AN IV 339,7 (translated by Bodhi 2012: 1232) and T 59 at T I 855c18; see also AN 9.14 at AN IV 385,22 and AN 10.58 at AN V 107,9 (translated by Bodhi 2012: 1269 and 1410).

73 AN 4.243 at AN II 244,7 (translated by Bodhi 2012: 611, given as number 245); no parallel to this discourse appears to be known.

74 EĀ 49.1 at T II 795a2 to 795a3, parallel to MN 33 at MN I 224,7 (translated by Ñāṇamoli 1995/2005: 317), AN 11.18 at AN V 352,25 (translated by Bodhi 2012: 1582, given as number 17), SĀ 1249 at T II 343a16 (translated by Anālayo 2015c: 46) and T 123 at T I 547a14; see also Anālayo 2011: 218.

> How does a monastic understand the ford? Here a monastic understands the four establishments of mindfulness. This is reckoned a monastic's understanding of the ford.

Parallels extant in Pāli and Chinese instead identify the four establishments of mindfulness with the proper "pasture" for the cows. In spite of differing in the respective image employed, the parallel versions could still be understood to converge on mindful discernment, which enables taking the proper ford to take the cattle across water or choosing the proper pasture for them. The ability to discern in turn relies on "receptivity" as an important dimension of mindfulness.

BARE AWARENESS (SĀ 312)

An intriguing perspective on the potential of "receptive" and "protective" mindfulness, cultivated on its own, emerges from an instruction given to the non-Buddhist practitioner Bāhiya and on another occasion to a monastic by the name of Māluṅkyaputta. These instructions appear to involve a "bare" form of awareness. This is of considerable importance for a proper appreciation of the range of applications of mindfulness in early Buddhist thought.[75] As the Bāhiya instruction is only extant in Pāli,[76] in what follows I take up the instruction related to Māluṅkyaputta:[77]

> The Buddha said to Māluṅkyaputta: "Suppose there are forms you have never seen with the eye [nor] will expect to see. Would you give rise to desire for those forms, give rise to craving, give rise to thoughts, and give rise to being defiled by attachment?"

---

75 According to Sun 2014: 399, such bare awareness or "'bare attention' was particularly influential in shaping Kabat-Zinn's conceptualisation of mindfulness"; see also Husgafvel 2018: 285.

76 Ud 1.10 at Ud 8,4 (translated by Ireland 1990: 20).

77 SĀ 312 at T II 90a9 to 90b26, parallel to SN 35.95 at SN IV 72,18 (translated by Bodhi 2000: 1175), Sanskrit fragments, SHT V 1311, Sander and Waldschmidt 1985: 215, SHT X 4097, Wille 2008: 265, and a Tibetan parallel, Up 4086 at D 4094 *ju* 241a7 or Q 5595 *tu* 275b7.

He replied: "No, Blessed One."

For sounds and the ear, odours and the nose, flavours and the tongue, tangibles and the body, and mental objects and the mind *it should also be recited in this way.*

The Buddha said to Māluṅkyaputta: "It is well, it is well, Māluṅkyaputta, see by way of being limited to seeing, hear by way of being limited to hearing, sense by way of being limited to sensing, and cognize by way of being limited to cognizing."[78]

Then he spoke in verse:

"If you are not in that,
And [from] that you also do not revert to being [in] this,[79]
And you also are not in between the two,
This then is the end of *dukkha*."

Māluṅkyaputta said to the Buddha: "I have understood, Blessed One, I have understood, Well-gone One!"

The Buddha said to Māluṅkyaputta: "How have you understood in detail the meaning of the teaching I have given herein in brief?"[80]

At that time Māluṅkyaputta spoke in verse to the Buddha:

"On having seen a form with the eyes,
If right mindfulness is lost,
Then in the form that has been seen
One grasps its marks (*nimitta*) with thoughts of craving.

"For one who grasps the marks with craving and delight
The mind will then be constantly in bondage to
attachment.
It will give rise to various kinds of craving
For the countless forms that manifest.

"Thoughts of lustful desire, ill will, and harming
Will bring about the mind's debasement

78 The original is somewhat cryptic; my translation is tentative.
79 My translation of this part of the verse is conjectural.
80 SN 35.95 reports no enquiry by the Buddha, as here Māluṅkyaputta on his own delivers a series of verses demonstrating his understanding.

And foster a host of afflictions;
One is forever far from Nirvāṇa.[81]

"[If] on seeing a form one does not grasp its marks,
And the mind conforms to right mindfulness
Craving will not defile the mind with what is detrimental,
And the bondage of attachment will also not arise.

"Not giving rise to cravings
For the countless forms that manifest,
Thoughts of lustful desire, ill will, and harming
Will be unable to afflict the mind.

"Diminishing [what] fosters a host of afflictions,
One gradually draws close to Nirvāṇa.
As taught by the kinsman of the sun:
'Being apart from craving is Nirvāṇa.'[82]

"If the ear has heard sounds
And the mind has lost right mindfulness,
The marks of sounds are grasped;
They are held firmly and not relinquished.

"With the nose and odours, with the tongue and flavours,
With the body and tangibles, and with the mind and
thoughts of mental objects,
Right mindfulness being forgotten
One also grasps the marks, it is just the same.

"The mind gives rise to craving and delight
And the bondage of attachment is firmly established;
Various kinds of craving arise
For countless mental objects that manifest.

---

81 The general thrust of the corresponding verses in SN 35.95 is similar, although the two versions differ in details. A difference in sequence is that SN 35.95 continues directly from seeing forms with attachment to the other senses, and only after that takes up the opposite case of seeing forms without attachment.

82 The expression "kinsman of the sun" refers to the Buddha. The last two lines have no counterpart in SN 35.95.

"Thoughts of lustful desire, ill will, and harming
Will debase and harm the mind,[83]
And increasingly nourish a host of afflictions;
One is forever far from Nirvāṇa.

"Not being defiled by mental objects,
Established in right knowledge and right mindfulness,
The mind is not contaminated
And no longer delights in them with attachment.

"Various kinds of craving are not aroused
For countless mental objects that manifest,
And thoughts of lust, ill will, and harming
Do not debase the mind.

"The host of afflictions consequently decreases
And one gradually draws close to Nirvāṇa.
'The eradication of craving is Nirvāṇa',
This has been taught by the Blessed One.[84]

"This describes my understanding in detail of the meaning of the teaching the Blessed One gave herein in brief."

The Buddha said to Māluṅkyaputta: "You truly understood in detail the meaning of the teaching I gave herein in brief. Why is that? It is as you said in verse:

"On having seen a form with the eyes
If right mindfulness is lost,
Then in the form that has been seen
One grasps its marks with thoughts of craving."

To be recited in detail as above.

At that time the venerable Māluṅkyaputta,[85] hearing what the Buddha had said, rejoiced and was delighted. He paid respect and left.

---

83 The translation is based on adopting a variant reading, in keeping with the formulation found previously and subsequently.
84 The last two lines have no counterpart in SN 35.95.
85 It is only from this point onwards that SĀ 312 qualifies Māluṅkyaputta as "venerable", whereas SN 35.95 uses the corresponding *āyasmant* right from the outset.

> At that time the venerable Māluṅkyaputta, having understood in detail the meaning of the teaching the Blessed One had herein given in brief, alone and in a quiet place reflected on it with energy. Being established in the absence of negligence ... *up to* ... his mind attained liberation and he became an arahant.

The detailed exposition given by Māluṅkyaputta of the implications of the brief instruction he had received points directly to mindfulness. The crucial contrast is between mindfulness being either established or else lost. If mindfulness is lost, the danger is that one gives attention to the pleasing characteristics of what is seen (etc.) and becomes attached and clings to it. The mind then becomes disturbed, one accumulates *dukkha*, and remains far from Nirvāṇa. This can be avoided by cultivating mindfulness in a way that appears to involve a bare form of awareness: what is experienced through any of the senses is simply received as such, without being further processed mentally by way of engaging with any mark or characteristic. It is in this way that it becomes possible to "see by way of being limited to seeing", etc.

The present discourse shows that "bare awareness" is already recognized in the early discourses.[86] This differs from related practices in some later traditions, which at times are based on the notion that the mind is intrinsically pure, even already awakened, a natural condition that just requires being recognized.[87] Such is not the case in early Buddhist thought, where the cultivation of bare awareness has the function of deconstructing the tendencies of the deluded mind.[88]

SUMMARY

In the context of the eightfold path to liberation, mindfulness has the monitoring function to oversee the cultivation of the other path factors. Here mindfulness builds on the preceding six path

---

86 See in more detail Anālayo 2018a.
87 See in more detail Anālayo 2017e.
88 See in more detail Anālayo 2019g.

factors and in turn supports concentration. The contrast between right and wrong forms of mindfulness does not preclude that there could be forms of mindfulness that do not easily fit either category, such as when certain celestials or a cowherd at work are described as having mindfulness. Despite requiring intentional cultivation to actualize its potential, mindfulness seems to have been considered, at least to some degree, a natural trait of humans (and celestials).

Already in early Buddhism mindful eating was cultivated for health purposes, leading to weight reduction. Mindfulness can also come to one's service when going to sleep, living in seclusion in a forest, and going into town to get food. In short, whatever the situation, one should best give priority to mindfulness. In support of mindfulness practice, it is helpful to associate with those who also cultivate it. Its cultivation is the path to follow, which can lead to mindfulness taking a leading role in one's activities and providing a function comparable to discerning the proper ford or pasture for cattle. Another dimension of mindfulness in early Buddhism is bare awareness, the ability to remain mindfully aware of what is experienced without proliferating it in any way.

VI

MINDFULNESS AND LIBERATION

Most of the passages surveyed in this chapter relate in one way or another to the "liberating" potential of mindfulness, be it temporary liberation from distractions or final liberation from defilements. I begin with descriptions of mindfulness practice geared at staying free of unwholesome thoughts (MĀ 198). Mindfulness, a quality similar to attention (MĀ 101), supports the development of concentration (SĀ 1305 and MĀ 210), leads to wisdom (MĀ 118), facilitates liberating insight (SĀ 983), and supports the cultivation of the divine abodes (MĀ 16). Moreover, mindfulness can lay the foundation for great mental powers (SĀ 537).

Mindful purification of the mind is productive of joy (DĀ 28). Mindfulness can counter confusion (SĀ 575), lead to mental balance (DĀ 18), facilitate facing a physical attack (MĀ 30), or criticism (MĀ 87), and enable one to remain aloof from clinging to views (DĀ 17 and MĀ 13). The cultivation of mindfulness can also aid in overcoming anger (SĀ 1319) and lustful desires (SĀ 586), thereby supporting a life of celibacy (SĀ 275). Mindfulness serves to overcome unwholesome thoughts (SĀ 272) and to remove the unwholesome influences in the mind (MĀ 10).

The awakening factors, the first of which is mindfulness, are like treasures (EĀ 42.4), discovered by the Buddha (MĀ 58). In order to undertake their cultivation, one should know what nourishes them (SĀ 715) and how they manifest (SĀ 713). Various aspects of the path to awakening depend on mindfulness (MĀ 51), which also supports contemplating the empty nature of the five aggregates (SĀ 265).

Mindfulness is indeed the path (SĀ 535): not only is it required for progress towards awakening (SĀ 542), but it also serves as a natural dwelling for one who has attained complete liberation of the mind (SĀ 543). All awakened ones are mindful (DĀ 10); in other words, arahants keep practising mindfulness (MĀ 12), and the Buddha was of course no exception to this (MĀ 133). The noble eightfold path, which sets the context for mindfulness practice, was already the topic of the Buddha's first discourse (EĀ 19.2). In sum, all Buddhas awaken through mindfulness (SĀ 498). An aspect of the Buddha's own practice is a specific set of three establishments of mindfulness, relevant in particular to the situation of giving a teaching (MĀ 163).

MINDFULNESS AND THINKING (MĀ 198)

The practice of mindfulness does not require keeping the mind free from all types of thought activity. This is evident in the exposition in the *Satipaṭṭhāna-sutta* and its parallels, whose instructions clearly involve the use of concepts. Nevertheless, the cultivation of mindfulness free from thought activity, in particular the one which is of an unwholesome nature, is also explicitly recognized and commended. Such practice already came up in the *Madhyama-āgama* parallel to the *Gaṇakamoggallāna-sutta*, discussed in a previous chapter (see above p. 142), although in that case it was absent from the Pāli version. An example where such a description occurs in both the Chinese and Pāli versions is the *Madhyama-āgama* parallel to the *Dantabhūmi-sutta*. The relevant passage sets in after the standard description of the cultivation of the four establishments of mindfulness:[1]

1 MĀ 198 at T I 758b15 to 758b19, parallel to MN 125 at MN III 136,20 (translated by Ñāṇamoli 1995/2005: 995).

> You should contemplate the body as a body internally and do not think thoughts associated with sensual pleasures ... *up to* ... contemplate feeling tones, the mind, and dharmas as dharmas and do not think thoughts associated with what is contrary to Dharma.
>
> When a noble disciple contemplates the body as a body internally and does not think thoughts associated with sensual pleasures ... *up to* ... contemplates feeling tones, the mind, and dharmas as dharmas and does not think thoughts associated with what is contrary to Dharma, then in this way the noble disciple follows the instructions of the Tathāgata.

The corresponding passage in the *Dantabhūmi-sutta* shows variations in different Pāli editions. In the case of contemplation of the body, according to some of these editions thoughts related to the body should be left behind, whereas others agree with the above passage from the *Madhyama-āgama* that the thoughts to be avoided are those related to sensual pleasures.[2] Given that the subsequent reference to thoughts associated with what is contrary to the Dharma concerns unwholesome thought, it seems more probable that the concern during contemplation of the body would have been to avoid sensual thoughts. In any case, the present passage clearly points to different modalities in cultivating the four establishments of mindfulness.

NO LONGER PAYING ATTENTION (MĀ 101)

The *Vitakkasanthāna-sutta* and its *Madhyama-āgama* parallel describe five methods to counter the presence of unwholesome thoughts in the mind. The third of these is not paying attention to whatever keeps triggering such thoughts:[3]

> One should not be mindful of those thoughts, which are the cause that made bad and unwholesome thoughts arise. Not being mindful of these thoughts, already arisen unwholesome thoughts will in turn come to cease. Bad thoughts having ceased, the mind

2 Anālayo 2011: 719n167.
3 MĀ 101 at T I 588b12 to 588b16, parallel to MN 20 at MN I 120,6 (translated by Ñāṇamoli 1995/2005: 212); see also Anālayo 2011: 141.

> will in turn be constantly established in inner tranquillity, it will become unified and gain concentration.
>
> It is just like a person with eyesight who, having no need to see visible forms that are in the light, were to close the eyes or turn the body away and leave.

The *Vitakkasanthāna-sutta* speaks of not being mindful (*asati*) and not paying attention (*amanasikāra*) to those thoughts. The suggestion that one should not be mindful of what happens in the mind might at first strike an unexpected note. Examination of the present injunction in its context helps to clarify the situation. The instructions in the *Vitakkasanthāna-sutta* and its parallel as a whole appear to set in at a point when mindful recognition of something unwholesome in the mind has not sufficed on its own to emerge from this condition. From the viewpoint of the noble eightfold path, the instructions given here fall into the realm of right effort. The two discourses agree that a first attempt to deal with the situation by taking up something wholesome has not worked, and a second attempt by examining the danger in those unwholesome thoughts has also not had the desired effect. When the issue at hand agitates the mind so much that, in spite of repeated attempts, one is unable to emerge from what is unwholesome, then the strategy of not paying any further attention becomes appropriate.

The two discourses continue by offering yet other strategies, in case not paying attention to the vexing matter should also be unsuccessful. This goes to show that the recommendation is not just to switch off mentally. The point is more specifically no longer to pay attention to the particular topic or incident that keeps triggering unwholesome reactions in the mind. But some degree of mindfulness of the overall condition of the mind must continue, otherwise one would be unable to recognize whether this approach has been successful or not. Such recognition is clearly expected in both versions, evident in their instruction on how to proceed, based on such recognition.

The Pāli version's reference to mindfulness (*sati*) and attention (*manasikāra*) operating in conjunction reflects a similarity in nature between these two qualities. A difference, from the viewpoint of early Buddhist thought, is that attention is present in any mental state, but mindfulness is not always present. Hence, whereas mindfulness needs to be established, attention needs to be directed in an appropriate manner so that it becomes penetrative or radical (*yoniso*), and thereby wise, instead of remaining superficial.[4] This distinction has not always remained the same in later tradition. Cox (1992/1993: 88) explains that

> for the Sarvāstivāda-Vaibhāṣikas, mindfulness is a mental event that occurs with regard to each object in every moment of psychic life. It enables the simultaneous insight or cognition of that object to occur and provides the necessary condition for later recollection ... in fixing or noting every present object, mindfulness performs an action essential for subsequent recollection.

This then led to the reasoning that, since in principle any moment of experience can be recalled, it follows that at least some degree of mindfulness must be present in every such moment. From the viewpoint of early Buddhist thought, however, a clear distinction can be drawn between mindfulness and attention. Whereas attention is present in any state of mind, mindfulness is not always present.

MINDFULNESS LEADS TO CONCENTRATION (SĀ 1305 AND MĀ 210)

Being with collected mindfulness leads to right concentration:[5]

> If one gains being collected with right mindfulness, unification of the mind will be well and rightly achieved.

The Pāli version indicates that those who have gained mindfulness become well and rightly concentrated. The main point made in both versions seems obvious: the more one is

4 On *manasikāra* as distinct from mindfulness see Anālayo 2020a and on *yoniso manasikāra* Anālayo 2009b.

5 SĀ 1305 at T II 358c6, parallel to SN 2.7 at SN I 48,34 (translated by Bodhi 2000: 143), and SĀ² 304 at T II 477a29 (which qualifies neither mindfulness nor concentration as "right").

with mindfulness, the easier it becomes to avoid distractions and experience an increasingly concentrated condition of the mind.

Another perspective on the same matter emerges from the *Cūḷavedalla-sutta*, its *Madhyama-āgama* parallel, and another parallel extant in Tibetan translation. The three versions group the factors of the noble eightfold path into three divisions, namely morality, concentration, and wisdom. Right mindfulness occurs in the second of these two:[6]

> Right mindfulness and right concentration, these two path factors are included in the aggregate of noble concentration.

The *Cūḷavedalla-sutta* differs from the above translated *Madhyama-āgama* statement in so far as it also includes right effort in the aggregate of concentration; the Tibetan parallel agrees with the *Madhyama-āgama* in placing right effort instead in the aggregate of wisdom.[7] Whatever may be the final word on the proper positioning of right effort, all versions clearly concur in placing right mindfulness under the heading of concentration.

This is significant in view of a tendency in some later traditions to combine mindfulness and wisdom. At times, this even goes so far as to consider mindfulness to be intrinsically a matter of wisdom.[8] Gethin (1992: 42) explains the reasoning that appears to have led to such considerations as follows:

> because *sati* "remembers" it knows how things stand in relation to one another; it, as it were, opens up one's view. In this way it tends towards a seeing of things that reflects what the Abhidhamma considers to be the way things truly are. This is the reason why *sati/smṛti* is so intimately bound up with wisdom.

From the viewpoint of the early discourses, it is not invariably the case that mindfulness is intimately bound up with

6 MĀ 210 at T I 788c11, parallel to MN 44 at MN I 301,8 (translated by Ñāṇamoli 1995/2005: 398) and Up 1005 at D 4094 *ju* 7b5 or Q 5595 *tu* 8b4.
7 See in more detail Anālayo 2011: 279–281.
8 See the discussion in Anālayo 2018c and 2018h.

wisdom. The present passage makes this quite clear, otherwise mindfulness would have been included under the aggregate of wisdom.

The same *Cūḷavedalla-sutta* and its parallels take up the potential of right mindfulness to lead to concentration:[9]

> The four establishments of mindfulness are reckoned a cause of concentration.

The translation "cause" renders *nimitta*, the term also found in the corresponding section of the *Cūḷavedalla-sutta*. This term can convey the sense of a "mark" or "sign" or else carry a causal nuance; in fact at times it can serve as an equivalent to other terms that translate "cause" and "condition".[10] This appears to be the sense relevant to the present context, in that the four establishments of mindfulness have a causal function in the cultivation of concentration. This was apparently considered such a significant dimension of mindfulness that the *Cūḷavedalla-sutta* and its parallels give precedence to it, rather than drawing attention to the relationship of mindfulness to wisdom.

At the same time, however, the statements of purpose in the *Satipaṭṭhāna-sutta* and its parallels list a range of benefits to be expected from cultivating the four establishments of mindfulness, none of which mentions concentration.[11] The benefits they list show that the overall orientation of the practice is towards liberating insight.[12] Implementing this orientation requires in particular that mindfulness be cultivated in combination with clear knowing (*sampajañña*). From this perspective, concentration is a by-product, although certainly an important one. It is important because it supports progress to liberation; it is a by-product because it is not the final aim of the practice.

In fact, the passage from the *Cūḷavedalla-sutta* and its parallels, quoted above, occurs in the context of a discussion of various

---

9 MĀ 210 at T I 788c25.
10 Anālayo 2003a.
11 Anālayo 2013b: 8–9.
12 See also above p. 126n9.

aspects of concentration. In other words, from the viewpoint of concentration, mindfulness is a crucial requirement, as its cultivation serves as the "cause" for concentration. Without mindfulness, it will hardly be possible to cultivate concentration.

THE SIMILE OF THE ELEPHANT (MĀ 118)

Mindfulness occurs in a simile that compares various qualities with parts of an elephant:[13]

> The great elephant has faith as its trunk
> And twofold virtue as its tusks;
> Mindfulness is its neck and wisdom its head,
> To reflect on and analyse the teachings.

The identification of mindfulness as the neck of the elephant points to its role in supporting the head of wisdom. The simile thereby confirms that in early Buddhist thought mindfulness makes a substantial contribution to, but is not the same as, wisdom.

The Pāli parallel differs in so far as in its presentation the elephant's tusks stand for equanimity, a quality also related to the tusks in the Tibetan version (here together with faith).

MINDFULNESS AND LIBERATING INSIGHT (SĀ 983)

The relationship between mindfulness and insight comes up in the following verse:[14]

---

13 MĀ 118 at T I 608c10 to 608c11, parallel to AN 6.43 at AN III 346,23 (translated by Bodhi 2012: 909), see also Th 695, a Sanskrit fragment parallel, SHT VIII 1981 R3, Wille 2000: 145, which has preserved a reference to wisdom as the head, and Up 4014 at D 4094 *ju* 211b6 or Q 5595 *tu* 241b4.

14 SĀ 983 at T II 256a13 to 256a14, parallel to AN 2.32.2 at AN I 134,10 (translated by Bodhi 2012: 230), and Sanskrit fragment SHT V 1171R9, Sander and Waldschmidt 1985: 167. The verse in AN 2.32.2 is a quote from Sn 1107 (translated by Bodhi 2017: 341); see also the discussion of this verse in Brough 1962/2001: 207f.

With purified equanimity and mindfulness,[15]
Being preceded by investigative contemplation of the Dharma,
I say, there is liberation by insight,
The eradication of the darkness of ignorance.

In the Pāli parallel, equanimity and mindfulness are preceded by "thought on the Dharma". In this way, both versions agree that progress to liberation requires combining equanimity and mindfulness,[16] informed by previously developed understanding (be this in the form of contemplation or thought).

The present illustration adds yet another perspective to the relationship between mindfulness and wisdom or insight. Not only is mindfulness merely the neck of the elephant, rather than its head, but it also requires being preceded by investigation in order to lead to liberation. With these two passages, the role of mindfulness in relation to insight emerges as a collaboration with other qualities, particularly the cultivation of clear knowing (*sampajañña*), a quality regularly mentioned alongside *sati*, and in the version translated above the arousing of investigation, which corresponds to the task of the second of the seven awakening factors. Both depend on the establishing of mindfulness to unfold their full potential, just as mindfulness in turn depends on them for engendering liberating insight.

MINDFULNESS AND THE DIVINE ABODES (MĀ 16)

Besides serving in the development of insight, mindfulness can also function as part of a meditative dwelling in any of the four divine abodes (*brahmavihāra*s). Whereas the development of insight aims at final liberation from defilements, a cultivation of

15 The translation is based on adopting a variant reading and on an emendation, by deleting a reference to aversion that appears to be the result of textual corruption; for other quotations whose formulation supports the impression that the reference to aversion in SĀ 983 is a textual corruption see Sanskrit fragment SHT V 1171 R9, Sander and Waldschmidt 1985: 167, SĀ^3 8 at T II 495b4 (see Harrison 2002: 9f), and the *Dharmaskandha*, T 1537 at T XXVI 489c2.

16 According to the commentary, Mp II 209,5, the reference here is to the fourth absorption.

the *brahmavihāras* leads to temporary liberation, in the sense that the mind is for the time being beyond the reach of defilements, whose roots in the mind, however, have not yet been eradicated. The first of the four divine abodes is benevolence (*mettā*), which should be cultivated in this way:[17]

> Being free from ill will and free from contention, discarding sloth-and-torpor, being without restlessness or conceit,[18] removing doubt and overcoming arrogance, with right mindfulness and right knowing, being without bewilderment, one dwells having accomplished pervasion of one direction with a mind endowed with benevolence, and in the same way the second, third, and fourth directions, [all] of the four directions, above and below, completely and everywhere being without mental shackles, without resentment, without ill will, and without contention; with a mind endowed with benevolence that is supremely vast and great, boundless and well developed, one dwells having accomplished pervasion of the entire world.

The above *Madhyama-āgama* version continues by applying the same description to the other three divine abodes of compassion, sympathetic joy, and equanimity. The Pāli parallel proceeds similarly.[19] The reference to "right mindfulness" in the *Madhyama-āgama* version has its counterpart in *paṭissato* in the Pāli parallel. In its general usage in Pāli discourses, this term carries similar connotations to *sati*, "mindfulness".[20]

Here and in a substantial number of other instances surveyed in this book, mindfulness is qualified as "right" in the Chinese *Āgamas*, but no such qualification is found in their Pāli parallels.

---

17 MĀ 16 at T I 439a29 to 439b5, parallel to AN 3.65 at AN I 192,3 (translated by Bodhi 2012: 282).

18 The translation "restlessness" is based on adopting a variant reading.

19 The same holds for a description of the cultivation of the *brahmavihāras* in MĀ 15 at T I 438a6 and its parallel to AN 10.208 at AN V 299,17 (translated by Bodhi 2012: 1542); see also Anālayo 2012: 489–514. In this case, however, another parallel extant in Tibetan, Up 4081 at D 4094 *ju* 238a2 or Q 5595 *tu* 272a1 (translated by Martini 2012: 65), does not explicitly refer to mindfulness.

20 See Anālayo 2018a: 11f.

Given the overarching concern in later exegesis with clear-cut categorization, in particular when it comes to contrasting "right" and "wrong", perhaps such concerns influenced some reciters of these discourses during oral transmission. This might have led to the addition of the qualification "right", in order to emphasize that the type of mindfulness under discussion fits into this category.

The association of mindfulness with the radiation of one or all of the divine abodes recurs in other Pāli discourses.[21] Such radiation without limit in all directions leads to the mind becoming "boundless" (*appamāṇa*), a qualification also employed in other discourses in relation to mindfulness of the body (see above p. 56).[22] This suggests that, in addition to the support mindfulness can offer to the meditative cultivation of the divine abodes by monitoring the practice, the divine abodes and the presence of mindfulness share the similar quality of broad-mindedness. Such broad-mindedness relates to the "receptive" quality of mindfulness and its ability to monitor a situation in such a way as to provide an overview of its various aspects.

GREAT MENTAL POWERS THROUGH MINDFULNESS (SĀ 537)

The potential of mindfulness emerges again in another passage, according to which one of the eminent disciples of the Buddha by the name of Anuruddha related his great supernormal mental power to his having cultivated the four establishments of mindfulness:[23]

> By cultivating the four establishments of mindfulness, cultivating them much, I accomplished such great supernormal power. What are the four establishments of mindfulness? They are the establishment of mindfulness by contemplating the body [in regard to] the body internally with diligent effort, right mindfulness, and

21 See, e.g., SN 42.8 at SN IV 322,4 (translated by Bodhi 2000: 1344), SN 42.13 at SN IV 351,8 (translated by Bodhi 2000: 1368), AN 8.1 at AN IV 150,19 (translated by Bodhi 2012: 1111), It 1.27 at It 21,5 (translated by Ireland 1991: 20), and Sn 151 (translated by Bodhi 2017: 180).

22 See also Anālayo 2019f.

23 SĀ 537 at T II 139c22 to 139c28, parallel to SN 52.6 at SN V 299,21 (translated by Bodhi 2000: 1755).

> right knowing, overcoming greed and discontent in the world.[24] In the same way with the body externally ... the body internally and externally ... feeling tones internally ... feeling tones externally ... feeling tones internally and externally ... the mind internally ... the mind externally ... the mind internally and externally ... dharmas internally ... dharmas externally ... and the establishment of mindfulness by contemplating dharmas [in regard to dharmas] internally and externally with diligent effort, right mindfulness, and right knowing, in this way overcoming greed and discontent in the world.

In the Pāli parallel, Anuruddha presents the four establishments of mindfulness as the basis for his having reached great direct knowledge (*abhiññā*). In this way, the capacity of mindfulness to empower the mind, potentially even leading to the acquisition of supernormal powers, is similarly evident in both parallels.

THE JOY OF PURIFICATION AND MINDFULNESS (DĀ 28)

The *Dīrgha-āgama* parallel to the *Poṭṭhapāda-sutta* clarifies that the eradication of defiled states and the growth of purified states lead to mindfulness and happiness:[25]

> Defiled states can be extinguished and purified states can be produced, [whereon] one dwells in a state of happy ease, with joy and delight, with mindfulness collected, with a unified mind, and with extensive wisdom.

The Pāli parallel speaks of a happy dwelling with delight, joy, tranquillity, mindfulness, and clear knowing. In both versions, the description serves to encourage the listener to feel inspiration for extinguishing what is defiled and cultivating what is purified.[26] For such purposes, mindfulness clearly has a crucial contribution to offer.

---

24 SN 52.6 does not explicitly mention the distinction between practice undertaken internally, externally, and both.

25 DĀ 28 at T I 112a6 to 112a8, parallel to DN 9 at DN I 196,7 (translated by Walshe 1987: 167).

26 On the contrast between the importance accorded in the early discourses to joy and happiness as integral aspects of the path of purification and

MINDFULNESS INSTEAD OF CONFUSION (SĀ 575)

Mindfulness could also serve to counter confused thoughts. This potential emerges from a *Saṃyukta-āgama* passage that reports an admonishment given by relatives to an accomplished lay practitioner. Mistakenly thinking him to be in a condition of confusion, they tell him:[27]

> You should collect your mindfulness; you should collect your mindfulness!

In agreement with its Pāli parallel, the *Saṃyukta-āgama* discourse clarifies that the lay practitioner was not in need of such instruction, as he had not been confused in the first place. Nevertheless, the instruction as such points to the potential of mindfulness as a way of countering confusion and thereby in a way "liberating" the mind from a confused condition.

THE BALANCE OF MINDFULNESS (DĀ 18)

Another aspect of the "liberating" dimension of mindfulness lies in remaining established in a state free from attraction and repulsion. A discourse in the *Dīrgha-āgama* and its Pāli parallel present such balance through mindfulness and equanimity as a culmination point of practice, after having first trained in countering perceptions related to attraction and to repulsion by cultivating their respective opposites. The two parallel versions agree in considering the final stage of mindful balance to be a noble type of supernormal power:[28]

> Having left behind both attractive appearances and unattractive appearances in this world, one cultivates equanimity with collected mindfulness that is not lost; this is then called a noble supernormal power.

---

the foregrounding of challenging experiences of fear and dread in later exegesis see Anālayo 2019h.

27 SĀ 575 at T II 153a9, parallel to SN 41.10 at SN IV 303,1 (translated by Bodhi 2000: 1330).

28 DĀ 18 at T I 78c10 to 78c12, parallel to DN 28 at DN III 113,6 (translated by Walshe 1987: 424), and a Sanskrit fragment, folio 294v3f, DiSimone 2016: 111 and 346.

Both versions deem such ability to be superior to supernormal feats like multiplication of oneself, levitation, diving into the ground, walking on water, etc. In other words, the balance that can be reached through mindfulness should be reckoned superior even to such spectacular achievements which, according to ancient Indian thought, could be achieved through mental training.

MINDFULLY FACING AN ATTACK (MĀ 30)

Mindfulness can also offer support when one has to endure being physically attacked by others. Such a situation should best be faced with the appropriate reflection:[29]

> One reflects: "I will be very diligent and not sluggish, with straight body and right mindfulness without loss and without delusion, with a stable and unified mind. I will endure this body being punched by fists, hurled at by stones, [even] to the extent of [being attacked] by swords or sticks, yet I shall diligently train in the teaching of the Blessed One."

The Pāli parallel proceeds similarly. In both versions, mindfulness provides support for being able to endure an attack. The implication here would not be that one should simply let others abuse one as they like. The description appears to take for granted that there is no possibility to avoid being physically attacked. In such a situation, the "protective" dimension of mindfulness can facilitate the type of mental stability to rely on in order to face what cannot be avoided with inner stability.

MINDFULNESS AND CRITICISM (MĀ 87)

After a rather stern teaching given by Sāriputta to others, his companion Mahāmoggallāna describes how those with good

---

29 MĀ 30 at T I 465a3 to 465a6, parallel to MN 28 at MN I 186,14 (translated by Ñāṇamoli 1995/2005: 280); see also Anālayo 2011: 195.

qualities, including the possession of mindfulness and clear knowing, will react on hearing Sāriputta's admonition:[30]

> Suppose there are persons who ... have right mindfulness and right knowing ... on hearing the teachings spoken by the venerable Sāriputta, from his mouth it reaches their minds just like the hungry who obtain food or the thirsty who obtain drink.

Although the illustration, found similarly in the Pāli parallel, is concerned with a range of qualities and not just the two mentioned explicitly in the extract translated above, it could nevertheless be taken to illustrate the potential of mindfulness and clear knowing for facing constructive criticism. The "receptivity" of mindfulness together with the clarity provided by clear knowing can counter the arising of strong negative reactions. Instead of being perceived as a personal attack, an admonition can thereby become an occasion to improve oneself.

MINDFUL ALOOFNESS FROM VIEWS (DĀ 17 AND MĀ 13)

The *Dīrgha-āgama* parallel to the *Pāsādika-sutta* takes up the need to go beyond various speculative views about the past and the future:[31]

> If one wishes to eliminate these wrong and bad views, one should cultivate the four establishments of mindfulness in three modes. How should a monastic, to eliminate these bad [states], cultivate the four establishments of mindfulness in three modes? Monastics, that is, one contemplates the body [in regard to] the body internally, with untiring energy and recollective mindfulness that is not lost, removing greed and discontent in the world. One contemplates the body [in regard to] the body

30 MĀ 87 at T I 569c1 to 569c5, parallel to MN 5 at MN I 32,16 (translated by Ñāṇamoli 1995/2005: 113), as well as EĀ 25.6 at T II 634a2, and T 49 at T I 842a12, both of which do not explicitly mention mindfulness; see also Anālayo 2011: 45.

31 DĀ 17 at T I 76b6 to 76b12, parallel to DN 29 at DN III 141,3 (translated by Walshe 1987: 438), Sanskrit fragments folio 290r1f, DiSimone 2016: 111 and 290, and SHT IV 32.66 folio 183V1, Sander and Waldschmidt 1980: 149.

> externally, with untiring energy and recollective mindfulness that is not lost, removing greed and discontent in the world. One contemplates the body [in regard to] the body internally and externally, with untiring energy and recollective mindfulness that is not lost, removing greed and discontent in the world.
>
> Contemplation of feeling tones, mind, and dharmas *is also again like that*. This is how one eliminates the mass of bad states by cultivating the four establishments of mindfulness in three modes.

The Pāli parallel makes basically the same point, although it does not explicitly mention the distinction into three modes of cultivating each establishment of mindfulness internally, externally, and both. In this way, the two passages agree in throwing into relief the potential of a systematic cultivation of the "liberating" potential of mindfulness to lead beyond speculations about the past and the future, presumably by directing attention to a direct apperception and understanding of the present.

A related perspective emerges in an examination of three types of view in a discourse in the *Madhyama-āgama*, which propose that all one does is just a result of the past, is due to a creator god, or is without any cause. When taken to their logical conclusion, each of these three views would deny personal responsibility for what one does. The resultant incorrect perspective is bereft of mindfulness:[32]

> If in relation to acting, together with not acting, one has no understanding in accordance with reality, one in turn has lost right mindfulness and is without right knowing.

The Pāli version similarly indicates that, once what should be done or should not be done is no longer seen as real, mindfulness is lost, and one dwells without protecting oneself.

Although this is not explicitly stated in either of the two versions, it would follow that the possession of mindfulness (or "right mindfulness" in the Chinese version) facilitates a

32 MĀ 13 at T I 435b12 to 435b13, parallel to AN 3.61 at AN I 174,11 (translated by Bodhi 2012: 267).

correct discernment of causality, in the sense of one's personal responsibility for one's actions and omissions. On this understanding, rather than adopting any of the three types of view, mentioned in these two discourses, one relies on the "receptive" quality of mindfulness and its broad-angled perspective as a means to observe things in relation to each other and thereby discern the workings of causality.

OVERCOMING ANGER THROUGH MINDFULNESS (SĀ 1319)

The potential of mindfulness for "liberating" the mind from anger is the topic of a set of verses addressed to the Buddha by a celestial being:[33]

The worthy and virtuous one has right mindfulness,
The worthy and virtuous one is continuously with right mindfulness.
With right mindfulness one sleeps in peace,
In this world and another world.

The worthy and virtuous one has right mindfulness,
The worthy and virtuous one is continuously with right mindfulness.
With right mindfulness one sleeps in peace,
And one's mind is always tranquil.

The worthy and virtuous one has right mindfulness,
The worthy and virtuous one is continuously with right mindfulness.
With right mindfulness one sleeps in peace
And one abandons defeating others in combat.

The worthy and virtuous one has right mindfulness,
The worthy and virtuous one is continuously with right mindfulness.

33 SĀ 1319 at T II 362a17 to 362a27, parallel to SN 10.4 at SN I 208,11 (translated by Bodhi 2000: 307), Sanskrit fragments, Minayeff and Oldenburg 1872/1983: 172f, and SĀ[2] 318 at T II 480b11 (translated by Bingenheimer 2020).

One neither kills nor incites [others] to kill,
One neither oppresses nor incites [others] to oppress,
One has a mind of *mettā* towards everyone,
A mind that does not harbour the bondage of enmity.

The *Saṃyukta-āgama* discourse continues by reporting that the Buddha approved, stating that it was as the celestial being had said. Another parallel preserved in Chinese conveys a similar impression of the potential of mindfulness to lead beyond anger.

The Pāli version proceeds differently, as here the celestial being speaks only a single verse and the Buddha then replies, apparently correcting what the deity had said. The Pāli version on its own conveys the impression that mindfulness is not enough to overcome anger.[34] In light of the above parallel, however, it seems possible that the Pāli version suffered from a textual corruption, where the conjunction *ca* was confused with the negative particle *na*.[35] On this assumption, the reply by the Buddha would originally have affirmed what the celestial being had said. In fact, the *Satipaṭṭhāna-sutta* and its parallels clearly envisage that the cultivation of mindfulness can lead to the higher two levels of awakening, with which anger is completely removed from the mind.

Alongside such differences on the potential of mindfulness, the parallel versions can nevertheless be seen to agree in so far as they similarly highlight the contribution of *mettā* (benevolence) in overcoming anger. The final outcome envisaged in the *Satipaṭṭhāna-sutta* and its parallels for a systematic cultivation of the four establishments of mindfulness certainly does not in any way put into question the potential of *mettā* in this respect. The point is only that such systematic cultivation of mindfulness is on its own able to erode the roots of anger in the

34 This was the conclusion I originally drew on consulting only the Pāli version; see Anālayo 2003b: 52n32. In view of the Chinese parallels, this conclusion needs to be revised.

35 See Anālayo 2018f. The Sanskrit fragment, Minayeff and Oldenburg 1872/1983: 173, has only preserved parts of the relevant passage and its import remains uncertain.

mind. Nevertheless, from the viewpoint of actual meditation practice a cultivation of both mindfulness and *mettā* is probably the best way to counter a tendency to anger.

MINDFUL REMOVAL OF LUST (SĀ 586)

Besides serving to counter anger, the "liberating" potential of mindfulness can also contribute to removing lustful desires:[36]

> Remove the fire of lustful desires,
> With right mindfulness seek to be far away from it.

Two Pāli parallels point to a similar relationship between mindfulness and overcoming sensuality. In the same vein, another discourse in the *Saṃyukta-āgama* enjoins removing dirty dust through right mindfulness, explaining that dust refers to lustful desires.[37] According to the Pāli parallel, the task of mindfulness here is in particular to overcome discontent, which can be a central condition for the arising of sensual desire.

Be it anger (mentioned in the previous passage) or lust, mindfulness can perform its liberating role and lead to a gradual diminishing and eventual removal of both types of defilement.

MINDFULNESS IN SUPPORT OF CELIBACY (SĀ 275)

A closely related perspective on the "liberating" potential of mindfulness emerges in the context of a description of the practices undertaken by the monastic Nanda, which enabled him to live a celibate life at ease, in spite of his lustful nature:[38]

---

36 SĀ 586 at T II 156a2, parallel to SN 1.21 at SN I 13,7 (translated by Bodhi 2000: 100) and SN 2.16 at SN I 53,26 (translated by Bodhi 2000: 149); another parallel, SĀ² 170 at T II 437a4, does not explicitly mention mindfulness.

37 SĀ 1333 at T II 368a26, parallel to SN 9.1 at SN I 197,15 (translated by Bodhi 2000: 294) and SĀ² 353 at T II 490a20.

38 SĀ 275 at T II 73b24 to 73b28 (already translated by Choong 2000: 99), parallel to AN 8.9 at AN IV 168,10 (translated by Bodhi 2012: 1122), SĀ² 6 at T II 375b9 (translated by Bingenheimer 2011: 69), and Up 2065 at D 4094 *ju* 91a3 or Q 5595 *tu* 103b6.

> The clansmen's son Nanda is aware of the arising of feeling tones, aware of the persisting of feeling tones, and aware of the cessation of feeling tones, being established in right mindfulness, without allowing for distractions. He is aware of the arising of perceptions, aware of the persisting of perceptions, and aware of the cessation of perceptions ... He is aware of the arising of thoughts, aware of the persisting of thoughts, and aware of the cessation of thoughts, being established in right mindfulness, without allowing for distractions.[39]
>
> This is reckoned the accomplishment of Nanda, the clansmen's son, in right mindfulness and right knowing.

The Pāli parallel proceeds similarly, although it does not explicitly mention that Nanda was undistracted. The description of the practice undertaken by Nanda suggests that a way to emerge from unwholesome thoughts of sensual lust can be found in mindful contemplation of impermanence.[40] Such a mode of cultivating mindfulness can enable even someone who experiences strong sensual lust to maintain a life of celibacy.

The above passage also offers an important reflection of the distinct early Buddhist perspective on impermanence. Later Buddhist traditions adopted the doctrine of momentariness, the notion that things cease immediately after having arisen.[41] Early Buddhist thought, however, clearly recognizes that feeling tones, perceptions, and thoughts can persist for some time (as changing processes, of course) before they cease.

COUNTERING UNWHOLESOME THOUGHTS (SĀ 272)

A discourse in the *Saṃyukta-āgama*, in agreement with its Pāli parallel, proposes the cultivation of the four establishments

39 The translation follows a variant reading, in keeping with the formulation employed for feeling tones.

40 On contemplation of impermanence in the cultivation of the four establishments of mindfulness see Anālayo 2003b: 102–107, 2013b: 16f, and 2018i: 40–42.

41 See in more detail von Rospatt 1995.

of mindfulness as the means to counter and remove any unwholesome thoughts:[42]

> Thoughts of lust, thoughts of hatred, and thoughts of harming; these are innumerable types of what is unwholesome. What is their complete cessation? [It is when] the mind is well settled in the four establishments of mindfulness.

The two versions add that the same can also be achieved through concentration on signlessness (*animitta*), an experience where perception no longer picks up the "signs" of phenomena required for their recognition and mental processing.[43]

The above passage in a way sums up the "liberating" quality of mindfulness that has already emerged with the previous three extracts, which showed the potential of mindfulness in relation to anger and lust. The present extract rounds off their presentation by pointing to the cultivation of the four *satipaṭṭhāna*s for this purpose.

MINDFULLY REMOVING UNWHOLESOME INFLUENCES (MĀ 10)

The topic of removing what is unwholesome appears again in the *Madhyama-āgama* parallel to the *Sabbāsava-sutta*. As part of a survey of different methods to counter the influxes (*āsava*), a term for unwholesome influences in the mind that are completely eradicated with full awakening, the relevant passage points to the cultivation of the awakening factors:[44]

> How are influxes abandoned through paying attention? Monastics, one gives attention to the first awakening factor of mindfulness in dependence on seclusion, in dependence on dispassion, in dependence on cessation, inclining to release.[45]

42 SĀ 272 at T II 72a25 to 72a26, parallel to SN 22.80 at SN III 93,21 (translated by Bodhi 2000: 920).

43 On signlessness see Harvey 1986.

44 MĀ 10 at T I 432c16 to 432c18, parallel to MN 2 at MN I 11,22 (translated by Ñāṇamoli 1995/2005: 95), EĀ 40.6 at T II 741b1, and Up 2069 at D 4094 *ju* 94a5 or Q 5595 *tu* 107b1; see also Anālayo 2011: 32.

45 The translation "inclining" is based on adopting a variant reading.

The *Madhyama-āgama* discourse continues by listing the other six awakening factors. The Pāli parallel similarly speaks of the cultivation of mindfulness (and of the other awakening factors), undertaken in dependence on seclusion, dispassion, and cessation, as "culminating in letting go". The expression "inclining to release" in the *Madhyama-āgama* passage appears to convey a similar sense. Given the overarching importance accorded to the abandoning of the influxes in early Buddhist thought, the present indication invests the cultivation of mindfulness and the other awakening factors with a crucial liberating potential.

The above extract also complements the previous passages, according to which the "liberating" potential of mindfulness can counter anger and lust, and the four *satipaṭṭhāna*s can serve to effectuate a cessation of unwholesome thoughts. The present passage directly addresses the roots of unwholesomeness in the mind, showing that to tackle them requires mindfulness in its role as an awakening factor.

THE TREASURES OF THE AWAKENING FACTORS (EĀ 42.4)

The awakening factors just mentioned, which have mindfulness as their foundation, are like treasures:[46]

> In my teaching there are many types of treasure, namely the treasure of the mindfulness awakening factor, the treasure of the [investigation-of-]dharmas awakening factor, the treasure of the energy awakening factor, the treasure of the joy awakening factor, the treasure of the tranquillity awakening factor, the treasure of the concentration awakening factor, and the treasure of the equipoise awakening factor.

Two parallels extant in Pāli and Chinese instead list the different practices and qualities pertinent to awakening, beginning with the four establishments of mindfulness and leading up to the

46 EĀ 42.4 at T II 753b5 to 753b7, parallel to AN 8.19 at AN IV 203,15 (translated by Bodhi 2012: 1144) and MĀ 35 at T I 476c20 (translated by Bingenheimer et al. 2013: 279).

noble eightfold path.[47] Since this listing includes the seven awakening factors, in this respect these parallels agree with the above passage. The treasures of the awakening factors in a way enrich the mind by enabling the breakthrough to liberation.

THE BUDDHA'S DISCOVERY OF THE AWAKENING FACTORS (MĀ 58)

The arising of a Buddha (here referred to as Tathāgata) results in the arising of the seven awakening factors:[48]

> [When] a Tathāgata, free from attachment and fully awakened, appears in the world, it should be known that the seven treasures of the awakening factors also appear in the world. What are the seven? They are the treasure of the mindfulness awakening factor, [the treasure] of the investigation-of-dharmas awakening factor, [the treasure] of the energy awakening factor, [the treasure] of the joy awakening factor, [the treasure] of the tranquillity awakening factor, [the treasure] of the concentration awakening factor, and the treasure of the equipoise awakening factor.

The Pāli parallel similarly relates the manifestation of the seven awakening factors to the arising of a Tathāgata. The point made with this presentation would be that it requires a Buddha to recognize the potential of these seven mental qualities for progress towards awakening. In other words, although mindfulness was already known in the ancient Indian setting, its potential to serve as the first and foundational awakening factor should be considered a distinct discovery of the Buddha.

---

47 The same listing occurs earlier and under a different heading in EĀ 42.4 at T II 753b2; on the list in general see also Anālayo 2020i.

48 MĀ 58 at T I 493a16 to 493a19, parallel to SN 46.42 at SN V 99,8 (translated by Bodhi 2000: 1595), Sanskrit fragment SHT VIII 1857, Bechert and Wille 2000: 50, T 38 at T I 822a29, SĀ 721 at T II 194a9, and EĀ 39.7 at T II 731b19.

NUTRIMENT FOR THE AWAKENING FACTOR OF MINDFULNESS (SĀ 715)

The awakening factor of mindfulness has its own nutriment, in the sense of the qualities or practices that nourish its arising and growth:[49]

> What is the nourishment for the mindfulness awakening factor? That is, having given attention to the four establishments of mindfulness, the not yet arisen mindfulness awakening factor arises and the already arisen mindfulness awakening factor is aroused further so as to increase and augment. This is called the nourishment for the mindfulness awakening factor.

The Pāli parallel is less specific, as it simply mentions "things that are the basis for the mindfulness awakening factor". A parallel extant in Tibetan agrees with the *Saṃyukta-āgama* version in stipulating the four *satipaṭṭhāna*s. Perhaps the two ways of presentation could be combined by considering a cultivation of the four establishments of mindfulness to be particularly suitable for stimulating the awakening potential of mindfulness, while at the same time leaving open the possibility that mindfulness can in principle also be cultivated as an awakening factor apart from formal *satipaṭṭhāna* practice.

MANIFESTATIONS OF THE AWAKENING FACTOR OF MINDFULNESS (SĀ 713)

Another perspective on the same awakening factor of mindfulness reveals in what way it can manifest:[50]

> There is the establishing of mindfulness in the mind in relation to internal phenomena and there is the establishing of mindfulness

---

49 SĀ 715 at T II 192c18 to 192c20, parallel to SN 46.51 at SN V 103,31 (translated by Bodhi 2000: 1598) and Up 5037 at D 4094 *ju* 286b1 or Q 5595 *thu* 31b5.

50 SĀ 713 at T II 191b21 to 191b24, parallel to SN 46.52 at SN V 110,30 (translated by Bodhi 2000: 1604) and Up 2022 at D 4094 *ju* 60b6 or Q 5595 *tu* 67a3 (whose presentation differs, as it instead brings in the distinction between what is wholesome and what is unwholesome).

> in the mind in relation to external phenomena. That establishing of mindfulness in relation to internal phenomena is the mindfulness awakening factor ... and that establishing of mindfulness in relation to external phenomena is the mindfulness awakening factor.

The Pāli parallel similarly relates mindfulness as an awakening factor to what is internal or else external. The distinction between internal and external comes up repeatedly in various passages on mindfulness, the present one highlighting in particular that the internal and the external domain are dimensions of mindfulness as an awakening factor. The relationship established in this way invests this distinction, which reflects the "receptive" dimension of mindfulness, with additional importance. I will discuss its implications in more detail below (p. 232) in relation to the Buddha's own practice of *satipaṭṭhāna*, as this conveniently exemplifies an external deployment of mindfulness.

LIBERATION DEPENDS ON MINDFULNESS (MĀ 51)

The next passage describes practices that lead to liberation. Several of these involve mindfulness, so the present exposition can be read as a complement to the *Dīrgha-āgama* discourse taken up at the outset of the second chapter (see above p. 48) with its emphasis on mindfulness among qualities to be cultivated. In agreement with its Pāli parallel, the *Madhyama-āgama* discourse translated below presents the subject matter by way of a series of questions and answers:[51]

> For knowledge and liberation there is also a practice, they are not without a practice. What is reckoned to be the practice for knowledge and liberation? The answer is: the seven factors of awakening are the practice.
>
> For the seven factors of awakening there is also a practice, they are not without a practice. What is reckoned to be the practice for the seven factors of awakening? The answer is: the four establishments of mindfulness are the practice.

---

51 MĀ 51 at T I 487b29 to 487c7, parallel to AN 10.61 at AN V 114,25 (translated by Bodhi 2012: 1416), T 36 at T I 820a21, and T 37 at T I 820c20.

> For the four establishments of mindfulness there is also a practice, they are not without a practice. What is reckoned to be the practice for the four establishments of mindfulness? The answer is: the three sublime types of conduct are the practice.[52]
>
> For the three sublime types of conduct there is also a practice, they are not without a practice. What is reckoned to be the practice for the three sublime types of conduct? The answer is: guarding the senses is the practice.
>
> For guarding the senses there is also a practice, they are not without a practice. What is reckoned to be the practice for guarding the senses? The answer is: right mindfulness and right knowing are the practice.

The Pāli parallel makes the same point, expressed in terms of each item having its specific nutriment. A minor difference is that the nutriment for guarding the sense doors is just mindfulness and clear knowing (*satisampajañña*),[53] without an explicit qualification of these as "right". This is in line with a recurrent pattern already noted earlier, where the Chinese parallels tend to qualify mindfulness additionally as "right".

The present passage covers three modalities of mindfulness. Besides serving as the first awakening factor and being the central quality cultivated with its four establishments, the text also mentions right mindfulness and right knowing as a separate quality. Such cultivation of mindfulness leads to sense restraint, which in turn builds the foundation for the four *satipaṭṭhāna*s (via facilitating proper conduct), and these in turn feed into the "liberating" dimension of mindfulness as the first awakening factor. In this way, from the basic to the profound, mindfulness can make a continuous contribution to progress on the path.

---

52 These are wholesome bodily, verbal, and mental conduct.

53 T 36 at T I 820b1 and T 37 at T I 820c28 do not mention clear knowing.

CONTEMPLATING THE AGGREGATES WITH MINDFULNESS (SĀ 265)

A whole set of similes serves to illustrate the nature of the five aggregates of clinging, singled out in early Buddhist thought as central dimensions of subjective experience to which the unawakened mind is prone to cling. In agreement with its Pāli parallel, the *Saṃyukta-āgama* discourse in question sums up the teaching in verse form:[54]

> Contemplate bodily form as a mass of foam,
> Feeling tones like bubbles on water,
> Perception like a glare in springtime,
> Formations like a plantain tree,
> And the nature of any consciousness like a magical illusion,
> As the kinsman of the sun has explained.
>
> Carefully attending to it from all sides,
> With right mindfulness examining it well,
> It is [found to be] insubstantial and without solidity

Although the parallels to the above verse do not explicitly mention mindfulness, they agree with the *Saṃyukta-āgama* version in referring to both mindfulness and clear (or right) knowing in a subsequent verse that describes how one should contemplate.[55] In this way, the parallel versions agree in conferring on mindfulness a central role in the cultivation of insight into the empty nature of the five aggregates of clinging. To fulfil its "liberating" role in this context, mindfulness collaborates with other mental qualities or factors, here in particular with examination.

---

54 SĀ 265 at T II 69a18 to 69a22, parallel to SN 22.95 at SN III 142,29 (translated by Bodhi 2000: 952), T 105 at T II 501b18, T 106 at T II 502a26, and Up 4084 at D 4094 *ju* 240b2 or Q 5595 *tu* 274b6 (translated by Dhammadinnā 2013: 78); on the similes employed to illustrate the nature of the five aggregates of clinging see also Anālayo 2015b: 77–82.

55 SN 22.95 at SN III 143,9, T 105 at T II 501c1, and Up 4084 at D 4094 *ju* 240b5 or Q 5595 *tu* 275a2 (T 106 does not have a counterpart to this last verse).

MINDFULNESS IS THE PATH (SĀ 535)

The four establishments of mindfulness are central to the path. This can be seen in another passage, which points out the dire consequences of neglecting their cultivation:[56]

> If one is apart from the four establishments of mindfulness, one is apart from the noble teaching. Being apart from the noble teaching, one is apart from the noble path. Being apart from the noble path, one is apart from the state of the deathless. Being apart from the state of the deathless, one is unable to become free from birth, old age, disease, death, worry, grief, vexation, and pain.

The Pāli parallel presents the matter in a more succinct manner, simply stating that those who neglect the four establishments of mindfulness neglect the noble path that leads to the destruction of *dukkha*. Alongside such differences, the parallel versions clearly reckon the cultivation of mindfulness (by way of its four establishments) as indispensable for the path to liberation.

MINDFULNESS AND THE QUEST FOR AWAKENING (SĀ 542)

Training in the four establishments of mindfulness is indeed crucial for progress towards awakening. This is explicitly formulated in another discourse in the *Saṃyukta-āgama* in the following manner:[57]

> If a monastic is at the state of a trainee, [proceeding] upwards, seeking to establish the mind in the peace of Nirvāṇa,[58] what should [such] a noble disciple cultivate, cultivating it much, so as to gain in this teaching and discipline the eradication of the

56 SĀ 535 at T II 139a23 to 139a26, parallel to SN 52.2 at SN V 296,26 (translated by Bodhi 2000: 1752) and Up 6029 at D 4094 *nya* 13a4 or Q 5595 *thu* 46b1 (translated by Dhammadinnā 2018: 25).

57 SĀ 542 at T II 141a4 to 141a8, parallel to SN 52.4 at SN V 298,27 (translated by Bodhi 2000: 1754).

58 The translation "seeking" is based on an emendation found in the Taishō edition, in line with an earlier occurrence of the otherwise equivalent formulation in the same discourse.

influxes, the influx-free liberation of the mind and liberation by wisdom, knowing here and now for oneself and realizing: "Birth for me has been eradicated, the celibate life has been established, what had to be done has been done, I myself know that there will be no receiving of any further existence"?

[Reply: Such a] one should dwell in the four establishments of mindfulness.

The discourse continues by describing the cultivation of the four establishments of mindfulness (with an abbreviated reference to the distinction between internal and external forms of such practice).[59] The question in the Pāli parallel is simply what a trainee should cultivate. Similar to the previous passage, the parallels agree in shining a spotlight on the importance of the four *satipaṭṭhāna*s for progress to liberation.

MINDFULNESS AND AWAKENING ATTAINED (SĀ 543)

In addition to being required for progress to liberation, dwelling in the four establishments of mindfulness is also the appropriate mode of meditative abiding for those who have successfully attained it:[60]

If a monastic has already eradicated the influxes, done what had to be done, relinquished the heavy burden, is apart from all fetters and well liberated in mind through right knowledge, such a one also cultivates the four establishments of mindfulness.[61] Why is that? [It is not] to gain what has not been gained, to realize what has not been realized, but for the sake of a pleasant dwelling in the here and now.

59 SN 52.4 at SN V 298,31 does not explicitly mention internal and external mindfulness and instead qualifies the practice undertaken as being "diligent, clearly knowing, and mindful, free from greedy desires and discontent in the world".
60 SĀ 543 at T II 141a22 to 141a25, parallel to SN 52.5 at SN V 299,10 (translated by Bodhi 2000: 1754).
61 SN 52.5 at SN V 299,12 qualifies the mindfulness meditation undertaken by fully awakened ones as being "diligent, clearly knowing, and mindful, free from greedy desires and discontent in the world".

The parallels agree that mindfulness practice continues even after full awakening has been successfully reached. In this way, mindfulness is not only the means for reaching the goal, but also the befitting expression of having reached the goal.

AWAKENED ONES ARE MINDFUL (DĀ 10)

The continued relevance of mindfulness for those who have reached awakening comes up again in a passage in the *Dasuttara-sutta* and its *Dīrgha-āgama* parallel, which present a list of seven powers of fully awakened ones. According to their description of one of these powers, fully awakened ones are cultivators of the four establishments of mindfulness:[62]

> [One who has eradicated the influxes] cultivates the four establishments of mindfulness, cultivating them much and practising them much.

The *Dasuttara-sutta* phrases its corresponding indication in such a way as to make it clearer that the cultivation of the four establishments is what led to the attainment of full awakening and its concomitant eradication of the influxes. The same practice then continues to be of relevance to fully awakened ones, who keep cultivating these four establishments of mindfulness. Their undertaking as a characteristic feature of arahants recurs in a listing of eight powers, found in a discourse in the *Aṅguttara-nikāya* and its *Saṃyukta-āgama* parallel.[63]

AN ARAHANT'S MINDFULNESS (MĀ 12)

Mindfulness is indeed a quality characteristic of those who have achieved the final goal:[64]

62 DĀ 10 at T I 54c14, parallel to DN 34 at DN III 283,29 (translated by Walshe 1987: 517).
63 AN 8.28 at AN IV 224,32 (translated by Bodhi 2012: 1156), parallel to SĀ 694 at T II 188b26 and Up 6067 at D 4094 *nyu* 37a5 or Q 5595 *thu* 74b8.
64 MĀ 12 at T I 434c18 to 434c20, parallel to AN 4.195 at AN II 198,24 (translated by Bodhi 2012: 574).

> One who has been rightly liberated in the mind in this way gains in turn being established in six wholesome abodes ... on seeing a form with the eye, one is neither delighted nor sad, but equanimous, seeking for nothing, being with right mindfulness and right knowing.

The *Madhyama-āgama* discourse continues with the same description for the other five senses. In each case, one who is fully liberated will remain in possession of right mindfulness and right knowing, without reacting with desire or aversion. The Pāli version makes the same point in terms of dwelling in equanimity with mindfulness and clear knowing.

Whereas the passages surveyed earlier were about the cultivation of the four establishments of mindfulness as characteristic of fully awakened ones, the present instance complements this by delineating how such possession of mindfulness plays out in daily-life situations. This takes the form of unshakeable mental balance, free from any delight or sadness, in relation to whatever is experienced.

THE BUDDHA'S MINDFULNESS AND INSIGHT (MĀ 133)

The Buddha's own mindfulness finds mention in the *Upāli-sutta* (MN 56) and its *Madhyama-āgama* parallel, occurring in a series of verses that eulogize the Buddha. One of these verses mentions his mindfulness:[65]

> Being with mindfulness well [established] and with sublime and right insight, he does not elevate and also does not demote himself, being imperturbable and with continuous mastery [of himself].

Instead of referring to elevating and demoting oneself, the Pāli parallel speaks of leaning neither forwards nor backwards, presumably in the same sense of neither favouring nor rejecting.

---

65 MĀ 133 at T I 632b10 to 632b11, parallel to MN 56 at MN I 386,22 (translated by Ñāṇamoli 1995/2005: 491), and a Sanskrit fragment, Waldschmidt 1979: 7; see also Anālayo 2011: 331.

The overall impression that emerges is the Buddha's superb inner balance, characterized by the presence of mindfulness and insight.

THE BUDDHA'S FIRST TEACHING (EĀ 19.2)

Mindfulness as a factor of the noble eightfold path already features in what according to tradition was the first teaching given by the Buddha, with which he set in motion the wheel of Dharma:[66]

> What is the essential path that leads to the attainment of full awakening, that arouses vision, arouses knowledge, [whereby] the mind attains appeasement, attains the penetrative knowledges, accomplishes the fruits of recluse-ship, and reaches Nirvāṇa? That is, it is this noble eightfold path, namely right view, right thought, right speech, right action, right livelihood, right effort, right mindfulness, and right concentration. This is reckoned to be the essential path that I have reached. I have now attained right awakening, arousing vision, arousing knowledge, the mind attaining appeasement, attaining the penetrative knowledges, accomplishing the fruits of recluse-ship, and reaching Nirvāṇa.

The Pāli parallel similarly identifies the path leading to the cessation of *dukkha* as the noble eightfold path, and then lists its factors. The role of mindfulness as one of the factors of the noble eightfold path in the first teaching by the Buddha could be related to his discovery of the awakening factors (see above p. 221) and of the four establishments of mindfulness (see above pp. 86 and 89). All of these appear to be central realizations that emerged during his quest for, and eventual attainment of, awakening. The roles of mindfulness as the seventh factor of the eightfold path, the first and foundational awakening factor, and the chief quality behind the cultivation

66 EĀ 19.2 at T II 593c2 to 593c7, parallel to SN 56.11 at SN V 421,10 (translated by Bodhi 2000: 1844) and a range of other parallels, for a survey of which see Anālayo 2015c: 348–350.

of the four establishments of mindfulness could thus all be considered outcomes of the Buddha's realization of awakening.

ALL BUDDHAS AWAKEN THROUGH MINDFULNESS (SĀ 498)

A discourse in the *Saṃyukta-āgama* and its *Saṃyutta-nikāya* parallel report Sāriputta describing the type of practice common to all Buddhas:[67]

> I know that all Buddhas of the past, being [Blessed Ones], Tathāgatas, arahants, rightly and fully awakened, completely abandoned the five hindrances, which afflict the mind, bring about a weakening of the power of wisdom, fall into the category of obstructions, and do not lead to Nirvāṇa; they dwelled in the four establishments of mindfulness and, cultivating the seven factors of awakening, attained unsurpassed right awakening.
>
> All Buddhas of the future, being Blessed Ones, [Tathāgatas, arahants, rightly and fully awakened], also will [completely] abandon the five hindrances, which afflict the mind, bring about a weakening of the power of wisdom, fall into the category of obstructions, and do not lead to Nirvāṇa; they will dwell in the four establishments of mindfulness and, cultivating the seven factors of awakening, will attain unsurpassed right awakening.
>
> All Buddhas of the present, being Blessed Ones, Tathāgatas, arahants, rightly and fully awakened, also [completely] abandon the five hindrances, which afflict the mind, bring about a weakening of the power of wisdom, fall into the category of obstructions, and do not lead to Nirvāṇa; they dwell in the four establishments of mindfulness and, cultivating the seven factors of awakening, attain unsurpassed right awakening.

In both versions Sāriputta explains that, even though he has no direct knowledge of Buddhas past, present, and future, he is able to make such a statement from inference. This is comparable to a gatekeeper at the only gate of a town, who would know

---

67 SĀ 498 at T II 131a11 to 131a20, parallel to SN 47.12 at SN V 160,28 (translated by Bodhi 2000: 1642).

that anyone entering or leaving the town will have to come through that gate.

The removal of the hindrances is an exercise in the *Satipaṭṭhāna-sutta* and its *Madhyama-āgama* parallel and would hardly be possible without any presence of mindfulness.[68] The same quality is of course central in the cultivation of the four establishments of mindfulness. It is also foundational as the first of the awakening factors, building on which the other awakening factors are cultivated. Their presence or absence is the topic of another exercise in the *Satipaṭṭhāna-sutta* and its parallels.[69]

In view of the central role of mindfulness for overcoming the five hindrances, dwelling in the four establishments of mindfulness, and cultivating the awakening factors, it follows that mindfulness is indeed a key aspect of the progress towards awakening for all Buddhas.

THE BUDDHA'S THREE ESTABLISHMENTS OF MINDFULNESS (MĀ 163)

The Buddha himself is on record for cultivating a set of three establishments of mindfulness. These three, listed only in the present context, do not correspond to the standard set of four concerned with the body, feeling tones, mind, and dharmas. Instead, they describe three different situations the Buddha might encounter when teaching an audience:[70]

> The Tathāgata teaches the Dharma to his disciples with thoughts of sympathy and consideration, seeking their benefit and welfare, seeking their peace and happiness, with a mind full of benevolence and compassion, [telling them]: "This is for your welfare, this is for your happiness, this is for your welfare and happiness."
>
> If the disciples are not respectful and do not act accordingly, do not become established in knowledge, their minds do not incline

68 Anālayo 2013b: 177–194.
69 Anālayo 2013b: 195–226.
70 MĀ 163 at T I 693c24 to 694a18, parallel to MN 137 at MN III 221,3 (translated by Ñāṇamoli 1995/2005: 1071) and Up 7015 at D 4094 *nyu* 59a2 or Q 5595 *thu* 101b; see also Anālayo 2017f: 171f.

> towards the Dharma and follow the Dharma, they do not accept the right Dharma, they disregard the Blessed One's instruction and are unable to attain certainty in it, then the Blessed One is not sad or sorrowful because of this. Instead, the Blessed One is equanimous and unaffected, constantly mindful and constantly knowing ...[71]
>
> If the disciples are respectful and act accordingly, become established in knowledge, their minds surrender and incline towards the Dharma and follow the Dharma, they accept and uphold the right Dharma, they do not disregard the Blessed One's instruction and are able to attain certainty in it, then the Blessed One is not glad or joyful because of this. Instead, the Blessed One is equanimous and unaffected, constantly mindful and constantly knowing ...
>
> [If] some disciples are not respectful and do not act accordingly, do not become established in knowledge, their minds do not incline towards the Dharma and follow the Dharma, they do not accept the right Dharma, they disregard the Blessed One's instruction and are unable to attain certainty in it; and some disciples are respectful and act accordingly, they become established in knowledge, their minds surrender and incline towards the Dharma and follow the Dharma, they accept and uphold the right Dharma, they do not disregard the Blessed One's instruction and are able to attain certainty in it, then the Blessed One is not sad or sorrowful and also not glad or joyful because of this. Instead, the Blessed One is equanimous and unaffected, constantly mindful and constantly knowing.

The three establishments of mindfulness described here reflect the need to remain balanced as a teacher, independent of whether members in the audience are attentive or not. The point made here is not a recommendation to ignore how one's way of teaching is received. It is in fact a task for mindfulness, while one is giving a talk, to monitor what is happening in order to be able to adjust to the situation and the audience. The

71 On the somewhat different presentation in MN 137, probably the result of a transmission error, see Anālayo 2011: 785–787.

passage translated above aptly reflects this by describing that the Buddha is continuously mindful and knowing.

However, such "receptive" mindfulness can be accompanied by inner balance and the absence of any negative reactions. In this way, one does not become dependent on the attitude of the audience by getting elated when they seem to be responsive and depressed when they do not seem to be attentive. Instead, with receptive mindfulness one does one's best and remains equanimous with whatever the results may be.

From the viewpoint of the cultivation of mindfulness, it is remarkable that the distinction between three types of audience is made the basis for an enumeration of three *satipaṭṭhāna*s. Here the emphasis is clearly on something external. In contrast, the enumeration of four establishments of mindfulness is based on distinguishing what are often internal conditions of the body, feeling tones, mental states, and dharmas, which can then lead over to discerning the same externally. In this way, in the present set of three *satipaṭṭhāna*s an external object forms the starting point for a practice that then leads over to being aware of the internal, namely equanimity in the face of each of the three types of audience.

This helps to appreciate the basic distinction between internal and external mindfulness. It also puts into perspective the variations repeatedly found between Pāli discourses and the Chinese *Āgama* parallels on whether the necessity to cultivate the four establishments of mindfulness internally and externally (and both) is explicitly mentioned (as well as the issue that these terms have led to various interpretations in later exegesis).[72] Even without any such explicit indication, the idea of three *satipaṭṭhāna*s already points to the need for interrelating what takes place in others to what takes place in oneself. This is a central implication to be taken away from the present discourse. Otherwise the Buddha's attitude towards three different

---

72 For instances of such variations see above p. 149n57, p. 152, p. 210n24, p. 214, and p. 227n59; on various interpretations in later tradition see Schmithausen 2012 and Anālayo 2020d.

audiences would not have been qualified as a distinct set of three *satipaṭṭhāna*s.

One of the body contemplations found under the set of four *satipaṭṭhāna*s proceeds to some degree similarly, showing that this pattern is not exclusive to the three establishments of mindfulness. This is contemplation of a corpse in different stages of decay, a practice found equally in the three parallel versions.[73] Comparable to observing the mental attitude of members of an audience and then attending to one's own mental attitude in relation to that, this contemplation requires observing the dead and decaying body of another and then attending to the fact that one's own body is destined to undergo the same fate.

The need to take into account what is external to oneself also finds reflection in the acrobat simile (see above p. 116). A central point of this simile is how to best take care of another, namely by first cultivating mindfulness in relation to oneself and, based on the balance established in this way, then taking care of another. Again, the simile of the cook (see above p. 111) illustrates how one should attend to one's own mind, an internal contemplation, with an example of external observation, in which the cook should assess how the food is being received by the master.

Given that the definition of the awakening factor of mindfulness mentions its internal and external dimensions (see above p. 222), it seems fair to assume that such broadening of perspective is indeed integral to *satipaṭṭhāna* meditation, independent of the degree to which this is mentioned explicitly. The predominant implications of this distinction can reasonably well be assumed to align with what is also evident in the Buddha's three *satipaṭṭhāna*s and the cemetery contemplations, as well as in the similes of the acrobats and the cook, namely to interrelate in some way what is internal to oneself with what takes place in others.[74]

---

73 Anālayo 2013b: 97–104.

74 See in more detail Anālayo 2003b: 94–102, 2013b: 17–19, 2018i: 35–40, and 2020d.

SUMMARY

Mindfulness can be cultivated in the presence of thought or else without it; it stands in close relationship to attention, but differs from it in needing to be aroused. Mindfulness leads to concentration and is not intrinsically a matter of wisdom. Instead, the role of mindfulness in relation to wisdom is comparable to how the neck of an elephant supports its head.

Mindfulness shares the quality of broad-mindedness with the divine abodes. It has the potential to lead to great mental power, mental purification, and the overcoming of anger and sensual lust. In this way, mindfulness is the tool for remaining free of attraction and repulsion; it enables one to face both physical attacks and criticism with inner balance, to stay aloof from speculative views, to emerge from unwholesome thoughts, and to remove unwholesome influences from the mind.

The awakening factors, the first of which is mindfulness, are like treasures, whose discovery is an outcome of the Buddha's awakening. The awakening factor of mindfulness has the four establishments of mindfulness as its nourishment; the same mental quality of mindfulness also facilitates guarding the senses and can lead to a contemplation of the empty nature of all aspects of subjective experience.

The four establishments of mindfulness are the path to inner nobility, being crucial for progress towards awakening. At the same time, they are the fitting expression of having become awakened. Fully awakened ones continue to practise mindfulness, being free from reacting with desire and aversion. The cultivation of mindfulness was already part of the first teaching delivered by the Buddha, and it forms an element common to the awakening of all Buddhas, past, present, and future. The Buddha himself cultivated three establishments of mindfulness when engaging in teaching activities. These reflect the presence of mindfulness and equanimity when teaching audiences that are either attentive, or else only partially attentive, or else not attentive at all. The distinction between internal and external mindfulness can reasonably well be assumed to refer to a broadening of perspective from oneself to others.

CONCLUSIONS

The material surveyed in the six chapters of this book reflects a range of nuances and applications of mindfulness attested in early Buddhist sources. Nevertheless, the resultant survey is in actual fact only meant to provide a starting point for further discussion and exploration. In particular, it is my hope that scholars of other Buddhist traditions will be inspired to compile similar surveys of the characteristics and functions of mindfulness in texts and practices reflecting those traditions, which will in turn enable a better appreciation of continuities and differences compared to the material examined here.

CHARACTERISTICS OF MINDFULNESS

As the nature of my survey in the preceding pages is inevitably somewhat preliminary, my identification of some key characteristics of mindfulness comes without any pretence that this is either an exhaustive or else a definitive way of understanding mindfulness. Given the inexhaustibility of teachings on mindfulness, to the extent that the Buddha would have been able to deliver teachings on this topic for a hundred years without running out of material (see above p. 103), any attempt at summarization can only be limited and provisory. With this caveat in place, I would like to present my personal understanding of mindfulness under the following five headings, already mentioned in the course of the preceding pages:

- protective,
- embodied,
- attentive,
- receptive,
- liberating.

PROTECTIVE

The establishing of mindfulness offers protection, in particular by introducing a pause before reacting. This enables a better assimilation of relevant information and a recognition of potential reactivity in the mind. Having established the protective dimension of mindfulness, safety is ensured within and without, both for oneself and for others.

Remaining in the field of protection afforded by mindfulness finds illustration in similes of animals that outwit their respective predators by staying on their home turf. Another relevant simile exemplifies how protecting oneself lays the foundation for being able to protect another with the example of an acrobatic performance. The protection afforded through mindfulness is like a gatekeeper of a town, whose presence ensures peace within. By enabling self-reliance, mindfulness can become one's true refuge.

EMBODIED

Mindfulness of the body in the form of proprioception presents a grounding quality that is characteristic of mindfulness in general. Such grounding helps to be fully in the here and now, rather than being carried away by associations and proliferations. Embodied mindfulness offers an inner centredness comparable to carrying a bowl of oil through a crowd watching a dancing spectacle. The cultivation of an embodied presence can become a firm post within that counters the tendency to mental fragmentation through the senses.

Mindfulness-related perspectives on the body range from deconstructions of notions of solidity and excessive concern with its external attractions to embodied bliss and happiness during deep meditative concentration. Taken together, they converge on the need for balance, which is indeed a central quality of mindfulness. Attending to the breath can serve as a convenient tool to come back to an embodied grounding in the here and now, as well as offering a doorway to a sophisticated meditation practice that covers all essential dimensions of the path to awakening.

ATTENTIVE

Mindfulness can be cultivated in such a way that what happens right now could easily be recalled later. Such close attentiveness can be directed to a mundane activity like eating in order to improve health and well-being, it can take place in the presence of conceptual thought or in its absence, and it can serve to lead the mind into deep concentration. Its central flavour is full presence of mind.

With further cultivation, the element of attentiveness nourishes a discerning and awake quality of mind. In this way, mindfulness can provide the foundation for the awakening factor of investigation. Such dwelling in the condition of being attentive and awake through mindfulness is a step towards awakening to a vision of reality as it really is.

RECEPTIVE

Comparable to a cowherd who just watches the cows from a relaxed distance, mindfulness is receptively aware without interfering. Such receptivity manifests in an ability to monitor what is taking place, just like a good charioteer has an overview of the whole traffic situation. Comparable to a cook who observes how the food is received, with receptive mindfulness it becomes possible to remain aware of the various repercussions of what is taking place.

The receptivity of mindfulness can take in information from the internal and the external dimensions of experience under an overarching objective to know and understand. It can manifest in the form of bare awareness as a way of countering the constructing tendency of the mind and its resultant projections.

LIBERATING

Mindfulness serves as a crucial quality in the Buddhist path to liberation, relevant for beginners and fully awakened ones alike. The liberative potential of the four establishments of mindfulness leads to a mental condition free from desire and discontent. Besides its liberating potential with regard to overcoming defilements, mindfulness can also be truly liberating in the face of pain and even death.

The nature of liberation through mindfulness is gradual but definite. Progress occurs in small steps, taken day by day in the cultivation of mindfulness, leading to eventual results that could hardly be more impressive.

PEARL

Taking the first letter of the above qualifications of mindfulness as Protective, Embodied, Attentive, Receptive, and Liberating leads me to the idea of mindfulness as a "p-e-a-r-l". A pearl results from something irritating that enters inside the shell of a mollusc and becomes surrounded with calcium carbonate. The result of this type of immune response is the formation of a beautiful pearl.

In the same vein, any irritant that has entered inside of our life can be surrounded with mindfulness. This mental immune response takes the form of facing any situation with mindfulness, a response that over time leads to the beauty of a mind ever more liberated from afflictions.

FUNCTIONS OF MINDFULNESS

The early Buddhist employment of mindfulness evolves from a quality already known in the ancient Indian setting, where it came prominently intertwined with aspects of memory. Nevertheless, from the outset such memory connotations were not confined to a recall of the past and could perhaps best be captured with an expression like "keeping in mind", in order to avoid restricting mindfulness to what is invariably related to the past. Instead, the memory connotation can more fruitfully be understood to convey an increased receptivity for information as well as an enhanced ability to retrieve that information at a later time, two mental functions that can be improved through mindfulness.

Out of the practices assembled under the first of the four establishments of mindfulness, of particular interest from a daily-practice perspective is mindfulness of bodily postures, which appears to rely on proprioceptive awareness. Such practice can engender a grounding and centring dimension of mindfulness that counters a tendency towards the fragmentation of experience often manifesting in ordinary living situations.

Cultivated in the form of four establishments, mindfulness has the overall purpose of purifying the mind from defilements and propelling progress to awakening. Such practice has an internal and an external dimension, probably implying a shift of mindful attention from what is experienced by oneself to the corresponding experiences of others. It also involves combining mindfulness with other qualities, in particular diligent effort and clear knowing as a basic form of practical wisdom. Only in later traditions do such qualities come to be seen as intrinsic to mindfulness itself. The same holds for the ethical qualification of being wholesome, which in early Buddhist thought is attributed not to mindfulness itself, but rather to its cultivation in the form of the four establishments.

As part of the path to liberation, mindfulness is considered to be "right", in contrast to what leads to mental bondage and affliction. Examples of distinctly wholesome manifestations of mindfulness are its cultivation in the form of the four establishments, as the first of the awakening factors, and as the seventh member of the eightfold path. Nevertheless, in early Buddhist thought the two opposing categories of "right" and "wrong" do not seem to function as an exhaustive account of all manifestations of mindfulness. Moreover, mindfulness appears to be seen as a natural trait of human and celestial beings, in the sense that, given the right conditions, it can manifest even without intentional meditative cultivation.

The practice of mindfulness stands in a close relationship with ethics as part of an overall gradual growth, where moral conduct and the presence of mindfulness mutually strengthen each other. Mindfulness has an important monitoring function, which enables an adjusting of meditation practice in accordance with what the present moment requires. Mindfulness also facilitates inner balance, which is in turn indispensable for facing the vicissitudes of life as well as for assisting others. The cultivation of mindfulness is relevant to all practitioners, from beginners to those who have walked the path to its final consummation.

The range of applications of this quality in Buddhist discourse includes mindful eating for improvement of health and the practice of bare awareness. Both are not merely later developments. Mindfulness offers substantial support to the meditative cultivation of both tranquillity and insight; it can come to one's aid when facing anger, sensual lust, criticism, and even physical attacks. Its continued cultivation is an element of practice common to all awakened ones; in fact, all Buddhas awaken in reliance on it. In sum, mindfulness can extend its transformative power from a mundane activity like eating all the way up to the attainment of Nirvāṇa.

As a complement to the "pearl" imagery employed in order to convey what I consider key qualities of mindfulness, here I would like to present my personal attempt to define mindfulness. This is not meant to compete in any way with existing definitions, but is much rather an attempt to complement them; in fact this whole book has as its purpose the addition of depth to existing definitions and understandings of mindfulness (Anālayo 2019a). Based on the present (and necessarily limited) state of my own research and practical experience, I would summarize key aspects of the function of mindfulness in this way:

An openly receptive presence that enables a full taking in of information, resulting in an awake quality of the mind that facilitates clarity and recollection by monitoring, in the present moment and without interfering, the internal and external repercussions of whatever is taking place.

ABBREVIATIONS

AN	*Aṅguttara-nikāya*
CBETA	Chinese Buddhist Electronic Text Association
D	Derge edition
DĀ	*Dīrgha-āgama* (T 1)
Dhp-a	*Dhammapada-aṭṭhakathā*
DN	*Dīgha-nikāya*
EĀ	*Ekottarika-āgama* (T 125)
It	*Itivuttaka*
It-a	*Itivuttaka-aṭṭhakathā*
MĀ	*Madhyama-āgama* (T 26)
MN	*Majjhima-nikāya*
Mp	*Manorathapūraṇī*
Nidd I	*Mahāniddesa*
Q	Peking edition
SĀ	*Saṃyukta-āgama* (T 99)
$SĀ^2$	*Saṃyukta-āgama* (T 100)
$SĀ^3$	*Saṃyukta-āgama* (T 101)
SHT	Sanskrithandschriften aus den Turfanfunden
Sn	*Sutta-nipāta*
SN	*Saṃyutta-nikāya*
Spk	*Sāratthappakāsinī*
Sv	*Sumaṅgalavilāsinī*
T	Taishō edition
Th	*Theragāthā*
Ud	*Udāna*
Ud-a	*Paramatthadīpanī*
Up	*Abhidharmakośopāyikā-ṭīkā*
〈〉	emendation
[]	supplementation

REFERENCES

Akanuma Chizen 1929/1990: *The Comparative Catalogue of Chinese Āgamas & Pāli Nikāyas*, Delhi: Sri Satguru.

Anālayo, Bhikkhu 2003a: "Nimitta", in *Encyclopaedia of Buddhism*, W.G. Weeraratne (ed.), 7.4: 177–179, Sri Lanka: Department of Buddhist Affairs.

— 2003b: *Satipaṭṭhāna, The Direct Path to Realization*, Birmingham: Windhorse Publications.

— 2007: "Sati & Samādhi", in *Preserving the Dhamma, Writings in Honor of the Eightieth Birthday of Bhante Henepola Gunaratana Mahā Thera*, Bh. Y. Rahula (ed.), 89–92, West Virginia: Bhavana Society.

— 2009a: "Yodhājīva Sutta", in *Encyclopaedia of Buddhism*, W.G. Weeraratne (ed.), 8.3: 798–799, Sri Lanka: Department of Buddhist Affairs.

— 2009b: "Yonisomanasikāra", in *Encyclopaedia of Buddhism*, W.G. Weeraratne (ed.), 8.3: 809–815, Sri Lanka: Department of Buddhist Affairs.

— 2010: *The Genesis of the Bodhisattva Ideal*, Hamburg: Hamburg University Press.

— 2011: *A Comparative Study of the Majjhima-nikāya*, Taipei: Dharma Drum Publishing Corporation.

— 2012: *Madhyama-āgama Studies*, Taipei: Dharma Drum Publishing Corporation.

— 2013a: "On the Five Aggregates (2) – A Translation of Saṃyukta-āgama Discourses 256 to 272", *Dharma Drum Journal of Buddhist Studies*, 12: 1–69.

— 2013b: *Perspectives on Satipaṭṭhāna*, Cambridge: Windhorse Publications.

— 2014: *The Dawn of Abhidharma*, Hamburg: Hamburg University Press.

— 2015a: "Āgama/Nikāya", in *Brill's Encyclopedia of Buddhism*, J. Silk, O. von Hinüber, and V. Eltschinger (ed.), 1: 50–59, Leiden: Brill.

— 2015b: *Compassion and Emptiness in Early Buddhist Meditation*, Cambridge: Windhorse Publications.
— 2015c: *Saṃyukta-āgama Studies*, Taipei: Dharma Drum Publishing Corporation.
— 2016a: "Early Buddhist Mindfulness and Memory, the Body, and Pain", *Mindfulness*, 7.6: 1271–1280.
— 2016b: *Ekottarika-āgama Studies*, Taipei: Dharma Drum Publishing Corporation.
— 2016c: *Mindfully Facing Disease and Death, Compassionate Advice from Early Buddhist Texts*, Cambridge: Windhorse Publications.
— 2017a: *Buddhapada and the Bodhisattva Path*, Bochum: Projektverlag.
— 2017b: *Dīrgha-āgama Studies*, Taipei: Dharma Drum Publishing Corporation.
— 2017c: *Early Buddhist Meditation Studies*, Barre: Barre Center for Buddhist Studies.
— 2017d: "The Healing Potential of the Awakening Factors in Early Buddhist Discourse", in *Buddhism and Medicine, An Anthology of Premodern Sources*, C.P. Salguero (ed.), 12–19, New York: Columbia University Press.
— 2017e: "The Luminous Mind in Theravāda and Dharmaguptaka Discourses", *Journal of the Oxford Centre for Buddhist Studies*, 13: 10–51.
— 2017f: *A Meditator's Life of the Buddha, Based on the Early Discourses*, Cambridge: Windhorse Publications.
— 2017g: "The 'School Affiliation' of the Madhyama-āgama", in *Research on the Madhyama-āgama*, Dhammadinnā (ed.), 55–76, Taipei: Dharma Drum Publishing Corporation.
— 2017h: "Some Renditions of the Term Tathāgata in the Chinese Āgamas", *Annual Report of the International Research Institute for Advanced Buddhology at Soka University*, 20: 11–21.
— 2018a: "The Bāhiya Instruction and Bare Awareness", *Indian International Journal of Buddhist Studies*, 19: 1–19.
— 2018b: "The Influxes and Mindful Eating", *Insight Journal*, 44: 31–42.
— 2018c: "Mindfulness Constructs in Early Buddhism and Theravāda, Another Contribution to the Memory Debate", *Mindfulness*, 9.4: 1047–1051.
— 2018d: "Once Again on Mindfulness and Memory", *Mindfulness*, 9.1: 1–6.
— 2018e: "Overeating and Mindfulness in Ancient India", *Mindfulness*, 9.5: 1648–1654.
— 2018f: "The Potential of Facing Anger with Mindfulness", *Mindfulness*, 9.6: 1966–1972.
— 2018g: *Rebirth in Early Buddhism and Contemporary Research*, Boston: Wisdom Publications.

— 2018h: "Remembering with Wisdom Is not Intrinsic to All Forms of Mindfulness", *Mindfulness*, 9.6: 1987–1990.
— 2018i: *Satipaṭṭhāna Meditation: A Practice Guide*, Cambridge: Windhorse Publications.
— 2019a: "Adding Historical Depth to Definitions of Mindfulness", *Current Opinion in Psychology*, 28: 11–14.
— 2019b: "Ancient Indian Education and Mindfulness", *Mindfulness*, 10.5: 964–969.
— 2019c: "Definitions of Right Concentration in Comparative Perspective", *Singaporean Journal of Buddhist Studies*, 5: 9–39.
— 2019d: "The Emphasis on the Present Moment in the Cultivation of Mindfulness", *Mindfulness*, 10.3: 571–581.
— 2019e: "How Mindfulness Came to Plunge Into Its Objects", *Mindfulness*, 10.6: 1181–1185.
— 2019f: "Immeasurable Meditations and Mindfulness", *Mindfulness*, 10.12: 2620–2628.
— 2019g: "In the Seen just the Seen: Mindfulness and the Construction of Experience", *Mindfulness*, 10.1: 179–184.
— 2019h: "The Insight Knowledge of Fear and Adverse Effects of Mindfulness Practices", *Mindfulness*, 10.10: 2172–2185.
— 2019i: "Meditation on the Breath: Mindfulness and Focussed Attention", *Mindfulness*, 10.8: 1684–1691.
— 2019j: *Mindfulness of Breathing: A Practice Guide and Translations*, Cambridge: Windhorse Publications.
— 2019k: "Open Monitoring and Mindfulness", *Mindfulness*, 10.7: 1437–1442.
— 2019l: "The Role of Mindfulness in the Cultivation of Absorption", *Mindfulness*, 10.11: 2341–2351.
— 2019m: "A Task for Mindfulness: Facing Climate Change", *Mindfulness*, 10.9: 1926–1935.
— 2019n: "On Time", *Insight Journal*, 45: 11–20.
— 2020a: "Attention and Mindfulness", *Mindfulness*, 11.
— 2020b: "Buddhist Antecedents to the Body Scan Meditation", *Mindfulness*, 11: 194–202.
— 2020c: "Clear Knowing and Mindfulness", *Mindfulness*, 11.
— 2020d: "External Mindfulness", *Mindfulness*, 11.
— 2020e: "Ichimura Shohei: The Canonical Book of the Buddha's Lengthy Discourses", *Indian International Journal of Buddhist Studies*.
— 2020f: *Introducing Mindfulness: Buddhist Background and Practical Exercises*, Cambridge: Windhorse Publications.
— 2020g: "'Mūlasarvāstivādin and Sarvāstivādin': Oral Transmission Lineages of Āgama Texts", in *Research on the Saṃyukta-āgama*, Dhammadinnā (ed.), Taipei: Dharma Drum Publishing Corporation.

— 2020h: "On the Six Sense-spheres (3) – A Translation of *Saṃyukta-āgama* Discourses 250 to 255", *Satyābhisamaya*.

— 2020i: "The Qualities Pertinent to Awakening: Bringing Mindfulness Home", *Mindfulness*, 11.

Aufrecht, Theodor 1877: *Die Hymnen des Ṛigveda, zweiter Theil, Maṇḍala VII–X*, Bonn: Adolph Marcus.

Bapat, P.V. 1957: "Atta-dīpa in Pali Literature", in *Liebenthal Festschrift, Sino-Indian Studies, Volume V Parts 3 & 4*, K. Roy (ed.), 11–13, Santiniketan: Visvabharati.

Bechert, Heinz and K. Wille 1989: *Sanskrithandschriften aus den Turfanfunden, Teil 6*, Stuttgart: Franz Steiner Verlag.

— 2000: *Sanskrithandschriften aus den Turfanfunden, Teil 8*, Stuttgart: Franz Steiner Verlag.

Bingenheimer, Marcus 2011: *Studies in Āgama Literature, with Special Reference to the Shorter Chinese Saṃyuktāgama*, Taiwan: Shin Weng Feng Print Co.

— 2020: "A Study and Translation of the Yakṣa Saṃyukta in the Shorter Chinese Saṃyukta Āgama", in *Research on the Saṃyukta-āgama*, Dhammadinnā (ed.), Taipei: Dharma Drum Publishing Corporation.

Bingenheimer, Marcus, Bh. Anālayo, and R. Bucknell 2013 (vol. 1): *The Madhyama Āgama (Middle Length Discourses)*, Berkeley: Numata Center for Buddhist Translation and Research.

Bodhi, Bhikkhu 2000: *The Connected Discourses of the Buddha, A New Translation of the Saṃyutta Nikāya*, Somerville: Wisdom Publications.

— 2011: "What Does Mindfulness Really Mean? A Canonical Perspective", *Contemporary Buddhism*, 12.1: 19–39.

— 2012: *The Numerical Discourses of the Buddha, A Translation of the Aṅguttara Nikāya*, Somerville: Wisdom Publications.

— 2017: *The Suttanipāta, An Ancient Collection of Buddha's Discourses, Together with Its Commentaries Paramatthajotikā II and Excerpts from the Niddesa*, Boston: Wisdom Publications.

Brough, John 1962/2001: *The Gāndhārī Dharmapada, Edited with an Introduction and Commentary*, Delhi: Motilal Banarsidass.

Brown, Kirk Warren and R.M. Ryan 2004: "Perils and Promise in Defining and Measuring Mindfulness: Observations from Experience", *Clinical Psychology: Science and Practice*, 11.3: 242–248.

Burlingame, Eugen Watson 1921: *Buddhist Legends, Translated from the Original Pali Text of the Dhammapada Commentary, Part 3: Translation of Books 13 to 26*, Cambridge, MA: Harvard University Press.

Choong Mun-keat 2000: *The Fundamental Teachings of Early Buddhism, A Comparative Study Based on the Sūtrāṅga Portion of the Pāli Saṃyutta-Nikāya and the Chinese Saṃyuktāgama*, Wiesbaden: Otto Harrassowitz.

Cone, Margaret 2001: *A Dictionary of Pāli, Part I, a-kh*, Oxford: Pali Text Society.

Cowell, E.B. and R.A. Neil 1886: *The Divyāvadāna, A Collection of Early Buddhist Legends, Now First Edited from the Nepalese Sanskrit Mss. in Cambridge and Paris*, Cambridge: Cambridge University Press.

Cox, Collett 1992/1993: "Mindfulness and Memory: The Scope of smṛti from Early Buddhism to the Sarvāstivādin Abhidharma", in *In the Mirror of Memory, Reflections on Mindfulness and Remembrance in Indian and Tibetan Buddhism*, J. Gyatso (ed.), 67–108, Delhi: Sri Satguru.

Dhammadinnā, Bhikkhunī 2013: "A Translation of the Quotation in Śamathadeva's Abhidharmakośopāyikā-ṭīkā Parallel to the Chinese Saṃyukta-āgama Discourse 265", *Dharma Drum Journal of Buddhist Studies*, 12: 71–84.

— 2018: "Discourses on the Establishment of Mindfulness (smṛtyupasthāna) quoted in Śamathadeva's Abhidharmakośopāyikā-ṭīkā", *Journal of Buddhist Studies, Sri Lanka*, 15: 23–38.

DiSimone, Charles 2016: *Faith in the Teacher: The Prāsādika and Prasādanīya Sūtras from the (Mūla-)Sarvāstivāda Dīrghāgama Manuscript, A Synoptic Critical Edition, Translation, and Textual Analysis*, PhD thesis, München: Ludwig-Maximilians-Universität.

Ditrich, Tamara 2016: "Situating the Concept of Mindfulness in the Theravāda Tradition", *Asian Studies*, 4.2: 13–33.

Enomoto, Fumio 1989: "Śarīrārthagāthā, A Collection of Canonical Verses in the Yogācārabhūmi", in *Sanskrit-Texte aus dem Buddhistischen Kanon: Neuentdeckungen und Neueditionen*, 1: 17–35, Göttingen: Vandenhoeck & Ruprecht.

— 1997: "Sanskrit Fragments from the Saṃgītanipāta of the Saṃyuktāgama", in *Bauddhavidyāsudhākaraḥ: Studies in Honour of Heinz Bechert on the Occasion of His 65th Birthday*, P. Kieffer-Pülz and J.-U. Hartmann (ed.), 91–105, Swisstal-Odendorf: Indica et Tibetica.

Fukita Takamichi 2003: *The Mahāvadānasūtra: A New Edition Based on Manuscripts Discovered in Northern Turkestan*, Göttingen: Vandenhoeck & Ruprecht.

Gethin, Rupert 1992: *The Buddhist Path to Awakening: A Study of the Bodhi-Pakkhiyā Dhammā*, Leiden: Brill.

Glass, Andrew 2007: *Four Gāndhārī Saṃyuktāgama Sūtras: Senior Kharoṣṭhī Fragment 5*, Seattle: University of Washington Press.

Griffith, Paul J. 1992/1993: "Memory in Classical Indian Yogācāra", in *In the Mirror of Memory, Reflections on Mindfulness and Remembrance in Indian and Tibetan Buddhism*, J. Gyatso (ed.), 109–131, Delhi: Sri Satguru.

Harrison, Paul 1992/1993: "Commemoration and Identification in Buddhānusmṛti", in *In the Mirror of Memory, Reflections on Mindfulness and Remembrance in Indian and Tibetan Buddhism*, J. Gyatso (ed.), 215–238, Delhi: Sri Satguru.

— 2002: "Another Addition to the An Shigao Corpus? Preliminary Notes on an Early Chinese Saṃyuktāgama Translation", in *Early Buddhism and Abhidharma Thought: In Honor of Doctor Hajime Sakurabe on His Seventy-seventh Birthday*, Sakurabe Ronshu Committee (ed.), 1–32, Kyoto: Heirakuji shoten.

— 2007: "A Fragment of the *Saṃbādhāvakāśasūtra from a Newly Identified Ekottarikāgama Manuscript in the Schøyen Collection", *Annual Report of the International Research Institute for Advanced Buddhology at Soka University*, 10: 201–211.

Harvey, Peter 1986: "'Signless' Meditations in Pāli Buddhism", *Journal of the International Association of Buddhist Studies*, 9.1: 25–52.

— 2009: "The Approach to Knowledge and Truth in the Theravāda Record of the Discourses of the Buddha", in *Buddhist Philosophy, Essential Readings*, W. Edelglass and J. Garfield (ed.), 175–184, Oxford: Oxford University Press.

Hecker, Hellmuth et al. 2003: *Die Reden des Buddha, Gruppierte Sammlung, Saṃyutta-nikāya, aus dem Pālikanon übsersetzt von Wilhelm Geiger, Nyānaponika Mahāthera, Hellmuth Hecker, Buch IV*, Herrnschrot: Beyerlein-Steinschulte.

Hirakawa Akira 1997: *Buddhist Chinese–Sanskrit Dictionary*, Tokyo: Reiyukai.

Hurvitz, Leon 1978: "Fa-Sheng's Observations on the Four Stations of Mindfulness", in *Mahāyāna Buddhist Meditation, Theory and Practice*, M. Kiyota (ed.), 207–248, Honolulu: University of Hawai'i Press.

Husgafvel, Ville 2018: "The 'Universal Dharma Foundation' of Mindfulness-based Stress Reduction: Non-duality and Mahāyāna Buddhist Influences in the Work of Jon Kabat-Zinn", *Contemporary Buddhism*, 19.2: 275–326.

Huyên-Vi, Thích 1986: "Ekottarāgama III", *Buddhist Studies Review*, 3.1: 31–38.

Ichimura Shohei 2015, 2016, and 2018: *The Canonical Book of the Buddha's Lengthy Discourses*, Berkeley: Bukkyo Dendo Kyokai America.

Ireland, John D. 1990: *The Udāna, Inspired Utterances of the Buddha, Translated from the Pali*, Kandy: Buddhist Publication Society.

— 1991: *The Itivuttaka, The Buddha's Sayings, Translated from the Pali*, Kandy: Buddhist Publication Society.

Jantrasrisalai, Chanida, T. Lenz, L. Quian, and R. Salomon 2016: "Fragments of an Ekottarikāgama Manuscript in Gāndhārī", in *Manuscripts in the Schøyen Collection, Buddhist Manuscripts, Volume IV*, J. Braarvig (ed.), 1–122, Oslo: Hermes Publishing.

Jones, J.J. 1956/1978 (vol. 3): *The Mahāvastu, Translated from the Buddhist Sanskrit*, London: Pali Text Society.

Kapstein, Matthew 1992/1993: "The Amnesic Monarch and the Five Mnemic Men: 'Memory' in Great Perfection (Rdzogs-chen) Thought", in *In the Mirror of Memory, Reflections on Mindfulness and Remembrance in Indian and Tibetan Buddhism*, J. Gyatso (ed.), 239–269, Delhi: Sri Satguru.

Klaus, Konrad 1993: "On the Meaning of the Root smṛ in Vedic Literature", *Wiener Zeitschrift für die Kunde Südasiens*, 36: 77–86.

— 2018: "Zu alt- und mittelindoarisch ekāyana", in *Festschrift für Jens-Uwe Hartmann zum 65. Geburtstag*, O. von Criegern et al. (ed.), 251–267, Wien: Arbeitskreis für Tibetische und Buddhistische Studien Universität Wien.

Kuan Tse-Fu 2008: *Mindfulness in Early Buddhism, New Approaches Through Psychology and Textual Analysis of Pali, Chinese and Sanskrit Sources*, London: Routledge.

Kudo Noriyuki 2009: "Or. 15009/101–150", in *Buddhist Manuscripts from Central Asia, The British Library Sanskrit Fragments, Volume II*, S. Karashima and K. Wille (ed.), 169–198, Tokyo: International Research Institute for Advanced Buddhology, Soka University.

— 2015: "The Sanskrit Fragments Or. 15009/351–400 in the Hoernle Collection", in *Buddhist Manuscripts from Central Asia, The British Library Sanskrit Fragments, Volume III*, S. Karashima, J. Nagashima, and K. Wille (ed.), 233–272, Tokyo: International Research Institute for Advanced Buddhology, Soka University.

Levman, Bryan 2017: "Putting smṛti Back into sati (Putting Remembrance Back into Mindfulness)", *Journal of the Oxford Centre for Buddhist Studies*, 13: 121–149.

— 2018: "Response to Ven. Anālayo's Once Again on Mindfulness and Memory in Early Buddhism", *Mindfulness*, 9: 1041–1046.

Luce, G.H. and B.B. Shin 1961: "Pagan Myinkaba Kubyauk-gyi Temple of Rājakumār (1113 A.D.) and the Old Mon Writings on Its Walls", *Bulletin of the Burma Historical Commission*, 2: 277–416.

Martini, Giuliana 2012: "The 'Discourse on Accumulated Actions' in Śamathadeva's Abhidharmakośopāyikā", *Indian International Journal of Buddhist Studies*, 13: 49–79.

Mattes, Josef 2019: "Are We Forgetting sati? Memory and the Benefits of Mindfulness from a Non-Buddhist Viewpoint", *Mindfulness*, 10: 1703–1706.

Melzer, Gudrun 2006: *Ein Abschnitt aus dem Dīrghāgama*, PhD thesis, München: Ludwig-Maximilians-Universität.

Minayeff, I.P. and S. Oldenburg 1872/1983: *Buddhist Texts from Kashgar and Nepal*, New Delhi: International Academy of Indian Culture.

Nagashima Jundo 2015: "The Sanskrit Fragments Or. 15009/501–600 in the Hoernle Collection", in *Buddhist Manuscripts from Central Asia, The British Library Sanskrit Fragments, Volume III*, S. Karashima, J. Nagashima, and K. Wille (ed.), 347–417, Tokyo: International Research Institute for Advanced Buddhology, Soka University.

Nakamura Hajime 2000 (vol. 2): *Gotama Buddha, A Biography Based on the Most Reliable Texts*, Tokyo: Kosei Publishing Co.

Ñāṇamoli, Bhikkhu 1995/2005: *The Middle Length Discourses of the Buddha, A Translation of the Majjhima Nikāya*, Bh. Bodhi (ed.), Somerville: Wisdom Publications.

Nattier, Jan 2003: "The Ten Epithets of the Buddha in the Translations of Zhi Qian支謙", *Annual Report of the International Research Institute for Advanced Buddhology at Soka University*, 6: 207–250.

— 2007: "'One Vehicle' (一乘) in the Chinese Āgamas: New Light on an Old Problem in Pāli", *Annual Report of the International Research Institute for Advanced Buddhology at Soka University*, 10: 181–200.

Norman, K.R. 1988: "Pāli Lexicographical Studies V", *Journal of the Pali Text Society*, 12: 49–63.

— 1990/1993: "Pāli Philology and the Study of Buddhism", in *Collected Papers Volume IV*, K.R. Norman (ed.), 81–91, Oxford: Pali Text Society.

Ohnuma Reiko 2017: *Unfortunate Destiny, Animals in the Indian Buddhist Imagination*, New York: Oxford University Press.

Okano Kiyoshi 1998: *Sarvarakṣitas Mahāsaṃvartanīkathā, Ein Sanskrit-Kāvya über die Kosmologie der Sāṃmitīya-Schule des Hīnayāna-Buddhismus*, Sendai: Tohoku University, Seminar of Indology.

Paṇḍita, Sayadaw U 1992/1993: *In This Very Life, The Liberating Teachings of the Buddha*, U Aggacitta (trsl.), Kandy: Buddhist Publication Society.

Pulleyblank, Edwin G. 1991: *Lexicon of Reconstructed Pronunciation in Early Middle Chinese, Late Middle Chinese and Early Mandarin*, Vancouver: UBC Press.

Radich, Michael David 2007: *The Somatics of Liberation: Ideas about Embodiment in Buddhism from Its Origins to the Fifth Century C.E.*, PhD thesis, Cambridge, MA: Harvard University.

Rhys Davids, T.W. and C.A.F. Rhys Davids 1910: *Dialogues of the Buddha, Translated from the Pali of the Dīgha Nikāya, Part II*, London: Oxford University Press.

Rhys Davids, T.W. and W. Stede 1921/1993: *Pali–English Dictionary*, Delhi: Motilal Banarsidass.

Salomon, Richard 2018: *The Buddhist Literature of Ancient Gandhāra, An Introduction with Translations*, Boston: Wisdom Publications.

Sander, Lore 1987: *Nachträge zu "Kleinere Sanskrit-Texte Heft III-V"*, Wiesbaden: Franz Steiner Verlag.

Sander, Lore and E. Waldschmidt 1980: *Sanskrithandschriften aus den Turfanfunden, Teil IV*, Stuttgart: Franz Steiner Verlag.

— 1985: *Sanskrithandschriften aus den Turfanfunden, Teil 5*, Stuttgart: Franz Steiner Verlag.

Schmithausen, Lambert 1981: "On Some Aspects of Descriptions or Theories of 'Liberating Insight' and 'Enlightenment' in Early Buddhism", in *Studien zum Jainismus und Buddhismus, Gedenkschrift für Ludwig Alsdorf*, K. Bruh and A. Wezler (ed.), 199–250, Wiesbaden: Franz Steiner Verlag.

— 2012: "Achtsamkeit 'innen', 'außen' und 'innen wie außen'", in *Achtsamkeit, Ein buddhistisches Konzept erobert die Wissenschaft, mit einem Beitrag S.H. des Dalai Lama*, M. Zimmerman, C. Spitz and S. Schmidt (ed.), 291–303, Bern: Hans Huber Verlag.

Senart, Émile 1897 (vol. 3): *Le Mahāvastu, texte sanscrit publié pour la première fois et accompagné d'introductions et d'un commentaire*, Paris: Imprimerie Nationale.

Sīlananda, U 1990: *The Four Foundations of Mindfulness*, Boston: Wisdom Publications.

Skilling, Peter 1993: "Theravādin Literature in Tibetan Translation", *Journal of the Pali Text Society*, 19: 69–201.

— 1994: *Mahāsūtras: Great Discourses of the Buddha*, Oxford: Pali Text Society.

Speyer, J.S. 1906/1970 (vol. 1): *Avadānaçataka, A Century of Edifying Tales Belonging to the Hīnayāna*, Osnabrück: Biblio Verlag.

Stache-Rosen, Valentina 1968: *Dogmatische Begriffsreihen im älteren Buddhismus II; Das Saṅgītisūtra und sein Kommentar Saṅgītiparyāya*, Berlin: Akademie Verlag.

Sujato, Bhikkhu 2005: *A History of Mindfulness, How Insight Worsted Tranquillity in the Satipatthana Sutta*, Taipei: The Corporate Body of the Buddha Educational Foundation.

Sun, Jessie 2014: "Mindfulness in Context: A Historical Discourse Analysis", *Contemporary Buddhism*, 15.2: 394–415.

Ṭhānissaro, Bhikkhu 2012: *Right Mindfulness, Memory & Ardency on the Buddhist Path*, California: Metta Forest Monastery.

von Gabain, Annemarie 1954: *Türkische Turfan-Texte VIII*, Berlin: Akademie Verlag.

von Rospatt, Alexander 1995: *The Buddhist Doctrine of Momentariness: A Survey of the Origins and Early Phase of This Doctrine up to Vasubandhu*, Stuttgart: Franz Steiner Verlag.

Waldschmidt, Ernst 1932: *Bruchstücke Buddhistischer Sūtras aus dem zentralasiatischen Sanskritkanon herausgegeben und im Zusammenhang mit ihren Parallelversionen bearbeitet*, Leipzig: F.A. Brockhaus.

— 1944: *Die Überlieferung vom Lebensende des Buddha, Eine vergleichende Analyse des Mahāparinirvāṇasūtra und seiner Textentsprechungen*, Göttingen: Vandenhoeck & Ruprecht.

— 1951 (vol. 2): *Das Mahāparinirvāṇasūtra, Text in Sanskrit und Tibetisch, verglichen mit dem Pāli nebst einer Übersetzung der chinesischen Entsprechung im Vinaya der Mūlasarvāstivādins, auf Grund von Turfan-Handschriften herausgegeben und bearbeitet*, Berlin: Akademie Verlag.

— 1956: *Das Mahāvadānasūtra, ein kanonischer Text über die sieben letzten Buddhas, Sanskrit, verglichen mit dem Pāli nebst einer Analyse der in*

Chinesischer Übersetzung Überlieferten Parallelversion, auf Grund von Turfan-Handschriften Herausgegeben, Berlin: Akademie Verlag.

— 1959/1967: "Kleine Brāhmī Schriftrolle", in *Von Ceylon bis Turfan, Schriften zur Geschichte, Literatur, Religion und Kunst des indischen Kulturraums. Festgabe zum 70. Geburtstag am 15. Juli 1967 von Ernst Waldschmidt*, 371–395, Göttingen: Vandenhoeck & Ruprecht.

— 1967: "Zu einigen Bilinguen aus den Turfan-Funden", in *Von Ceylon bis Turfan, Schriften zur Geschichte, Literatur, Religion und Kunst des indischen Kulturraums, Festgabe zum 70. Geburtstag am 15. Juli 1967 von Ernst Waldschmidt*, 238–257, Göttingen: Vandenhoeck & Ruprecht.

— 1979: "The Varṇaśatam, An Eulogy of One Hundred Epitheta of Lord Buddha Spoken by the Gṛhapati Upāli", *Nachrichten der Akademie der Wissenschaften in Göttingen, Philologisch-Historische Klasse*, 1: 3–19.

Walshe, Maurice 1987: *Thus Have I Heard; The Long Discourses of the Buddha*, London: Wisdom Publications.

Weller, Friedrich 1934: *Brahmajālasūtra, Tibetischer und Mongolischer Text*, Leipzig: Otto Harrassowitz.

Wille, Klaus 2000: *Sanskrithandschriften aus den Turfanfunden Teil 8*, Stuttgart: Franz Steiner Verlag.

— 2006: "The Sanskrit Fragments Or. 15003 in the Hoernle Collection", in *Buddhist Manuscripts from Central Asia, The British Library Sanskrit Fragments, Volume I*, S. Karashima and K. Wille (ed.), 65–153, Tokyo: International Research Institute for Advanced Buddhology, Soka University.

— 2008: *Sanskrithandschriften aus den Turfanfunden Teil 10*, Stuttgart: Franz Steiner Verlag.

— 2009: "The Sanskrit Fragments Or. 15004 in the Hoernle Collection", in *Buddhist Manuscripts from Central Asia, The British Library Sanskrit Fragments, Volume II*, S. Karashima and K. Wille (ed.), 73–104, Tokyo: International Research Institute for Advanced Buddhology, Soka University.

— 2012: *Sanskrithandschriften aus den Turfanfunden Teil 11*, Stuttgart: Franz Steiner Verlag.

— 2015: "The Sanskrit Fragments Or. 15007 in the Hoernle Collection", in *Buddhist Manuscripts from Central Asia, The British Library Sanskrit Fragments, Volume III*, S. Karashima, J. Nagashima, and K. Wille (ed.), 13–198, Tokyo: International Research Institute for Advanced Buddhology, Soka University.

Woodward, F.L. 1927/1980 (vol. 4) and 1930/1979 (vol. 5): *The Book of the Kindred Sayings (Saṃyutta-Nikāya) or Grouped Suttas*, London: Pali Text Society.

Wright, J.C. 2000: "Pāli dīpam attano and attadīpa", in *Harānandalaharī, Volume in Honour of Professor Minoru Hara on His Seventieth Birthday*,

R. Tsuchida and A. Wezler (ed.), 481–503, Reinbek: Dr. Inge Wezler Verlag für Orientalistische Fachpublikationen.

Zhang Tieshan 2002: "An Uighur Fragment of the Za-ahanjing from Dunhuang Preserved in the Library of the Beijing University", *Journal of the Central University for Nationalities, Philosophy and Social Sciences Edition*, 4: 108–112.

INDEX OF SUBJECTS

INTRODUCTORY NOTE

References such as '178–9' indicate (not necessarily continuous) discussion of a topic across a range of pages. Wherever possible in the case of topics with many references, these have either been divided into sub-topics or only the most significant discussions of the topic are listed. Because the entire work is about 'mindfulness', the use of this term (and certain others which occur constantly throughout the book) as an entry point has been minimised. Information will be found under the corresponding detailed topics.

Abhidharma 5, 44, 157
  definitions 36
  thought 35–6
absence of mindfulness 181, 188
absorptions 26–7, 72, 74–5, 81, 139, 145–6, 159
  attainment 79, 159
  bodily dimensions of 72–5, 140
  experience 73–4
  first 72–3, 110
  fourth 73–4, 145–6, 207
  second 72–3
  third 73–4, 145
access roads 38–9
acrobatics 116–17, 238
acrobats simile 86, 116–20, 235
activities 12, 15, 68–9, 80, 82, 84, 144, 190–1
  bodily 69, 72, 82–3, 140
  daily 138
  mundane 239, 242
  verbal 72
  warrior 176
affection 148, 151, 176
afflictions 87, 95, 138, 150–1, 194–5, 240–1
Āgamas 2–5, 7–8, 27, 32, 36, 41, 186
  see also Index Locorum

aggregates, contemplating with mindfulness 225
alarm clock 143, 182
alms 108, 185
aloofness from views, mindful 213–15
amanasikāra 60, 202
Ambapālī 126–8
Ānanda 108–9, 124–5, 133, 135, 147–9, 152, 156
anatomical constitution 54, 75, 78
ancestral domain 114–16, 122–3
anger 102, 105–6, 114–15, 219–20, 236, 242
  overcoming through mindfulness 215–17
Aṅguttara-nikāya see Index Locorum
animals 62–4, 68, 77, 84, 173, 175
Anuruddha 122, 132, 153–4, 209–10
apilāpana 43–5
appamāda 180–1
arahants 130, 132–3, 135, 137, 165–6, 178, 228, 231
arousing knowledge 90, 230
arrogance 66–7, 208
Asoka, King 4–5
assemblies 128, 148, 150, 177
attachment 17, 21–2, 64, 68, 115–16, 192–5
  bondage of 194
  defilement of 123
attacks
  mindfully facing 212
  physical 199, 236, 242
attainment 81, 87, 136–7, 139, 145, 228, 230
  meditative 74, 155
attention 41, 44, 97–9, 119, 129, 182–3, 202–3, 205
  bare 192
attentive dimension 8, 11, 53, 99
attentiveness 16, 41, 46, 182, 239
attraction 57, 211, 236
attractiveness 64, 78, 211
audiences 232–5
authority 162, 190–1
aversion 139, 190, 207, 229, 236
awakening 31–4, 51–2, 78–9, 85–7, 126, 137, 156–7, 165–7, 219–23, 230–2
  attained and mindfulness 227–8
  factors 33, 51–2, 98, 219–23, 230–2, 236, 239, 242
    Buddha's discovery of 221
    healing through 155–9
    treasures of 220–1
  mindfulness and quest for 226–7
awareness, bare 162, 192–7, 240, 242
axle of mindfulness of the body 65–6

bad conduct 105
Bāhiya 131, 192
balance 61, 118, 120, 211–12, 235, 239
  inner 230, 234, 236, 242
  of mindfulness 211–12
bare awareness 162, 192–7, 240, 242
beauty 57–8, 126, 240
begging 108, 123, 185–6
beginners 240, 242
benefits 17–18, 47, 121, 126, 129, 134, 205
benevolence 208, 216, 232
Bhadda 133–5
birds 62, 113–14, 140
birth 95, 131, 174, 226–7
bodily activity 69, 72, 82–3, 140
bodily condition 178–9
bodily dignity 59, 61
bodily dimensions of absorption 72–5, 140
bodily experience 72–4
bodily pains 153–5
bodily postures 48, 55, 79, 91, 241
  mindfulness of 68–72, 241
body 89–94, 96–7, 106–7, 109, 123–5, 132–4, 138–42, 151–4, 201–2, 212–14
  constitution of the 54, 75–81, 84
  contemplations 69, 149, 235

mindfulness of the 8, 40, 47–84, 209, 238
straight 139, 144, 156, 212
and tangibles 64, 123, 194
bondage 123–4, 138, 193, 216, 241
of attachment 194
bones 75, 77–8
boundless conditions 47, 56, 62, 84, 104, 208–9
boundless mind 56, 81
boundless mindfulness of the body 56–7
bowl of oil 47, 57–62, 68, 84, 128, 238
brahmavihāra 56, 207–8
brahmins 13, 33, 59, 81, 146
brain 75
brain stem 75
breath 45, 48, 71, 82–3, 177, 239
breathing, mindfulness of 48, 53–4, 70, 72, 81–3
Buddha *see Introductory Note*
buddhānusmṛti 18
Buddha's awakening and the direct path 86–9
Buddha's awakening through mindfulness 231–2
Buddha's first teaching 230–1
Buddha's mindfulness and insight 229–30
Buddha's mindfulness at conception 174
Buddhist monastics 21, 69–70, 171, 187
Buddhist traditions 1, 3, 5, 7, 218, 237
bulkiness 177, 179

calming 72, 82–3
of mental activity 82
care 117–19, 235
cattle 162, 172, 191–2, 197
causality 205, 215
ceasing 17–18, 96–7
nature of 97
celestials/celestial beings 17–18, 43, 158, 162, 170–2, 197, 215–16
celibacy 199, 217–18
celibate life 66, 130, 138, 191, 217, 227
censure 184–5
cessation 34, 51–2, 83, 96–7, 146, 156, 218–20
complete 219
of nutriment 96
of pain 146
of perceptions 23, 218
characteristics of mindfulness 237–40
charioteer simile 17, 161, 167–8, 239
chariots 47, 65–6, 80, 127, 167
charnel ground 77–8
Chinese
Āgama 2–5, 8, 27, 32, 36, 41
characters 18, 21, 51, 170, 174
parallels 85, 88, 91, 142–3, 145, 176, 179–80
translations 5, 7, 17, 65, 88, 173
translators 67, 98, 170
circumspect behaviour 70, 186
circumspection 55, 80, 84, 153
clarity of perception 156, 181
climatic conditions 3
clinging 39, 96–8, 103, 166, 199
five aggregates of 225
cognition 24, 203
cognitive psychology 46
coins 178–9
collected mind 108, 127–8, 158
collected mindfulness 58, 89, 147, 156, 203, 211
collectedness 108–9, 127
collecting oneself, mindfully 25
comparative study 4, 14, 45, 68, 126
compassion 119, 178, 208, 232
concentration 26–7, 51–2, 71–2, 80–1, 90–1, 125–6, 156–7, 164–6, 187–8, 203–6
awakening factors 220–1
cultivation of 125, 205
degrees of 91, 125
and mindfulness 107–13
mindfulness leading to 203–6
right 29, 51–3, 164–6, 169, 190, 203–4

concentration (*cont.*)
  wrong 169
conditionality 98–9
conduct 59, 69, 129, 137, 139, 141
  bad 105
  ethical 34, 133–4, 141, 159
  mental 105, 224
  moral 100, 134, 138, 140–1, 242
  unwholesome 140
  wholesome 25
confidence 29–30, 109
confusion 55, 173, 211
consciousness 24, 39, 76–7, 97, 166, 225
constitution of the body 54, 75–81, 84
contemplating dharmas 92–4, 127, 130, 133–4, 136, 139, 149, 151
contemplation(s) 48, 50, 54–5, 79–80, 98–9, 109–12, 201, 235–6
  body 69, 149, 235
  of feeling tones 49, 89, 106–7, 113, 124–5, 132
  internal 149, 235
continuity of mindfulness 101, 116, 183
conventions 7–9
cook 111–13, 120, 235, 239
cooperation 118–19
corpses 54, 69, 77–9, 235
cowherd simile 162, 171–2, 191, 197, 239
craving 42, 82, 166, 192–5
criticism 184, 199, 212–13, 236, 242
crowds 57–8, 62, 128, 238
Cūḷavedalla-sutta 204–5
cultivation 99–101, 103, 105–8, 134–7, 166–7, 196–7, 199–200, 206–8, 217–19, 226–30
  of concentration 125, 205
  of insight 40, 68, 225
  meditative 41, 172, 175, 209, 242
  of mindfulness 34, 52–4, 81, 120–2, 131, 133–4, 188–90, 199–200, 220
    modalities 48–53
daily-life situations 65, 113, 187, 229
Dantabhūmi-sutta 200–201
Dasuttara-sutta 48–9, 51–3, 228
death 95, 131, 140, 147, 150–1, 153, 159
  facing with mindfulness 153
  of others 150–3
decay 48, 54, 69, 77–9, 235
defilements 111–12, 123, 126, 163–4, 187, 207–8
delight 42, 48–9, 56, 138, 140, 193–5, 210
delusion 105, 212
dependence 34, 51–2, 116, 123, 141, 219–20
desires, greedy 93–4, 107, 123, 227
Dharmaguptaka 5–6
dharmas 17–20, 92–7, 106–8, 123–5, 132–6, 148–52, 156–8, 190, 201, 232–4
  contemplating 92–4, 127, 130, 133–4, 136, 139, 149, 151
  right 91, 157, 233
Dīgha-nikāya see Index Locorum
dignity, bodily 59, 61
diligence 29, 60, 93–4, 100–101, 105, 107, 132, 227
diligent effort 93, 99, 124–5, 127–8, 130, 132, 151, 209–10
dimensions of mindfulness 50, 52–3, 66–8, 81, 98–100, 161–97, 211–12, 223–4
direct knowledge 210, 231
direct path 86–9, 119, 126
Dīrgha-āgama see Index Locorum
disciples 49, 59, 103–4, 117–18, 150, 232–3
  noble 17, 34, 37, 42, 132, 201
discipline 21, 132, 157, 226
discontent 49–50, 89, 93–4, 127–8, 132, 138–9, 151–2, 210, 213–14, 227
disease 1, 95, 156–7, 226
disgust 63–4
dispassion 21, 51–2, 82–3, 156, 169, 219–20
distant past 14, 27, 30, 32–3, 41, 55

distractions 16, 57, 60–2, 126, 128, 199, 218
sensual 116, 128
divine abodes 199, 207–9, 236
doors, sense 56–7, 224
drinking 69, 144
dukkha 34, 94–5, 136, 193, 196, 226, 230
dust 78, 217
Dvedhāvitakka-sutta 171–2
dwelling 59, 96–100, 111–12, 123–5, 133–4, 136, 138–40, 147–9, 153–4, 184
in dependence 187
in equanimity 145, 229

ear 64, 115, 123, 138, 193–4
faculty 63
early discourses 2, 57, 60, 126, 157, 161, 175
eating 69, 144, 162, 181, 239, 242
mindful 143, 175, 179, 197, 242
effort 20–1, 25, 27, 29, 126–8, 163–4, 184–5
diligent 93, 99, 124–5, 127–8, 130, 132, 151, 209–10
right 52–3, 162–4, 166–7, 169, 202, 204
strong 61, 100
wrong 169
eightfold path *see* noble eightfold path
ekayāna 87–8
ekāyana 87–8
Ekottarika-āgama see Index Locorum
elephants 19, 115, 206–7, 236
emancipating effect 121, 135
emancipation, through mindfulness 135–7
embodied form 55, 57, 62, 64–5, 67, 69, 73
embodied mindfulness 70, 80, 128, 238
energy 29–30, 33, 45, 50, 52, 127, 156–7
awakening factor 220–1
untiring 49, 89, 213–14
equanimity 145–6, 206–8, 211, 229, 234, 236
and mindfulness 211, 236
purified 207
equipoise 33, 51–2, 157
awakening factor 156, 220–1
establishing mindfulness 28, 85–159, 189
establishments 36, 39–40, 93, 166–7, 224, 226, 228, 241–2
Buddha's teaching of 89–92
cultivating 99–101
of mindfulness 29–33, 47–50, 85–97, 99–110, 116–26, 130–7, 139–42, 151–4, 226–32, 234–6
potential of 134–5
training in 92–4
wholesome nature 101–3
ethical conduct 34, 133–4, 141, 159
ethical foundation 52, 131, 140, 166
ethics 169, 242
exaggerations 179
exegesis 5, 27, 44, 46, 209, 211
exercises 31, 68–72, 74–9, 98, 144, 232
experience 19–20, 71, 74, 82, 203–4, 240, 243
bodily 72–4
fragmentation of 64, 241
somatic 68, 79
subjective 77, 191, 225, 236
external dimensions 61, 86, 235, 240–1
external marks 111–13
external mindfulness 50, 227, 234, 236
external objects 123, 234
eye faculty 63, 138

faculties 11, 28–34, 51, 63, 138, 186
ear 63
eye 63, 138
five 29–30, 47, 51, 147, 167
of mindfulness 28–33
nose 63
sense 142, 186
spiritual 28, 30
tongue 63

faeces 75–6
faith 29, 206
  right 129, 138
  serene 138
falling asleep with mindfulness of the Buddha 22–3
fate 78, 235
fear 11, 19–20, 61, 81, 139, 211
feeling tones 49–50, 89–94, 96–7, 133–4, 142, 151–2, 177–8, 201, 210, 218
  contemplation 49, 89, 106–7, 113, 124–5, 132
  painful 154
female monastics 38, 186
fetters 125, 227
final goal 89, 165–6, 228
final Nirvāṇa 150, 158
five faculties 29–30, 47, 51, 147, 167 *see also* faculties
five hindrances *see* hindrances
five mental qualities *see* mental qualities
five powers *see* powers
five precepts *see* precepts
flavours 63–4, 115, 123, 157, 193–4, 239
floating 44–5
flowers 73, 148, 150
focus 31, 36, 83, 119
  exclusive 62, 83
  narrowed 57
food 13, 143–4, 162, 178–9, 235, 239
  mindful begging for 185–7
fords 162, 189, 191–2, 197
forests 62, 81, 162, 187, 197
  dwelling in a forest with mindfulness 184–5
formal meditation 113, 140
foundations 34, 100, 129–31, 133–4, 159, 161, 238–9
  ethical 52, 131, 140, 166
  moral 121, 129–31
  in morality 129, 133, 146
four establishments *see* establishments
fragmentation of experience 64, 241
freedom 96, 131, 150
  path to 96, 131
fruits of recluse-ship 53–4, 230
fulfilment 127, 166–7
functions 14–15, 18, 70, 73, 76, 162–3, 166, 196–7
  of mindfulness 14–15, 40, 137, 241–3
  monitoring 40, 168, 196, 242
  protective 9, 120, 159
  psychological 55–6
  of recollection 17–18

Gaṇakamoggallāna-sutta 141–6, 200
Gāndhārī fragments 3, 54–5, 190
gatekeeper simile 12, 31–2, 36–41, 231, 238
generosity 17–18, 51, 128
girls 57–8, 61–2, 128
goal, final 89, 165–6, 228
gradual path 69–70, 121, 159
  and mindfulness 137–49
great mental powers 199, 209–10, 236
greedy desires 93–4, 107, 123, 227
growth 73, 134, 210, 222
  gradual 242
guardedness 60

hair 20, 75–6, 129, 138
happiness 72–3, 79, 82, 109–10, 112, 145–6, 210, 232
harming 106, 118, 169, 193–5
  thoughts of 106, 219
hawk 86, 113–16
healing 159
  through awakening factors 155–9
health 122, 152, 158, 239, 242
  bodily 155
healthcare 175, 181
heedfulness 180–1
hindrances 98, 102–3, 105–6, 139–40, 144–5, 183, 231–2
homelessness 129, 138
humility 47, 66–7

illness 153, 157
imagery 38, 40, 42–3, 74, 80, 86
immune response 240
impermanence 54, 82–3, 98, 218
of the objects of mindfulness 96–9
India 3–4, 13, 37, 57, 73–4, 141
Indic 4, 6, 88, 172, 177, 179
inexhaustibility 86, 120, 237
of teachings on mindfulness 103–6
influxes 106–7, 125, 132, 165, 219–20, 227–8
inner balance 230, 234, 236, 242
insight 29, 39–40, 67–8, 206–7, 225, 230
and Buddha's mindfulness 229–30
liberating 126, 131, 199, 205–7
meditation 1, 31, 44–5, 167
right 29, 39, 158, 229
inspiration 18–19, 22, 110, 210
instructions 39–40, 83, 98, 100–101, 125–6, 128–30, 177–81, 192, 200–202, 233
intensive practice 121, 129
intention(s) 31–2, 63, 163–4, 169
right 52, 163–4, 166, 169
wrong 163, 169
internal contemplation 149, 235
internal phenomena 222–3
intestines 75
iron 42–3

jackals 62, 77
Janavasabha-sutta 89–91
jhāna 74
joy 49, 52, 72–3, 109–10, 145–6, 156–8, 210
awakening factor 220–1
earlier cessation 146

Kāyagatāsati-sutta 68–72, 74–6, 79–81, 144
killing 140, 163–4
kings 23, 36, 38, 175–80
knowing, right 105, 124, 127–8, 130, 132, 138–9
knowledge 90–1, 133, 137, 147–8, 166, 223, 232–3
arousing 90, 230
direct 210, 231
right 165, 195, 227

lake 62, 73
laxity 101, 152
laypeople 173, 187
liberating dimension of mindfulness 52, 67–8, 81, 83, 96, 98
liberating insight 126, 131, 199, 205–7
liberation 26–7, 56, 94–6, 130–1, 141–3, 147, 187–8, 199–236, 240–1
depending on mindfulness 223–4
final 199, 207
by insight 207
and mindfulness 94–6
path to 11, 26–7, 29, 40, 65, 80
right 165
temporary 199, 208
by wisdom 56, 227
lifestyle 24, 184, 190
limbs 69, 124, 144, 178
lineages
reciter 6, 28
transmission 2–7
livelihood
right 52, 138, 163–4, 166–7, 169, 230
wrong 169
longevity 177–8
loss 20, 28, 37, 62, 170, 172
of mindfulness 14, 16, 20, 43–4, 46, 170–1
lust 105–7, 169, 185, 190, 195, 217, 219–20
mindful removal 217
sensual 185, 218, 236, 242
thoughts of 169, 195, 219
lustful desires 199, 217
mindful protection against 126–31

Madhyama-āgama see Index Locorum
Mahāmoggallāna 132, 148, 150–1, 212
Mahāsāṅghika 5
Majjhima-nikāya see Index Locorum
male monastics 128, 185–6
Māluṅkyaputta 192–3, 195–6
manasikāra 21, 61, 98, 202–3
Māra 80–1, 115, 123, 131
marks 70, 165, 193–6, 205
 external 111–13
 inspiring 109–10
meals 128, 177–8
meditation 14, 16, 48–9, 93–4, 96, 99–101, 103, 166–7
 formal 113, 140
 insight 1, 31, 44–5, 167
 mindfulness 79, 98, 111, 120, 126, 227
 practice 79–80, 84, 86, 108, 110, 113, 118, 120
 walking 181, 183
meditative cultivation 41, 172, 175, 209, 242
meditative practices 40, 45, 81, 134, 187
meditative training 31, 173
memory 8, 55–6, 241
 connotation 31, 38, 241
 dimension 19, 25, 46
 dimensions of mindfulness 11–46
 nuance 12, 16, 30, 41, 45–6, 98
 semantic 16, 46
mendicant life 141, 187
mental condition 18, 38, 47, 53, 84, 119
mental conduct 105, 224
mental objects 63–4, 193–5
mental purification 87, 89, 94, 119, 236
mental qualities 28, 30, 35–6, 40, 44–5, 221, 225
mental reactivity 64, 66–7
mental states 98, 109, 119, 154, 203, 234
 unwholesome 18, 127
 wholesome 127
merriment 58, 162
mettā 118–19, 208, 216–17
mind 56–62, 82–3, 89–94, 106–7, 109–13, 123–7, 138–43, 193–6, 199–204, 208–11
 collected 108, 127–8, 158
 sensual 115–16
 unified 210, 212
mindful aloofness from views 213–15
mindful ascent to a higher heaven 20–2
mindful company 189–90
mindful dwelling of a trainee 131–3
mindful eating 143, 175, 179, 197, 242
mindfully collecting oneself 25
mindfulness *see also Introductory Note*
 absence of 181, 188
 attentive dimension 8, 11, 53, 99
 of awakened ones 228
 as awakening factor 33–4, 223
 balance of 211
 and being reminded of the Buddha 23–5
 of bodily postures and activities 68–72, 241
 of the body 8, 40, 47–84, 209, 238
  axle of 65–6
  boundless 56–7
  to counter sensuality 67–8
  and humility 66–7
  potential 53–6
 boundless 56
 of breathing 48, 53–4, 70, 72, 81–3
 characteristics 237–40
 collected 58, 89, 147, 156, 203, 211
 and concentration 107–13
 continuity of 101, 116, 183
 cultivation 34, 47–8, 52–4, 81, 120–2, 131, 133–4, 189–90, 199–200, 220

before teaching others 188–9
definitions 11, 15, 25, 28, 36
dimensions 50, 52–3, 66–8, 81, 98–100, 161–97, 211–12, 223–4
embodied 70, 80, 128, 238
establishing 28, 85–159, 189
establishments 29–33, 47–50, 85–97, 99–110, 116–26, 130–7, 139–42, 151–4, 226–32, 234–6
external 50, 227, 234, 236
faculties of 28–30
as form of authority 190–1
functions 14–15, 40, 137, 241–3
giving priority to 187–8
and the gradual path 137–49
great person practising 106–7
liberating dimension 52, 67–8, 81, 83, 96, 98
and liberation 94–6
loss of 14, 16, 20, 43–4, 46, 170–1
meditation 79, 98, 111, 120, 126, 227
and memory 11, 22, 41, 44
modalities 48, 53, 68, 78, 162, 224
in noble eightfold path 34–6
as path of Dharma 190
possession of 66, 173–4, 213–14, 229
practice 34–5, 50, 52–3, 100, 134, 151–2, 180–2, 199–200
protective dimension 8, 116, 121–2, 128, 143, 149
quality of 35, 38, 187, 209, 215, 219
receptive dimension 50, 86, 92, 100, 234, 239–40
recollective 49, 152, 213–14
right 34–5, 127–8, 132, 138–9, 161–9, 186–7, 193–5, 203–5, 214–15, 217–18
role 14–15, 45, 47, 81, 83, 162, 230
slow arising 12, 41–5
wrong 26, 103, 169–71, 185–7, 197
misconduct, sexual 140, 163–4
misfortunes 113–15
modalities of mindfulness 48, 53, 68, 78, 162, 224
moderation 143
monastics 57–9, 105–7, 115–16, 123–4, 127–9, 131–3, 141–2, 149–52, 156, 182–8
Buddhist 21, 69–70, 171, 187
female 38, 186
male 128, 185–6
monitoring function 40, 168, 196, 242
monkey simile 62, 121–4, 159
moral conduct 100, 134, 138, 140–1, 242
moral foundation 121, 129–31
morality 17–18, 129–31, 133, 139–40, 146, 191
for mindfulness 133–4
noble 133, 138
training in 139–40, 191
mortality 78–9
mother's womb 173–5
mountains 73, 122, 148, 151
mucus 75–6
Mūlasarvāstivāda 5–6, 116, 155, 176

neck 206–7, 236
bones 77
negligence 60, 102, 124–5, 129, 196
newcomers 121, 124–6
nimitta 110, 112, 193, 205
Nirvāṇa 40, 53–4, 139, 147–8, 194–6, 230–1
final 150, 158
peace of 112, 124, 132, 226
no longer paying attention 201–3
noble disciples 17, 34, 37, 42, 132, 201
noble eightfold path 34–5, 40, 52, 161–2, 200, 202, 204, 230
in meditation 166–7
mindfulness in 162–6
noble morality 133, 138
nose 64, 115, 123, 138, 193–4
faculty 63

nuns 108–9 *see also* female monastics
nutriment 96–7, 99, 119, 222, 224

objects 15, 19, 24, 44–6, 59, 64, 96–7, 203
  external 123, 234
  mental 63–4, 193–5
  of mindfulness, impermanence 96–9
ocean 78–80
odours 63–4, 193–4
offerings 127, 141
oral transmission 2, 4–5, 27–9, 34, 71, 74–5, 77
  lineages 4–7
overeating 175–81

pain 14, 94–5, 146, 151, 154–5, 159
  bodily 153–5
  Buddha bearing pain with mindfulness 154–5
  facing with mindfulness 153–4
pajānāti 101
Pāli parallels 18–21, 64–6, 90–2, 135–6, 167–9, 172–4, 206–8, 210–14, 217–18, 220–7
Paṇḍita 45
Pasenadi, King 162, 175–81
past 11–14, 16, 18–19, 23–5, 27–8, 30–1, 33–4, 45–6, 100, 213–14
  distant 14, 27, 30, 32–3, 41, 55
past lives, recollection of 11–14, 16
pasture 191–2, 197
path 25–7, 31–2, 34, 40, 87, 138, 165–6, 169, 187–90, 230
  of Dharma 17, 162, 190
  factors 35, 53, 163–8, 196, 204
  to freedom 96, 131
  gradual 69–70, 121, 137, 139–41, 143, 146
  to liberation 11, 26–7, 29, 40, 65, 80
  mindfulness as 226
  for one who is mindful 26–7
  of purification 210
  right 168–9
  wrong 161, 163, 168–9, 189
peace 35–6, 40, 147, 154, 215, 232, 238
  of Nirvāṇa 112, 124, 132, 226
pearl, beautiful 240
perceptions 23, 25, 53–4, 106, 109, 154–6, 181–2, 218–19
  clarity of 156, 181
  sensual 185
perfection 24, 141, 165
persecution 3
personal responsibility 214–15
phenomena 25, 90, 219, 222–3
physical attacks 199, 236, 242
physical body 71, 74, 159
pilāpana 44
poisonous snakes 39, 62
possession of mindfulness 66, 173–4, 213–14, 229
postures, bodily 48, 55, 68, 70, 79, 91
powers 29–34, 114, 122, 147, 157, 228
  great mental 199, 209–10, 236
  supernormal 53–4, 209–12
  of wisdom 82, 139, 231
practice 47–8, 54–5, 68–9, 78–9, 83, 86–8, 110–11, 140–3, 222–4, 241–2
  foundational 70, 79
  intensive 121, 129
  of recollection 8, 11, 20, 45, 51
  of wakefulness 143, 183
practitioners 1, 23, 69–70, 108, 110, 211
praise 68, 128, 180
precepts 141, 147, 163–4, 173
progression 48, 83, 142, 164
  meditative 81
proprioception 68, 84, 238, 241
protective dimension of mindfulness 8, 116, 121–2, 128, 143, 149
protective function 9, 120, 159
psychological functions 55–6
psychology, cognitive 46
purification 88, 94, 100, 130–1, 138–9, 159
  joy of 210

mental 87, 89, 94, 119, 236
path of 210
purified equanimity 207
purity 138, 141, 146
mental 73

quail simile 86, 113–16, 120, 122–3, 179
qualities
bad 146, 173
mental 28, 30, 35–6, 40, 44–5, 221, 225
protective 86, 187
unwholesome 103

reactivity
mental 64, 66–7
potential 238
rebirth 11, 20–1, 43, 173
receptive dimension of mindfulness 9, 86, 92, 100, 234, 239–40
receptivity 111, 113, 119–20, 168, 192, 239–41
recitation 19, 28, 71, 155, 158, 178
reciter traditions 6, 12, 143
reciters 5, 7, 100, 209
recluse-ship, fruits of 53–4, 230
recollection 8, 11, 13–21, 24, 51, 54–5, 88, 203
of celestial beings 51
countering fear 20
and mindfulness 19
of past lives 11–19
practice of 8, 11, 20, 45, 51
recollective mindfulness 49, 152, 213–14
refuge 147, 149, 151–3, 159, 173, 238
relationships 8–9, 11, 16, 31–3, 41, 44–6, 133, 206–7
close 12, 21, 51, 236, 242
reliance 149, 151, 238, 242
remembering 13, 18–19, 23–5, 27–30, 32–4, 36–7, 40–1, 43
repercussions 50, 106, 177, 240, 243
repulsion 211, 236
resin 122–3
responsibility
active 41
personal 214–15
taking 134
restlessness 82, 102, 139, 208
restraint 86, 134, 138–9, 141
sense 56, 86, 140, 142–3, 162, 185–6
retreats 1, 45, 184–5
right action 52, 163–4, 166–7, 169, 230
right concentration 29, 51–3, 164–6, 169, 190, 203–4
right Dharma 91, 157, 233
right effort 52–3, 162–4, 166–7, 169, 202, 204
right faith 129, 138
right insight 29, 39, 158, 229
right intention 52, 163–4, 166, 169
right knowing 105, 124, 127–8, 130, 132, 138–9
right knowledge 165, 195, 227
right liberation 165
right livelihood 52, 138, 163–4, 166–7, 169, 230
right mindfulness 127–8, 132, 138–9, 161–9, 186–7, 193–5, 203–5, 208–10, 214–15, 217–18
definition 34–5
right path 168–9
right speech 52, 163–4, 166–7, 169, 230
robes 108, 123, 127, 144, 147, 185, 187
double 69, 144
roots 73, 81, 139, 208, 216, 220

Sakkapañha-sutta 20–1, 170
sampajañña 100–101, 175, 205, 207
Sampasādanīya-sutta 90–1
Saṃyukta-āgama see Index Locorum
Saṃyutta-nikāya see Index Locorum
Sāriputta 66, 107, 147–8, 150, 157, 212–13
Sarvāstivāda 5–6, 203
sati 24, 31, 44–5, 172, 202, 204, 207–8

satipaṭṭhāna 93–4, 96–7, 99–101, 103, 105–8, 126, 219–20, 222–4, 234–5
Satipaṭṭhāna-sutta 27, 69, 71–2, 98–9, 101, 216, 232
seasoned practitioners 121, 124–6
seclusion 23, 51–2, 72, 144, 147, 156, 219–20
semantic memory 16, 46
sense doors 56–7, 224
sense faculties 142, 186
sense restraint 56, 86, 140, 142–3, 162, 185–6
sensual distractions 116, 128
sensual lust 185, 218, 236, 242
sensual mind 115–16
sensual perceptions 185
sensuality 21–2, 42, 84, 106, 142, 158
  mindfulness of the body to counter 67–8
  overcoming 47, 67, 217
sentient beings 87, 94, 135–6, 170
sexual misconduct 140, 163–4
shame 30, 179
signlessness 219
signs 74–5, 90, 205, 219
similes 57, 65, 68, 80, 119–20, 225, 235, 238 *see also individual similes*
sinews 75, 77
singing 58, 61
six animals bound to a post 62–5, 68
sleep 22, 104, 197
  going to sleep with mindfulness 181–4
slow arising of mindfulness 12, 41–5
sluggishness 52, 107, 109, 212
smṛti 12–13, 24, 55–6, 145, 170
snakes, poisonous 39, 62
somatic experience 68, 79
sorrow 87, 94–5, 99, 149–51
source material 2–3
speech 90, 117, 130, 140–1, 185–6
  right 52, 163–4, 166–7, 169, 230
  wrong 169
spiritual faculty 28, 30
Sri Lanka 3–4
śruti 12–13
stilling the mind 112, 124–5
stones 45, 80, 212
straight body 139, 144, 156, 212
strength 63, 66, 103, 114–15
subjective experience 77, 191, 225, 236
sun 74, 192, 194, 225
supernormal powers 53–4, 209–12
swords 58–60, 212
synonyms 44, 180–1

tangibles 63–4, 123, 193–4
tastes 111–12
Tathāgata 17, 20–1, 30, 89, 103–4, 133, 148–50, 178, 221, 231–2
teeth 70, 75–6
temporary liberation 199, 208
terminology 12, 61, 87, 98
textual corruption 207, 216
textual error 72, 87
Theravādins 4–6, 12, 71
thinking 200–201
through mindfulness, emancipation 135–7
Tibetan versions 3, 7, 38–40, 167, 170, 204, 206
tones, feeling *see* feeling tones
tongue 64, 70, 115, 123, 138, 193–4
  faculty 63
torpor 82, 102, 139, 145, 208
towns 40, 108, 162, 185, 231–2, 238
  border 36–8
traditions 2, 5, 91, 101–3, 203–4, 234, 237
  Buddhist 1, 3, 5, 7, 218, 237
trainees 124–5, 131–2, 226–7
  mindful dwelling 131–3
training 28, 70, 82, 132, 134, 141, 165–6, 188–9
  in the four establishments 92–4
  meditative 31, 173
  moral 121
  in morality 139–40, 191

tranquillity 29, 33, 39–40, 51–2, 109–10, 156–8, 210
transcendence 94, 136
transmission
  errors 233
  lineages 2–7
  oral 2, 4–5, 27–9, 34, 71, 74–5, 77
trees 81, 87, 139, 144, 148, 150–1
truth 40, 78–9, 87, 94–5
Tusita Heaven 173–4

unified mind 210, 212
untiring energy 49, 89, 213–14
unwholesome conditions 102, 106
unwholesome conduct 140
unwholesome influences 199, 219–20, 236
unwholesome states 18, 56, 81, 102, 127, 138
unwholesome thoughts 42, 70, 141–2, 199, 201–2, 218–20
  countering 218–19
Uttara 177–9
Uttiya 129–31

variations 12, 28, 30, 40, 143–4, 234
verbs 37, 43, 101, 177
vicissitudes 66, 81, 151, 242
villages 62, 123, 155, 162, 185–6
virāga 83

wakefulness 143, 162, 183
walking meditation 181, 183
watchfulness 168
water 42–3, 72–4, 80, 191–2, 212, 225
wealth 2, 8, 117, 138, 150, 180
wholesome states 70, 78, 82, 100, 102, 127
wisdom 29, 31, 101, 104, 115, 147–8, 191, 204–7
  liberation by 56, 227
  power of 82, 139, 231
womb, mother's 173–5
worry 82, 87, 94–5, 99, 102, 139
wrong action 163–4, 169
wrong concentration 169
wrong effort 169
wrong eightfold path 169
wrong intentions 163, 169
wrong livelihood 169
wrong mindfulness 26, 103, 169–71, 185–7, 197
wrong path 161, 163, 168–9, 189
wrong speech 169

INDEX LOCORUM

Abhidharmakośopāyikā-ṭīkā
Up 1005 204n6
Up 2022 222n50
Up 2065 217n38
Up 2069 219n44
Up 3050 170n15
Up 4006 166n7
Up 4014 206n13
Up 4081 208n19
Up 4084 225n54, 225n55
Up 4086 192n77
Up 5010 67n33
Up 5037 222n49
Up 6027 92n17
Up 6028 99n34, 101n36
Up 6029 88n5, 226n56
Up 6031 96n27
Up 6066 42n76
Up 6067 228n63
Up 6078 38n67, 39n68, 39n69, 39n70, 39n71, 40n73, 40n75
Up 6080 162n1, 164n3
Up 7015 232n70
Up 9006 62n26

Aṅguttara-nikāya
AN 1.20 53n15
AN 2.32.2 206n14
AN 3.16 183n56
AN 3.61 214n32
AN 3.65 208n17
AN 3.70 17n8, 17n9
AN 3.74 88n8
AN 4.35 32n56
AN 4.122 186n62
AN 4.127 174n24
AN 4.191 43n78
AN 4.195 228n64
AN 4.243 191n73
AN 5.7 180n48
AN 5.14 30n51
AN 5.15 30n51
AN 5.34 128n11
AN 5.76 185n59
AN 5.114 142n37
AN 5.120 187n63
AN 5.197 180n49
AN 5.210 182n54
AN 5.213 180n49
AN 6.26 88n8
AN 6.29 54n16
AN 6.43 206n13
AN 6.54 29n40
AN 7.4 30n51
AN 7.63 36n62, 37n64, 145n47
AN 8.1 209n21
AN 8.9 217n38
AN 8.19 220n46
AN 8.28 228n63
AN 8.30 26n32, 27n33
AN 8.83 191n72
AN 9.11 66n32
AN 9.14 191n72
AN 10.17 32n55
AN 10.18 32n55
AN 10.50 32n55
AN 10.58 191n72
AN 10.61 223n51
AN 10.77 172n20
AN 10.208 208n19
AN 11.18 191n74

Dīrgha-āgama
DĀ 1 5n4, 162, 173n21, 174n23
DĀ 2 11, 28n35, 122, 126n10, 152n64, 174n23
DĀ 4 85, 89n10, 90n12, 91n16
DĀ 9 11–12, 14n4, 32n55, 162, 190n69
DĀ 10 11, 25n27, 26n28, 32n55, 47, 48n1, 49n6, 51n10, 51n11, 51n12, 52n13, 228n62
DĀ 14 11, 20, 21n15

DĀ 17 199, 213n31
DĀ 18 90n13, 199, 211n28
DĀ 21 5n4, 162, 170n15, 170n16
DĀ 28 11, 23n22, 199, 210n25

Dīgha-nikāya
DN 1 170n15, 170n17
DN 9 23n22, 210n25
DN 16 28n36, 126n10, 152n64, 174n23
DN 18 90n11, 90n12, 91n16
DN 21 21n16, 21n18, 21n19
DN 24 170n16
DN 28 90n13, 211n28
DN 29 213n31
DN 33 14n4, 32n55, 190n69
DN 34 25n27, 26n29, 32n55, 48n2, 49n6, 51n10, 51n11, 51n12, 52n13, 228n62

Ekottarika-āgama
EĀ 2.19 47, 53n15
EĀ 12.1 77n52, 98n31
EĀ 19.2 7n9, 200, 230n66
EĀ 21.6 162, 183n56
EĀ 24.1 20n14
EĀ 25.6 213n30
EĀ 27.1 34n58
EĀ 33.4 162, 185n59
EĀ 35.9 67n33
EĀ 37.6 66n32
EĀ 38.8 62n26
EĀ 38.10 23n26
EĀ 39.4 36n62
EĀ 39.6 158n83
EĀ 39.7 221n48
EĀ 40.6 219n44
EĀ 41.1 19n11
EĀ 42.4 199, 220n46, 221n47
EĀ 42.6 27n32
EĀ 47.9 188n65, 189n66
EĀ 49.1 162, 191n74

Itivuttaka
It 1.27 209n21

Madhyama-āgama
MĀ 3 12, 36n62, 37n64, 145n47
MĀ 10 199, 219n44
MĀ 12 200, 228n64
MĀ 13 199, 213, 214n32
MĀ 16 199, 207, 208n17
MĀ 24 47, 66n32
MĀ 26 162, 184n58
MĀ 30 199, 212n29
MĀ 31 11, 34n58
MĀ 32 162, 174n25
MĀ 35 220n46
MĀ 51 200, 223n51
MĀ 58 199, 221n48
MĀ 69 38n66
MĀ 74 11, 26n30, 26–7n32
MĀ 76 99n34, 101n36
MĀ 81 48, 68n35, 69n36, 70n38, 71n39, 71n40, 72n44, 74n46, 75n47, 76n51, 77n53, 78n54, 80n56, 80n57
MĀ 87 199, 212–13, 213n30
MĀ 91 162, 188n65, 189n66, 189n67,
MĀ 98 71n39, 98n31
MĀ 101 71n39, 199, 201n3
MĀ 102 162, 171n19
MĀ 107 162, 187n64
MĀ 113 162, 190–1, 191n72
MĀ 118 199, 206n13
MĀ 133 200, 229n65
MĀ 134 21n17
MĀ 144 121n1, 141n32, 141n33, 142n34, 144n40, 144n42,145n47, 146n50
MĀ 163 6n5, 200, 232n70
MĀ 179 164n3
MĀ 189 6n5, 161, 162n1, 164n3, 165n5
MĀ 192 12, 41, 42n77
MĀ 194 165n5
MĀ 198 6n5, 199–200, 200n1
MĀ 201 47, 56n18
MĀ 202 11, 17n8
MĀ 210 199, 203, 204n6, 205n9
MĀ 211 101n37
MĀ 213 23n25, 176n34

Majjhima-nikāya
MN 2 219n44
MN 5 213n30
MN 8 188n65, 189n66, 189n67
MN 10 98n31
MN 12 103n41, 157n80
MN 17 187n64
MN 19 171n19
MN 20 71n39, 201n3
MN 28 212n29
MN 33 191n74
MN 38 56n18
MN 43 101n37
MN 44 204n6
MN 53 32n55
MN 65 165n5
MN 66 42n77
MN 67 186n62
MN 69 184n58
MN 89 23n25, 176n34
MN 117 162n1, 164n3
MN 119 68n35, 69n36, 71n39, 71n40, 72n44, 75n47, 76n51, 77n53, 78n54, 80n56, 80n57
MN 129 65n30

MN 137 232n70, 233n71
MN 141 34n58
MN 149 166n7

Saṃyukta-āgama (T 99)
SĀ 98 11, 20n14, 168n10, 199, 206n14, 207n15
SĀ 255 56n19
SĀ 265 6n7, 200, 225n54
SĀ 271 6n7, 161, 168–9, 169n13
SĀ 272 6, 199, 218–19, 219n42
SĀ 275 199, 217n38
SĀ 305 161, 166n7
SĀ 312 6n7, 162, 192n77, 195n85
SĀ 450 162, 189n68
SĀ 498 200, 231n67
SĀ 535 88n5, 200, 226n56
SĀ 537 199, 209n23
SĀ 540 153n68
SĀ 541 6n7, 122, 153n68
SĀ 542 200, 226n57
SĀ 543 200, 227n60
SĀ 550 88n7
SĀ 561 88n7
SĀ 563 88n7
SĀ 566 47, 65n29
SĀ 575 6n7, 199, 211n27
SĀ 586 199, 217n36
SĀ 587 65n31
SĀ 592 11, 22n21
SĀ 605 85n2, 86, 92n17, 96
SĀ 605 to 615 85n2
SĀ 605 to SĀ 639 92
SĀ 606 86, 92n17, 96
SĀ 607 86, 94n20, 96
SĀ 608 86, 94–6, 95n24, 95n26
SĀ 609 86, 96n27, 98n31, 103
SĀ 610 86, 93, 99n34, 103, 130n15
SĀ 611 86, 102n38, 103, 105
SĀ 612 86, 103n41
SĀ 613 105n43
SĀ 614 86, 106n44
SĀ 615 6n7, 86, 107–8, 108n46
SĀ 616 6n7, 86, 111n52
SĀ 617 6n7, 86, 113n59, 114n60
SĀ 618 116n68
SĀ 619 6n7, 86, 116n69, 117n73
SĀ 620 6n7, 121–2, 122n2
SĀ 621 121, 124n7
SĀ 622 121, 126n10
SĀ 623 6n7, 47, 57n21, 58n24, 128
SĀ 624 121, 129n12
SĀ 626 131
SĀ 627 121, 131n18
SĀ 628 121, 133n21
SĀ 629 121, 134n24
SĀ 630 135
SĀ 631 135
SĀ 632 135
SĀ 633 135n27
SĀ 634 121, 135n28
SĀ 635 136n29
SĀ 636 137n30
SĀ 637 121n1, 137, 139n31
SĀ 638 6n7, 121n1, 147n51, 149n57
SĀ 639 6n7, 92, 121, 148n55, 150n59
SĀ 646 11, 28–9, 29n41
SĀ 647 11, 28–9, 29n43
SĀ 655 30n48
SĀ 658 30n48
SĀ 659 30n48
SĀ 675 30n50
SĀ 691 30n50
SĀ 694 228n63
SĀ 698 30n50
SĀ 711 11, 33n57
SĀ 713 6n7, 200, 222
SĀ 715 6, 200, 222n50
SĀ 721 221n48
SĀ 727 6n7, 122, 155n71, 157n81
SĀ 769 161, 167n9
SĀ 784 11, 34–5, 35n61
SĀ 785 35n61
SĀ 803 6n7, 48, 81n59
SĀ 930 11, 19n11
SĀ 981 11, 20n14
SĀ 1028 122, 153n66
SĀ 1087 162, 181n51, 182n53
SĀ 1144 49n4
SĀ 1145 176n33
SĀ 1148 176n31
SĀ 1150 6n7, 162, 175, 177n37, 177n38, 179n43
SĀ 1171 6n7, 47, 62n26
SĀ 1173 12, 41–2, 42n76
SĀ 1175 6n7, 12, 36, 38n67, 39n68, 39n70, 40n73
SĀ 1176 56n19, 182n53
SĀ 1189 85, 86n3, 94n22
SĀ 1191 162, 185, 186n60
SĀ 1214 47, 67n33
SĀ 1234 175n29
SĀ 1235 175n30
SĀ 1236 176n32
SĀ 1237 176n32
SĀ 1238 180n46
SĀ 1239 180n47
SĀ 1249 191n74
SĀ 1260 162, 185, 186n61
SĀ 1289 122, 154n69
SĀ 1305 199, 203n5
SĀ 1319 6n7, 199, 215n33
SĀ 1333 217n37

Saṃyukta-āgama (T 100)
SĀ² 6 217n38
SĀ² 26 168n10, 181n51
SĀ² 61 175n29
SĀ² 62 175n30
SĀ² 63 176n32
SĀ² 64 176n32
SĀ² 65 180n46
SĀ² 66 180n47
SĀ² 68 176n33
SĀ² 71 176n31
SĀ² 73 177n37, 177n38, 179n42
SĀ² 102 86n3, 88n6
SĀ² 104 186n60
SĀ² 119 49n5
SĀ² 155 19n11
SĀ² 170 217n36
SĀ² 186 22n21
SĀ² 230 67n33
SĀ² 264 168n10
SĀ² 287 154n69
SĀ² 304 203n5
SĀ² 318 215n33
SĀ² 353 217n37

Saṃyukta-āgama (T 101)
SĀ³ 1 168n10
SĀ³ 4 86n3, 88n6
SĀ³ 8 207n15
SĀ³ 20 189n68

Saṃyutta-nikāya
SN 1.21 217n36
SN 1.38 154n69
SN 1.46 65n31
SN 2.7 203n5
SN 2.16 217n36
SN 3.9 175n29
SN 3.10 175n30
SN 3.11 176n31
SN 3.13 177n37, 177n38, 178n39, 178n40, 178n41, 179n43
SN 3.14 176n32
SN 3.15 176n32
SN 3.17 180n47
SN 3.18 180n46
SN 3.24 176n33
SN 4.7 181n51
SN 6.13 186n60
SN 7.11 168n10
SN 8.4 67n33
SN 9.1 217n37
SN 10.4 215n33
SN 10.8 22n21
SN 11.3 20n14
SN 14.17 189n68
SN 16.11 49n3
SN 20.10 186n61
SN 22.80 219n42
SN 22.84 169n13
SN 22.95 225n54, 225n55
SN 35.89 131n16
SN 35.95 192n77, 193n80, 194n81, 194n82, 195n84, 195n85
SN 35.132 56n19
SN 35.202 56n19, 182n53
SN 35.203 42n76
SN 35.204 38n67, 39n68, 39n69, 39n70, 39n71, 40n72, 40n73, 40n74
SN 35.206 62n26, 64n28
SN 36.7 153n66
SN 41.5 65n29
SN 41.10 211n27
SN 42.8 209n21
SN 42.13 209n21
SN 45.4 167n9
SN 45.8 35n61
SN 45.21 35n61
SN 46.7 114n63, 115n65, 115n66
SN 46.14 158n82
SN 46.15 158n82
SN 46.16 155n71, 155n72, 155n73, 156n75, 156n76, 156n77
SN 46.42 221n48
SN 46.51 222n49
SN 46.52 222n50
SN 46.56 33n57
SN 47.1 94n20, 94n23
SN 47.2 126n10
SN 47.3 99n34, 100n35, 130n15
SN 47.4 124n7, 125n8
SN 47.5 102n38
SN 47.6 113n59, 114n60, 114n61, 114n62
SN 47.7 122n2, 122n3, 122n4, 123n5, 123n6
SN 47.8 111n52, 111n53, 111n54, 112n55, 112n57
SN 47.9 152n64
SN 47.14 148n55
SN 47.18 86n3
SN 47.20 57n21, 58n22, 58n23, 58n24, 60n25
SN 47.24 92n17, 93n18
SN 47.33 95n24, 95n26
SN 47.41 95n26
SN 47.42 96n27
SN 47.43 86n3
SN 48.8 29n42
SN 48.9 29n45
SN 48.10 29n46
SN 48.11 30n47
SN 48.50 30n48
SN 51.15 88n8
SN 52.2 226n56
SN 52.4 226n57, 227n59
SN 52.5 227n60, 227n61
SN 52.6 209n23, 210n24
SN 52.10 153n68
SN 54.1 81n59
SN 55.21 19n11
SN 56.11 230n66

Sutta-nipāta
Sn 77 168n10
Sn 151 209n21
Sn 1107 206n14

Taishō edition
T 2 173n21

T 5 28n38, 126n10, 174n23
T 6 28n38, 126n10, 152n64, 174n23
T 7 28n38, 126n10, 174n23
T 9 91n16
T 15 21n20
T 21 170n15
T 32 34n58
T 36 223n51, 224n53
T 37 223n51, 224n53
T 46 26n32
T 49 213n30
T 59 191n72
T 70 141n32, 141n33, 142n35, 144n41, 145n43, 145n47, 146n50
T 87 17n8
T 105 225n54, 225n55
T 106 225n54, 225n55
T 111 189n68
T 112 35n61
T 123 191n74
T 150A 7
T 212 36n62, 114n61, 176n32
T 757 157n80
T 1448 116n69, 117n70, 117n72, 117n75, 118n76, 118n77
T 1451 155n73, 176n34
T 1536 14n4
T 1537 207n15
T 1545 170n16

WINDHORSE PUBLICATIONS

Windhorse Publications is a Buddhist charitable company based in the UK. We place great emphasis on producing books of high quality that are accessible and relevant to those interested in Buddhism at whatever level. We are the main publisher of the works of Sangharakshita, the founder of the Triratna Buddhist Order and Community. Our books draw on the whole range of the Buddhist tradition, including translations of traditional texts, commentaries, books that make links with contemporary culture and ways of life, biographies of Buddhists, and works on meditation.

As a not-for-profit enterprise, we ensure that all surplus income is invested in new books and improved production methods, to better communicate Buddhism in the 21st century. We welcome donations to help us continue our work – to find out more, go to windhorsepublications.com.

The Windhorse is a mythical animal that flies over the earth carrying on its back three precious jewels, bringing these invaluable gifts to all humanity: the Buddha (the 'awakened one'), his teaching, and the community of all his followers.

Windhorse Publications
info@windhorsepublications.com

Perseus Distribution
210 American Drive
Jackson TN 38301
USA

Windhorse Books
PO Box 574
Newtown NSW 2042
Australia

THE TRIRATNA BUDDHIST COMMUNITY

Windhorse Publications is a part of the Triratna Buddhist Community, an international movement with centres in Europe, India, North and South America and Australasia. At these centres, members of the Triratna Buddhist Order offer classes in meditation and Buddhism. Activities of the Triratna Community also include retreat centres, residential spiritual communities, ethical Right Livelihood businesses, and the Karuna Trust, a UK fundraising charity that supports social welfare projects in the slums and villages of India.

Through these and other activities, Triratna is developing a unique approach to Buddhism, not simply as a philosophy and a set of techniques, but as a creatively directed way of life for all people living in the conditions of the modern world.

If you would like more information about Triratna please visit thebuddhistcentre.com or write to:

London Buddhist Centre
51 Roman Road
London E2 0HU
UK

Aryaloka
14 Heartwood Circle
Newmarket NH 03857
USA

Sydney Buddhist Centre
24 Enmore Road
Sydney NSW 2042
Australia